ISOLATIONISM
IN AMERICA
1935–1941

ISOLATIONISM
IN AMERICA
1935-1941

>>>>>>>>>>>>>>>>>>><<<<<<<<<<<<<<<<<<<

By Manfred Jonas

Cornell Paperbacks

CORNELL UNIVERSITY PRESS

Ithaca and London

First Published 1966 by Cornell University Press.
Published in the United Kingdom by Cornell University Press Ltd.,
2-4 Brook Street, London W1Y 1AA.

First printing, Cornell Paperbacks, 1969
Second printing 1972

International Standard Book Number 0-8014-9078-2
Library of Congress Catalog Card Number 66-16289

Printed in the United States of America by Vail-Ballou Press, Inc.

To Nancy

PREFACE

AMERICAN isolationism before the Second World War has deservedly been the subject of careful scrutiny in recent years. The anomaly of a great nation in the twentieth century intently avoiding responsibility for world events, and striving to insulate itself by domestic legislation against disasters it was unwilling to help prevent, has been treated from complementary viewpoints in Robert E. Osgood's *Ideas and Self-Interest in American Foreign Relations* (1953) and Selig Adler's *The Isolationist Impulse* (1957). It also received considerable attention in *Isolation and Security* (1957), edited by Alexander De Conde. The "battle against isolation" is described in great detail both in *The Challenge to Isolation, 1937–1940* (1952) by William L. Langer and S. E. Gleason, and in Donald F. Drummond's *The Passing of American Neutrality, 1937–1941* (1955). The controversy over neutrality legislation is examined by Robert A. Divine in *The Illusion of Neutrality* (1962). Wayne S. Cole has treated one of the principal isolationist organizations in *America First* (1953) and one of the leading isolationist spokesmen in *Senator Gerald P. Nye and American Foreign Relations* (1962).

No attempt has been made here to go over in detail the

ground covered in these studies. Nor is it the purpose of this work to utilize the conclusions they offer for a synthesis that might try to be the definitive historical treatment of isolationism in the thirties. Instead, this analysis seeks to define an aspect of isolationism previously glossed over or completely ignored. Nowhere in the works cited, nor in any others dealing with this subject, is the nature and content of isolationist thought adequately described, nor are its basic assumptions carefully examined. This is an effort to remedy the lack.

The isolationist viewpoint, as expressed from 1935 to 1941, cannot be elevated to the level of political philosophy, yet it cannot be dismissed as simple obstructionism based on ignorance and folly. Isolationism was the considered response to foreign and domestic developments of a large, responsible, and respectable segment of the American people. This response can be understood and evaluated only by examining the validity of the assumptions on which it was based.

By extracting these basic premises from the mass of isolationist letters, speeches, and writings and examining them in the light of the events to which they were applied, one can go far in explaining not only the survival of isolationism until the attack on Pearl Harbor, but also its subsequent disappearance.

Because so many persons, knowingly or not, have helped to make this book possible, I can specifically acknowledge only my major indebtednesses. The task of collecting the necessary material was made less arduous through the generous assistance provided by the staffs of the Franklin D. Roosevelt Library, the Yale University Library, the library of the John F. Kennedy–Institut at the Free University of Berlin, the Peace Collection of the Swarthmore College Library, the Manuscript Division of the Library of Congress, the Legislative Records Division of the National Archives, and, above all, the Harvard University Library. I am indebted to the Honorable Ralph R. Roberts, Clerk of the U.S. House of Representatives, for permission to examine the records of various House committees and to the Honorable Leo W. O'Brien, M.C., for securing this permission for me.

Arthur M. Schlesinger, Jr., encouraged me to undertake this project and throughout its earlier stages contributed suggestions and advice that have proved invaluable. Frank Freidel and Ernest R. May of Harvard University, and my colleague in Berlin, Ursula Brumm, read the original manuscript and offered much-needed criticism. The perceptive judgment of Donald Fleming of Harvard University aided me in eliminating various errors and inconsistencies, though he is in no way responsible for those that may remain.

I owe a special debt of gratitude to Bernard Roshco, who graciously gave of his time and talent. The nimble fingers and cheerful goodwill of Nancy Petersen Gibbons were essential to the final preparation of the manuscript.

Grants from the Penrose Fund of the American Philosophical Society and from the Union College Faculty Research Fund made the completion of this book possible.

My heaviest obligation is to my wife, Nancy Greene Jonas, whose contributions are too varied to permit enumeration here, and who bore the strains involved in the preparation of this book with fortitude, if not always with patience.

M. J.

Schenectady, New York
August, 1965

CONTENTS

I

THE ISOLATIONISM
OF THE THIRTIES

IN 1935 it became evident that Germany's expansionist ambitions included more than the reoccupation of the Rhineland, that Italy hoped to carve for herself an extensive North African empire, and that Japan sought nothing less than the complete conquest of China. The threat of a major war once more confronted the world, and public opinion in the United States responded with near unanimity. "Ninety-nine Americans out of a hundred," estimated the *Christian Century*, "would today regard as an imbecile anyone who might suggest that, in the event of another European war, the United States should again participate in it." A year later, a poll conducted by the American Institute of Public Opinion set the exact figure at 95 per cent.[1]

This attitude reflected both a general abhorrence of war and the clear assumption that the coming struggle involved no vital interests of the United States and could be settled in Europe and Asia. The Japanese attack on Pearl Harbor on December 7, 1941, disproved this assumption and launched

[1] "A Peace Policy for 1935," *Christian Century*, LII (January, 1935), 40; George Gallup and Claude Robinson, "American Institute of Public Opinion—Surveys, 1935–38," *Public Opinion Quarterly*, II (July, 1938), 388.

this country into the Second World War as an active belligerent. But it did more than that. It led the United States to
change its foreign policy fundamentally, to assume global
political and economic commitments, and to accept consciously a large share of the responsibility for the maintenance of
world peace. The Pearl Harbor attack was not merely the
beginning of a war. It was also the end of a bitter political
and ideological struggle.

The controversy over foreign policy which raged from 1935
to 1941 has frequently been described as a battle over American isolation.[2] This characterization is somewhat misleading.
As a nation devoted to the expansion of its foreign commerce,
as a haven for immigrants, and as a country firmly convinced
that its institutions were to serve as a model for the world,
the United States had never been truly isolated. The relative
geographic isolation it originally enjoyed was steadily dimin-
ished by advances in transportation and communication.
Whatever degree of political isolation existed in the
eighteenth and early nineteenth centuries was destroyed by
America's growth in economic and naval power and its acqui-
sition of overseas colonies.

"The isolation of the United States is at an end," Woodrow
Wilson had already pointed out in 1919, "not because we
chose to go into the politics of the world, but because by the
sheer genius of this people and the growth of our power we
have become a determining factor in the history of mankind
and after you have become a determining factor you cannot
remain isolated, whether you want to or not."[3]

[2]See, for example, Walter Johnson, *The Battle against Isolation*
(Chicago, 1944); William L. Langer and S. E. Gleason, *The Challenge
to Isolation, 1937–1940* (New York, 1952); Donald F. Drummond, *The
Passing of American Neutrality, 1937–1941* (Ann Arbor, 1955).

[3]*The Public Papers of Woodrow Wilson,* Ray Stannard Baker and
W. E. Dodd., eds. (New York and London, 1925–1927), VI, 18–19. The
point that this view was also shared by Wilson's opponents in the

Even though the United States failed during the 1920's to assume the responsibilities that went with its new position and power, it consciously took part in world politics. By participating in various League of Nations conferences, assuming the initiative in efforts at naval disarmament, attempting to maintain the *status quo* in the Far East, and making semiofficial efforts to solve the reparations problem, America demonstrated its awareness that genuine isolation was neither possible nor desirable. This awareness remained. The battle over foreign policy in the thirties was not fought over the continuance or restoration of American isolation. At issue was an isolationism that had narrower, more specific aims.

The bitterness of this conflict and subsequent world events have obscured the isolationist position of the Roosevelt Era by highlighting only its negative aspects: its opposition to certain aspects of foreign trade, to the creation of a military force strong enough to fight a global war, and to those policies of the Roosevelt Administration that aligned the United States increasingly with Great Britain and France. To regard isolationism as pure obstructionism, however, is unfruitful and misleading. Most of the men who fought against American "entanglement" in what they considered to be the affairs of other nations had a positive view of the world and of the role that should be played in it by the United States. They based their arguments on a thorough, if erroneous, analysis of the nature of the crises confronting Europe and Asia, and they carefully considered America's internal problems.

Many isolationist leaders owed their reputations to the vigor with which they had previously supported positive programs:

League fight and by most so-called isolationists during the 1920's is made with considerable force in William A. Williams, "The Legend of Isolationism in the 1920's," *Science and Society*, XVIII (Winter, 1954), 1–20.

John Bassett Moore, whose writings provided much material for Congressional debates on neutrality and whose testimony exerted considerable influence on the deliberations of the Senate Committee on Foreign Relations, had spent a lifetime trying to strengthen and expand the scope of international law.

Senator William E. Borah of Idaho, ranking Republican member of the Foreign Relations Committee and outspoken opponent of all policies he regarded as interventionist, had been instrumental in calling numerous international conferences and had led the fight for ratification of the Kellogg-Briand Pact in 1928.

Senator Gerald P. Nye of North Dakota, whose investigation of the munitions industry provided material effectively used in isolationist argument and propaganda, was heir to the traditions of the Nonpartisan League and of agrarian radicalism in general.

Norman Thomas, a tireless witness before Congressional committees and author of numerous books and pamphlets urging the strictest neutrality in any future war, was, as a Socialist, committed both to programs of internal reform and to the advancement of the international working class.

Charles A. Beard, who lent the weight of his enormous scholarly prestige and the services of his practiced pen freely to the isolationist cause, had devoted much of his life to expounding the necessity for the reorganization of the United States into a democratic commonwealth.

Such men did not approach American foreign policy from a purely negative and obstructionist viewpoint.

Moore, Borah, and Thomas had devoted much of their energy to international problems. Their appearance as spokesmen for isolationism during the thirties strongly suggests that the movement did not aim at literal isolation of the United States from the rest of the world. The cultural ties binding America to Europe were never challenged by the isolationists; nor was the necessity for maintaining diplomatic relations with other countries. No American isolationist made a principle out of cutting off all foreign trade nor seriously advocated trying to attain economic self-sufficiency. None sought to close this country's doors to immigrants or foreign travelers.

True isolation, as maintained by China or Japan in the early nineteenth century, would have required all of these steps. The isolationists of the thirties, however, sought only to preserve the American government's absolute control over its foreign policy by avoiding any long-term political commitments, either actual or implied, to other nations. They advocated a form of unilateralism, a policy of independence in foreign relations which would leave the United States free at all times to act according to the dictates of national self-interest. Speaking before the Council on Foreign Relations in New York on January 8, 1934, Senator Borah stated this case clearly:

In matters of trade and commerce we have never been isolationist and never will be. In matters of finance, unfortunately, we have not been isolationist and never will be. When earthquake and famine, or whatever brings human suffering, visit any part of the human race, we have not been isolationists, and never will be. . . . But in all matters political, in all commitments of any nature or kind, which encroach in the slightest upon the free and unembarrassed action of our people, or which circumscribe their discretion and judgement, we have been free, we have been independent, we have been isolationist.[4]

Not all isolationists shared Borah's views entirely, but none contradicted his basic premises. Some advocated restrictions on wartime trade and commerce because they believed eco-

[4]William E. Borah, *Bedrock* (Washington, 1936), 58.

nomic factors were the major cause of military involvement. "I would rather temporarily abandon all our world commerce," Senator Homer T. Bone, Democrat of Washington and prominent member of the Nye Committee, declared in August, 1935, "than to have this Republic, which my father fought to preserve, destroyed or irreparably injured by another great war."[5] Such sentiments were echoed many times during the ensuing years, but they do not demonstrate the existence of a belief in the intrinsic value of economic isolation.

Some anti-interventionists were more willing than Senator Borah to cooperate with foreign nations or consult with the League of Nations, but none were willing to tie American foreign policy to the decisions reached by international agencies or multinational conferences. Norman Thomas, while urging the United States to cooperate with European efforts to prevent another general war, cautioned at the same time that "we should support no consultative pact that goes beyond the promise to confer."[6]

The isolationists adopted their foreign policy views for a wide variety of reasons that were often contradictory, and never fully agreed among themselves on the methods for implementing these views. They were united, however, by their basic conviction that political commitments tying American policy to the policies of other nations were unnecessary and dangerous. In a world drawing closer together because of interlocking economic interests and military necessity, they sought to preserve for the United States the same independence in foreign affairs it had maintained with relative success during the nineteenth century. In their view, adherence to the foreign policy of the past did not cause the

[5]*Congressional Record,* 74th Cong., 1st sess., 13784 (August 20, 1935).
[6]Norman Thomas, *The Choice Before Us* (New York, 1934), 179.

United States to withdraw from the world nor force it to relinquish its position as defender of the ideals embodied in the Constitution.

It does not [said Borah], and it never has, shrunk from its duty to civilization. It will not disown any obligation which human liberty and human justice impose upon a free people. But it does propose, I venture to prophesy, to determine for itself when civilization is threatened, when there may be a breach of human rights and human liberty sufficient to warrant action, and it proposes also to determine for itself when to act and in what manner it shall discharge the obligations which time and circumstances impose.[7]

The isolationists may therefore be regarded as the true heirs to the American tradition to which they constantly appealed. The attitude of the colonists and the Founding Fathers toward other nations was also based on a belief in the desirability of unilateral action and reflected no desire to cut America off entirely from the Old World. The majority of the early immigrants had, to be sure, crossed the Atlantic in order to turn their backs on the political and religious problems troubling Europe in the seventeenth and eighteenth centuries. "After I had sufficiently seen the European provinces and countries, and the threatening movements of war, and had taken to heart the dire changes and disturbances of the Fatherland," wrote the German Pietist leader Francis Pastorius, "I was impelled through a special guidance from the Almighty, to go to Pennsylvania."[8]

Although the settlers separated themselves from their old homes by three thousand miles of ocean and confronted new problems requiring radically altered methods, they remained

[7]Borah, *op. cit.*, 159.
[8]Quoted in J. Fred Rippy and Angie Debo, "The Historical Background of the American Policy of Isolation," *Smith College Studies in History*, IX (1924), 71.

bound to Europe by ties of kinship, language, law, literature, and trade. They also recognized that ultimately their welfare depended on the outcome of the world-wide struggle between Great Britain and France, in which they consequently played an important and by no means involuntary part. The successful expedition organized independently by Massachusetts in 1745 against the French fortress of Louisbourg on Cape Breton Island, and the military operations in the Ohio Valley that began the Seven Years' War are ample evidence that the majority of colonists believed they had an important stake in "European" wars.[9]

When the American Revolution severed the direct ties of the colonies to Europe, the result was a feeling of independence and national pride and a consequent denigration of the political and social institutions of the Old World. In such an atmosphere a policy of literal isolation could possibly have found favor, and various statements by John Adams, Thomas Jefferson, George Washington, and other leaders of the period are often cited to support the conclusion that such was the case.[10]

Yet Washington's Farewell Address, the most frequently quoted document, does not bear out this contention. Having observed that all the wars of the eighteenth century had been fought for dynastic and imperialist reasons, Washington pointed out that "Europe has a set of primary interests which to us have none or a very remote relation." He therefore urged his countrymen "to steer clear of permanent alliances" and involvement "by artificial ties in the ordinary vicissitudes

[9]For brief but stimulating discussions of this question, see Max Savelle, *Seeds of Liberty* (New York, 1948), 343–351, and Thomas A. Bailey, *A Diplomatic History of the American People,* 3rd ed. (New York, 1946), 2–6.

[10]Compare, J. Fred Rippy, *America and the Strife of Europe* (Chicago, 1938), Chap. I and *passim.*

of her politics and the ordinary combinations and collisions of her friendships and enmities."

The choice of adjectives is significant. Washington did not suggest that the United States shared no interests with the nations of Europe, nor that this country should avoid agreements with European powers to defend common interests. On the contrary, Washington strongly favored the expansion of American commerce through treaties negotiated by the Federal Government, and envisaged future situations in which the new nation might "safely trust to temporary alliances for extraordinary emergencies." The whole address reflects, in fact, the outgoing President's effort to urge caution and self-restraint on a people in no way isolated from Europe's quarrels. He warned of the danger of "inveterate antipathies against particular nations and passionate attachment for others" on the grounds that "an attachment of a small or weak toward a great and powerful nation dooms the former to be the satellite of the latter."[11]

Washington merely drew hardheaded inferences from two circumstances: the United States was too weak to induce any major power of which it might become an ally to consider American interests more than incidentally; and this country's favorable geographic position did not require it to join defensive alliances. Consequently, he felt certain, this country could best serve its interests by adopting a policy of independence which would leave it free to make foreign policy decisions on an *ad hoc* basis.

In the first draft of the Farewell Address, sent by Washington to Alexander Hamilton on May 15, 1796, the President announced his intention to urge upon his countrymen the proposition that "we ourselves are now a distinct Nation the

[11]James D. Richardson, *A Compilation of the Messages and Papers of the Presidents, 1789–1897* (Washington, 1889), I, 221–223.

dignity of which will be absorbed, if not annihilated, if we enlist ourselves (further than our obligations may require) under the banner of any Nation whatsoever." He pointed out that "Nations as well as individuals, act for their own benefit, and not for the benefit of others, unless both interests happen to be assimilated (and when that is the case there requires no contract to bind them together)." Washington concluded that "if there be no engagements on our part, we shall be unembarrassed, and at liberty at all times, to act from circumstances, and the dictates of Justice—sound policy—and our essential Interests."

Hamilton's abstract of points to form an address contains as Point XVI: "The greater rule of our foreign politics ought to be to have as little political connection with foreign Nations" and as a possible addition to it, the phrase "& Cherish the sentiment of *independence.*"[12]

"Avoidance of foreign alliances and entanglements" in Washington's time was, as Samuel Flagg Bemis has pointed out, nothing more than "a question of independence and national sovereignty."[13] It was part of an attempt to secure American freedom of action against the pressures exerted by more powerful European states, but it was not a refusal to play any part in world politics. Far from committing the new nation to permanent isolation, it merely sought to endow the United States with the ability to chart its future foreign policy on the basis of unilateral decisions.

The same basic unilateralism is evident in the Jeffersonian

[12]Felix Gilbert, *To the Farewell Address* (Princeton, 1961), 138–139, 141 (italics in the original). Both Washington's draft and Hamilton's abstract are reprinted in their entirety in the appendix to Gilbert's book.

[13]Samuel Flagg Bemis, "Washington's Farewell Address: A Foreign Policy of Independence," *American Historical Review*, XXXIX (January, 1934), 268; Gilbert sees the address as an idealistic document incorporating the principles of a "new diplomacy." See Gilbert, *op. cit.*, 134–136.

dictum that the key principle of American foreign policy was "peace, commerce and honest friendship with all nations, entangling alliances with none."[14] When Jefferson proclaimed a general embargo on shipments to belligerents in 1807, his purpose was not to isolate America by cutting off its foreign trade. He hoped, rather, to coerce foreign governments into recognition of the traditional rights of an independent nation through the application of economic pressure. The restrictions on trade were thus part of an active policy and, in effect, an instrument for intervening in world affairs. The intervention was, however, unilateral, and did not involve direct cooperation with other nations. Jefferson's action conformed to American tradition, but it was not indicative of a policy of isolation.

Fifteen years later, to be sure, Jefferson, in reply to President Monroe's request for advice on whether to join Great Britain to counter the threat of the Holy Alliance against the newly independent nations of Latin America, wrote these often quoted words:

Our first and fundamental maxim should be, never to entangle ourselves in the broils of Europe. Our second, never to suffer Europe to meddle with cis-Atlantic affairs. America, North and South, has a set of interests distinct from those of Europe, and peculiarly her own. She should therefore have a system of her own, separate and apart from that of Europe. While the last is laboring to become the domicile of despotism, our endeavors should surely be, to make our hemisphere that of freedom.[15]

Yet, in the same letter, Jefferson drew from these maxims

[14]Richardson, *op. cit.*, I, 323.

[15]Jefferson to Monroe, dtd October 24, 1823, in Adrienne Koch and William Peden, eds., *The Life and Selected Writings of Thomas Jefferson*, Modern Library Edition (New York, 1944), 708. This passage is quoted, for example, with insignificant omissions, in Marcus Cunliffe, *The Nation Takes Shape, The Chicago History of American Civilization*, Daniel J. Boorstin, ed., (Chicago, 1959), 65–66, as summing up "underlying American attitudes to foreign policy."

the conclusion that the United States should, under then
existing circumstances, ally herself with Great Britain.

Great Britain [he insisted] is the nation which can do us the
most harm of any one, or all on earth; and with her on our side
we need not fear the whole world. With her then, we should most
sedulously cherish a cordial friendship; and nothing would tend
more to knit our affections than to be fighting once more, side
by side, in the same cause.

The author of the Declaration of Independence was not
motivated by concern for the British Empire. He saw clearly
that "the war in which the present proposition might engage
us should that be its consequence, is not her war, but ours,"
and that its object would be "to introduce and establish the
American system of keeping out of our land all foreign
powers." "And if, to facilitate this," he added, "we can effect
a division in the body of the European powers, and draw over
to our side its most powerful member, surely we should do it."

Not only did this alliance seem to Jefferson to increase
America's chances to further its own interests in a potential
future war, but it also offered a good chance to prevent the
war itself. "With Great Britain withdrawn from their scale
and shifted into that of our two continents, all Europe combined would not undertake such a war."[16]

Jefferson was certainly not arguing for isolation, for he
was willing to engage in power politics to attain American
ends. As long as the United States could maintain its freedom
of choice, its capacity to continue acting unilaterally over the
long term, even a temporary military alliance did not appear
to Jefferson to be an entanglement.

In the specific matter of the British alliance, Monroe and
Secretary of State John Quincy Adams overruled Jefferson.
In general, however, the United States acted in the spirit of

¹⁶Koch and Peden, eds., *op. cit.*, 709.

Washington and Jefferson throughout the nineteenth century. It did not isolate itself from world affairs. On the contrary, it encouraged revolutions in the Spanish colonies and sought to protect their new independence with the Monroe Doctrine. It attempted to conquer Canada in 1812 and vied with Great Britain for the Oregon Territory in the 1840's. It followed the progress of the European revolutions of 1830 and 1848 with sympathetic interest and treated the Hungarian revolutionary Louis Kossuth to a hero's welcome. It joined in the imperialist scramble of the late nineteenth century and went to war with Spain over the independence of Cuba. It was instrumental in bringing Japan, a truly isolated nation, into contact with the world. It enunciated the Open Door Policy, which directly affected the colonial ambitions of the powers then engaged in establishing spheres of influence in China.

In all these enterprises, the United States acted alone. Although it fought Great Britain at the close of the Napoleonic Wars, it did so without allying itself with France. Despite dependence on the British navy for making the Monroe Doctrine effective, it never made certain of the support of that fleet by formal treaty. It refused, despite Kossuth's eloquent pleas, to give more than lip service to the oppressed Magyars.

During the entire nineteenth century, the United States limited its treaty making to the settlement of disputes concerning boundaries, immigration, fishing and sealing rights, and similar matters. The only possible exception, the Clayton-Bulwer Treaty of 1850 with Great Britain, which limited this country's freedom of action in regard to the construction of a canal across the Isthmus of Panama, has been called "the most persistently unpopular pact ever concluded by the United States."[17]

[17]Bailey, *op. cit.*, 292.

The geographic position of the United States and the distribution of power among the nations of the world during the nineteenth century made it possible for this country to pursue what it considered its best interests without directly aligning itself with any nation or bloc. In a limited sense, such a course may be regarded as one of isolation. But it can be more accurately defined as the achievement, to an enviable degree, of the ability to act independently in foreign affairs.

"It is," as President Grover Cleveland explained in 1885, "the policy of independence, favored by our position and defended by our known love of justice and by our power. It is the policy of peace suitable to our interests. It is the policy of neutrality, rejecting any share in foreign broils and ambitions upon other continents and rejecting their intrusion here. It is the policy of Monroe and of Washington and Jefferson—'Peace, commerce and honest friendship with all nations; entangling alliances with none.' "[18]

The isolationists of the 1930's believed that the conditions of their time were still suitable for such a policy. They realized that some things had changed. The United States had developed into a major power and acquired overseas possessions. Rapid means of transportation and communication posed problems that had not existed in the nineteenth century, and military technology had made frightening progress. But they were convinced that the possible effects of these changed conditions could be neutralized by adopting precautionary domestic legislation and cultivating proper attitudes in the American people.

In the course of adapting their concept of foreign policy to the requirements of the twentieth century, they were compelled to espouse schemes tending to abridge the commercial ties which Washington and Jefferson had deemed essential

[18]Richardson, *op. cit.*, VIII, 301.

and to surrender rights the United States had vigorously defended since its founding. Nonetheless they held fast in principle to the traditional American concept of unilateralism. At the same time, the isolationists of the thirties modified their determination to retain full freedom of choice in foreign policy decisions by their conviction that the domestic crisis and the course of world events made the primary foreign policy interest of the United States the avoidance of war.

These two principles—unilateralism in foreign affairs and the avoidance of war as the *sine qua non* of a beneficial foreign policy—are not necessarily interconnected. It is quite possible to regard preservation of peace as the ultimate purpose of foreign policy and favor, at the same time, a system of collective security or the establishment of supranational organizations. On the other hand, a belief in unilateralism is perfectly consistent with an aggressive foreign policy that accepts war as one of its chief instruments.

It is easier, in fact, to argue that the two principles are incompatible. One insists on freedom of choice while the other predetermines the choice on the most important issue of all, peace or war. One establishes the primacy of a goal while the other limits the steps that can be taken toward that goal to those which can be taken unilaterally. This incompatibility became apparent in the years after 1935, as the isolationists sought to apply both principles to specific situations. Ultimately, it was a major factor in the decline of isolationism.

In 1935, however, the combination of unilateralism and *ad hoc* pacifism seemed logical. Washington had expressed the hope that, if the advice contained in the Farewell Address was followed, the time would not be far distant "when we may choose peace or war, as our interest, guided by justice, shall counsel."[19] The isolationists believed the thirties to be such a time and they chose peace. They did so partly from pacifist principle, but more generally because they foresaw that participation in the coming war would lead to permanent entanglement in world affairs. They were afraid that the progress of technology would subject the United States to the horrors of modern warfare which some of them had experienced in the trenches of France twenty years earlier. They feared that American institutions, already weakened by the economic crisis, could not withstand the shock of total mobilization. They believed that the United States could best fulfill its historic mission by becoming an unscarred island of sanity in the shell-shocked postwar world.

Washington had never ruled out war as an instrument of American foreign policy and Jefferson had favored joining Great Britain in a war against the Holy Alliance. The United States had fought France in 1798, Great Britain in 1812, Mexico in 1846, and Spain in 1898. A man so clearly within the isolationist tradition as Grover Cleveland had threatened Great Britain with war over the Venezuela boundary as late as 1895. But the isolationists of the thirties regarded war and entanglement as virtually synonymous terms. By opposing both, they were able to appeal simultaneously to national egotism and humanitarian sentiments. They could attract support from genuine pacifists, from the politically apathetic who accepted isolationism as a way to remain uninvolved in world affairs without sacrificing either their sense of virtue or their security, and from those who, though primarily concerned with maintaining America's freedom of action and thus adhering to the unilateralist tradition of Washington and Jefferson, were happy to accept noninvolvement in war as an unexpected bonus.

[19]*Ibid.*, I, 222.

American isolationism during the thirties was basically "the nation's insistence upon the sole authorship of its legal acts" and thus "the non-judicial counterpart of sovereignty,"[20] combined with a policy of subordinating virtually all other interests to that of avoiding war. It was a general American sentiment; not, as sometimes pictured, simply a Midwestern phenomenon born of the insularity of the American interior. Nor was it merely a partisan movement aimed at undermining the popularity and prestige of President Franklin D. Roosevelt. Isolationist leaders had diverse backgrounds, advocated varied courses of action, and shared few domestic interests. But men from New York and California, from Idaho and Texas, men whose political creeds ranged from the socialism of Norman Thomas to the conservative Republicanism of Herbert Hoover, made common cause in the field of foreign policy because they believed in unilateralism and feared the effects of war on the United States.

Geographic insularity and political partisanship help to explain why anti-interventionist sentiment was more prevalent in the Republican Middle West than in any other section of the country, and why a disproportionate number of spokesmen for isolationism came from that region. At the same time, the affinity between the tenets of isolationism and the presuppositions underlying various forms of agrarian radicalism colored the Midwestern response to the wars in Europe and Asia.[21] In the final analysis, however, the basic assump-

[20] Albert K. Weinberg, "The Historical Meaning of the American Doctrine of Isolation," *American Political Science Review,* XXXIV (June, 1940), 540.

[21] Ray Allen Billington, "The Origins of Middle Western Isolationism," *Political Science Quarterly,* LX (March, 1945), 63–64; the data compiled by Billington also indicate that while the Congressional delegations from the Midwest were markedly more isolationist than those from other sections, the sectional differences in public opinion, while present, were less pronounced. Wayne S. Cole, while recognizing the

tions of those who opposed greater American participation in
world affairs were more comprehensive and more complex,
transcending both regional and partisan interests.

Isolationist legislators were elected in all sections of the
country and represented both major parties. Democratic
Senators Bone of Washington and Bennett C. Clark of
Missouri were among the most ardent champions of neutrality legislation designed to make involvement in war impossible. Their Democratic colleague, Representative Louis
Ludlow of Indiana, was the chief sponsor and most persistent
advocate of a constitutional amendment that, in his view,
would have prevented the United States from ever engaging
in a foreign conflict. Democratic Congressman Maury
Maverick of Texas was also for some years an isolationist
spokesman of note. Although many Republicans holding isolationist views came from the Midwest, Senator Hiram W.
Johnson of California and Representatives Hamilton Fish,
Jr., of New York and George Holden Tinkham of Massachusetts spoke for areas far removed from the American
interior. And the largely pro-Roosevelt *New Republic,* as
much as the bitterly anti-Roosevelt *Saturday Evening Post,*
can be classified as an isolationist publication.[22]

---

importance of other elements, places great stress on the agrarian bias
in isolationism. See his *Senator Gerald P. Nye and American Foreign
Relations* (Minneapolis, 1962), 6–13, 227–235. The predisposition to
isolationism of an agricultural area threatened with rapid industrializa-
tion is suggested in Charles O. Lerche, Jr., *The Uncertain South* (Chicago, 1964), 288–290.

[22]A Gallup Poll released on April 14, 1939, showed that 57 per cent
of those asked "Do you think the law should be changed so that we
could sell war materials to England and France in case of war?"
answered in the affirmative. Results were very nearly the same in all
sections of the country, and Republicans responded much like Democrats. A copy of the results was sent to Senator Key Pittman by the
editor of the *Daily Republic* of Mitchell, S.D. See Ronald to Pittman,
dtd April 14, 1939, in Senate Records (Committee on Foreign Relations),

The impossibility of explaining isolationism fully in terms of geography or political partisanship has led to an effort to account for it on the basis of ethnic considerations. The researches of Samuel Lubell into the statistics of the presidential elections of 1920, 1940, and 1948 led him to the conclusion that the factors primarily responsible for American isolationism were "the existence of pro-German and anti-British ethnic prejudices" and the exploitation of these prejudices by an opposition political party.[23] If applied to the entire isolationist tradition, this explanation is clearly inadequate. Washington's Farewell Address shows a strong anti-French bias and must therefore be regarded, at least by implication, as pro-British. Moreover, isolationism antedates both the arrival of the majority of the German settlers in America and the formation of the German Empire. Even when applied only to the period which Lubell has investigated, his thesis is more useful for explaining the support given isolationist candidates by many German-Americans and Irish-Americans than for revealing the bases of the movement itself.

After 1933, it was apparent that if the United States joined in a future European war, it would inevitably be on the side of Great Britain and France against Germany. This fact greatly concerned German diplomats in America and they constantly reflected it in their reports to Berlin.[24] Many Americans of German descent, regardless of their views

---

File 76A-F 9. Editorials from 42 newspapers in 20 states and all sections of the country taking the same view are collected in House Foreign Affairs Committee, *American Neutrality Policy; Editorials,* 76th Cong., 1st sess. (1939).

[23]Samuel Lubell, *The Future of American Politics,* 2nd ed., rev. (New York, 1956), 141.

[24]See, for example, Dieckhoff to Foreign Office, dtd December 7, 1937, or Thomsen to Foreign Office, dtd September 12, 1938, in *Akten zur deutschen auswärtigen Politik, 1918–1945,* Series D, I *(Von Neurath zu Ribbentrop,* Baden Baden, 1951), 593–594.

concerning Hitler's Third Reich, retained family ties and
sentimental attachments that made such a course seem undesirable. Similarly, a large percentage of Irish-Americans
preferred nonentanglement to war on the side of England.
However, such persons did not constitute a large part of the
majority holding isolationist views in 1935 and the years
immediately thereafter. A poll conducted by the American
Institute of Public Opinion in October, 1937, found 69 per
cent of the population in favor of stricter neutrality legislation giving less discretion to the President. They were, therefore, at least implicit supporters of the isolationist position.
Yet, six months later, 55 per cent chose England as the European country they liked best and another 11 per cent chose
France. Only 8 per cent expressed a preference for Germany
and 4 per cent for Ireland.[25]

Lubell himself has cited economic and educational factors
that influenced votes and perhaps helped to produce an isolationist response.[26] It is likely that these were more important than ethnic considerations, and that emotional judg-
ments unrelated to ethnic background also played a prominent role.[27] Moreover, none of the elections examined by
Lubell turned solely, or even largely, on the issue of isolationism. In 1920, the "solemn referendum" that Wilson had
called for did not materialize. In 1948, both candidates were
confirmed internationalists. In the most relevant election,
that of 1940, many German-American voters probably preferred the Republican candidate Wendell Willkie not for his
views on foreign policy, which differed little from those of

[25]Gallup and Robinson, *op. cit.*, 388, 389.
[26]Lubell, *op. cit.*, 145–146, 155–161.
[27]Emotional and psychological bases for isolationism are examined in
Bernard Fensterwald, Jr., "The Anatomy of American 'Isolationism'
and Expansionism. II," *Journal of Conflict Resolution*, II (December,
1958), 280–307.

President Roosevelt, but rather for his German-American background.

An examination of isolationist policies and the statements of the movement's leading spokesmen confirms that isolationism during the period just before the Second World War was not essentially an ethnic matter. The two-year cash-and-carry provisions of the Neutrality Act of 1937, as well as other measures accepted willingly by the isolationists, were favorable to Great Britain. The attitude of Senator Nye and some of his isolationist colleagues toward the Spanish Civil War was significantly more anti-German and anti-Italian than the official policy of the United States Government.[28] Although the isolationist movement was supported by the German government and its agents in this country, and even though some American isolationists, notably Charles A. Lindbergh, had a distinct pro-German bias, most anti-interventionists were friendly to Great Britain. They favored helping her as much as possible, so long as the risk of involvement in war could be avoided.

"We wish to aid Britain," wrote Herbert Hoover in an article strongly urging the United States to remain out of the war and painting a dire picture of the domestic results of American intervention. "I am for aid to Britain. I am against naval or military intervention in this war," added Robert Maynard Hutchins, then Chancellor of the University of Chicago and prominent member of the America First Committee. And Senator Burton K. Wheeler, Democrat of Montana who has often been charged with harboring pro-German sentiments, stated at the same time: "No blood but English flows through my veins or any of my family. And next to being pro-American I am pro-English."[29]

[28]See below, Chapter VI.
[29]Herbert C. Hoover, "The Immediate Relation of the United States to this War," Robert Maynard Hutchins, "War and the Four Freedoms,"

American isolationism was obviously not limited to a single geographic area or one major political party and cannot be considered merely the product of the prejudices of large ethnic groups. Any attempt to define it in socioeconomic terms must also prove futile. It is possible that isolationist organizations derived much of their support from certain segments of the business community and that most of the votes received by isolationist candidates were cast by farmers and owners of small businesses. Attempts to document such a thesis would require an organization by organization and county by county investigation. Were it undertaken, it would only show the socioeconomic groups to which isolationism had the greatest appeal, without necessarily yielding an explanation for the sentiment itself.[30]

Isolationism transcended socioeconomic divisions and was supported by Americans of widely divergent status. On the subject of America's relationship to the conflicts in Europe

---

and Burton K. Wheeler, "What If Germany Seizes the British Fleet?" in Nancy Schoonmaker and Doris Fielding Reid, eds., *We Testify* (New York, 1941), 10, 37, 187–188. The question of Wheeler's bias is discussed at some length in Arthur M. Schlesinger, Jr., *The Politics of Upheaval, The Age of Roosevelt*, III (Boston, 1960), 141–142. Although it is implied there that Wheeler was pro-German, the evidence presented is of the "hearsay" variety. In an open letter addressed "Dear Friend" and written during the Lend-Lease debate in 1941, Wheeler stated "I am perfectly willing to aid Great Britain." A copy of this letter is in the Amos Pinchot Papers, Box 69. Representative Hamilton Fish and Senator Robert A. Taft expressed the same sentiment in speeches delivered on January 21, and January 25, 1941. Copies in Amos Pinchot Papers, Box 69, and Charles L. McNary Papers, Box 14.

[30]The only thorough study of an isolationist organization is Wayne S. Cole, *America First* (Madison, Wisconsin, 1953). Cole has investigated the leadership of the Committee, the sources of its financial support and the geographical distribution of its membership. He points out, however, that other isolationist organizations had different bases of support and, in any case, makes no attempt to analyze the socioeconomic status of the rank and file. See especially 30–33 and 69–74.

and Asia, Socialist intellectuals shared the views of the American Legion. The Chicago Federation of Labor agreed with Henry Ford. Midwestern Progressives who had spent their lives fighting against Eastern banking interests espoused ideas on neutrality legislation first expounded by Bernard Baruch. Herbert Hoover's arguments were supported in the pages of the *New Republic*.

Isolationism owed whatever unity it had during the thirties not to geography, nor politics, nor class structure, nor ethnic background, but to faith in unilateralism and fear of war. On the one hand, isolationism was a symptom of national egotism and the universal aspiration for complete freedom of action, buttressed by the unique experience of the United States during the nineteenth century. On the other hand, it was a fearful response to a modern technology that made involvement in a new world conflict appear hopelessly entangling and fatal to American institutions.

The isolationists' basic unilateralism is clearly shown by the difference in their attitudes toward the crises in Europe and in Asia. They opposed American involvement in both areas, but their major fears arose out of the European situation. In part this was undoubtedly due to their assumption that a Far Eastern war could never be a land war for the United States and would thus not require a degree of mobilization which might threaten American democracy. More significantly, however, a war in Asia was only conceivable against Japan, the single major power in the area. In such a war the United States could function quite independently and ran no risk of having its wartime or postwar policies "dictated" by powerful allies. In Europe, on the other hand, war would mean a *de facto* alliance with Great Britain and France, and thus raise the specter of substantial and perhaps permanent entanglement in European affairs. Most isolationists, therefore, agreed with Senator Taft that "it is not nearly so dangerous to become involved in a war in the Pacific as in the European war," though they sought to avoid even the former out of fear that a war in the Pacific might soon become part of a more general conflict.[31]

The great resurgence of overt isolationism in the thirties resulted from an unusual combination of political, military, economic, and ideological factors. Foremost was the widespread realization that the activities of Germany, Italy, and Japan would probably lead to a major war in the near future and that, unless appropriate measures were taken, the United States would ultimately be involved. Japan's advance into China and the appointment, in October, 1931, of an American representative to join the Council of the League of Nations in its consideration of the Manchurian crisis seemed to presage such a development. Isolationist newspapers immediately raised the alarm and voiced strong objections to the State Department's action. The steps Germany took toward rearmament in 1933 and 1934 indicated that future trouble would not be limited to the Far East. In August of the following year, Senator Nye found the world "topsy-turvy and quite definitely headed for more war."[32]

The second important factor was the Great Depression. A relationship between isolationism and economic difficulties was observed by Lubell, and Ray Allen Billington has pointed out that it was during the last, crisis-ridden decade of the nineteenth century that isolationism came to the Midwest along with Populism and the demand for the free coinage of silver.[33]

    [31]Robert A. Taft, "Our Foreign Policy," *Vital Speeches of the Day*, VI (March, 1940), 348. See also Borchard to Senator George W. Norris, dtd January 7, 1938, Norris Papers, Tray 104, Box 4.
    [32]Bailey, *op. cit.*, 724–725; *Congressional Record*, 74th Cong., 1st sess., 14535 (August 24, 1935).
    [33]Lubell, *op. cit.*, 145–146; Billington, *op. cit.*, 50–53.

The links between depression and isolationism are not difficult to find. People confronted by widespread unemployment, lengthening breadlines, and increasing poverty understandably pay little attention to questions of foreign policy, but tend to demand that the nation's entire energy be devoted to the solution of domestic problems. Faced with an immediate crisis at home, few persons consider carefully the future dangers being generated in distant places.

A poll conducted in December, 1936, to determine "the most vital issue before the American people today" ranked unemployment first and economy in government second. When Republican voters were asked in December, 1937, on what issue they would appeal for support if they were candidates for public office, economy in government spending, restoration of business prosperity, and reduction of taxes were the most frequently mentioned. Not until May, 1939, was the problem of keeping out of war, let alone any other issue involving foreign policy, listed as the most serious American problem. By that time, the worst of the Depression had passed.[34]

Foreign policy problems were not a primary interest of the American people when isolationist sentiment was strongest. Even when the activities of other nations posed a potential threat to the security of the United States, they were regarded by many as distractions diverting the Administration from the country's "real" problems. In view of the existing economic distress, it seemed proper to most Americans to consider America first and to ignore the dangerous world situation as long as possible. When this could no longer be done, the simplest course appeared to be that of insulating the United States against these dangers by means of restrictive neutrality

[34]Gallup and Robinson, *op. cit.*, 381, 383; "American Institute of Public Opinion—Surveys, 1938–1939," *Public Opinion Quarterly*, III (October, 1939), 595–596.

legislation designed to reduce direct contact with belligerent powers.

The Depression also tended to deflate confidence in the strength of the United States and the effective carrying out of its historic mission. Faced with evidence that much was wrong at home, many persons abandoned the traditional belief that American institutions should serve as a model for the world. Others reasoned that the economic crisis had so sapped the nation's strength it would be futile to intervene in international affairs. Both lines of thought led to isolationist conclusions, which appeared all the more attractive because it could be argued that refraining from intervention abroad and concentrating on the solution of domestic problems would enable the United States to regain its influence and fulfill its historic mission in a postwar world requiring aid and guidance.

Finally, the Depression increased popular distrust of bankers and big business. Since these two groups had the largest direct stake in foreign trade and in maintaining active relations with other nations, some of their members were among the leading supporters of a foreign policy designed to safeguard America's overseas economic interests. The line of action they favored risked more general entanglement in European and Asian affairs. Advocacy of this policy by these basically unpopular interest groups helped discredit the policy they supported. The isolationists were able to use the effective, though specious, argument that meddling in world affairs merely insured profits for bankers and businessmen who were war's chief beneficiaries, and therefore its chief advocates.

Any additional impetus besides the threat of war and the misery of the Depression needed to produce a resurgence of isolationism was provided by the spread of so-called revisionist thinking about America's role in the First World War.

The entry of the United States into the war of 1914–1918 was not necessarily a reversal of traditional policy. In 1917, most Americans believed war against Germany was justified by the U-boat attacks on American shipping and by a whole series of atrocities which, though not directed against this country, still violated many of the nation's basic principles. American entry into the war, of its own volition and to defend its rights and beliefs, could be regarded as a unilateral act even though the situation required close association with Great Britain and France to achieve the swiftest possible victory. No such unilateralist construction could be put on President Wilson's plan for joining the League of Nations. Significantly, opposition to this permanent commitment to international cooperation was far more widespread, and ultimately more effective, than opposition to going to war.

Almost as soon as the war was over, however, the idea that America had participated of its own free will and in defense of its own interests was challenged. In July, 1920, Sidney B. Fay began a series of articles in the *American Historical Review* controverting the prevailing opinion that Germany had been primarily responsible for the First World War. His revelations undermined the belief that the United States had fought for good and against evil and gave rise to the idea that this country had been tricked by other nations into participating in the conflict. Fay's further examination of material from Russian, Austrian, German, and British archives ultimately resulted in his *The Origins of the World War,* published in 1928. This influential work demonstrated that the causes and purposes of the war were quite different from those the American people were led to accept in 1917.[35]

[35]Sidney B. Fay, "New Light on the Origins of the World War," *American Historical Review,* XXV (July, 1920), 616–639 and XXVI (October, 1920, and January, 1921), 37–53, 225–234; *The Origins of the World War* (New York, 1928), *passim.*

Fay did not use his findings to reassess the policies of the
Wilson Administration, but others did. Frederick Bausman,
a Washington jurist, bitterly blamed France for the outbreak
of the war in a volume that also asserted American intervention had been due entirely to Allied trickery. John Kenneth
Turner based a book on a re-evaluation of the war-guilt
question and blamed both President Wilson and "Wall
Street" for what was to him the unwarranted and unwise
declaration of war by the United States. Under the pen name
"Historicus," Albert Jay Nock, writing in the *Freeman*, of
which he was editor, absolved Germany of all blame and
implied that American efforts on behalf of the guilty Allies
had been a grievous error. Published in pamphlet form in
1922 under the title *The Myth of a Guilty Nation*, his articles
were widely distributed and uncommonly effective in shaping
public opinion.[36]

Chief among those who used Fay's conclusions to discredit
the role played by the United States in the First World War
was Harry Elmer Barnes. In two book reviews written for the
New Republic, he took sharp issue with the position, taken
by E. R. Turner in *Europe since 1870* and Charles Downer
Hazen in a new edition of *Europe since 1815*, that this
country had fought to protect itself against further depreda-
tions by German submarines and to rid the world of the
specter of German militarism. Allied propaganda and unwise
economic entanglements had so confused the United States,
he maintained, that the country yielded to the prodding of
pro-British officials like Secretary of State Robert Lansing
and foolishly entered the war. This thesis was expanded in

[36]Frederick Bausman, *Let France Explain* (London, 1922), *passim;*
John Kenneth Turner, *Shall It Be Again?* (New York, 1922), esp. 20–25
and 256–271; Selig Adler, "The War-Guilt Question and American
Disillusionment, 1918–1928," *Journal of Modern History*, XXIII
(March, 1951), 11–12.

subsequent articles appearing in *Current History* and *Christian Century*, and was put into definitive form in Barnes's *The Genesis of the World War*, published in 1926.[37]

Amid the general disillusionment of the twenties, these views were widely accepted. Bausman's second book pictured not only France, but all European nations, as unscrupulously selfish and pursuing aims inimical to the best interests of the United States. His conclusions were based largely on his interpretation of the lesson provided by the First World War. "The Allies beguiled us into this war by false propaganda, concealing both the origins of the war and their secret profits," he wrote, "while we did everything we could to aid them and got nothing by way of compensation."[38]

C. Hartley Grattan, a student of Barnes's, expressed in *Why We Fought* the opinion that America had been duped into entering the war through ignorance of the true aspirations of the Allies, that American bankers had been pro-British from the outset and had actively wanted war for their own purposes in 1917, and that false and misleading propaganda had played a crucial role in molding public opinion to favor United States entry.[39]

The revisionists generally argued that America's entry into the war had been brought about by direct and indirect Allied pressure and by the machinations of bankers, brokers, and businessmen who had unwisely tied American prosperity to the cause of Great Britain and France. To those who accepted this thesis, Wilson seemed to have abandoned the

[37]Drummond, *op. cit.*, 2–23; Harry Elmer Barnes, "Why America Entered the War," *Christian Century*, XLII (November, 1925), 1441–1444 and *The Genesis of the World War* (New York, 1926), *passim*.

[38]Frederick Bausman, *Facing Europe* (New York and London, 1926), 321.

[39]C. Hartley Grattan, *Why We Fought* (New York, 1929), *passim*, esp. Chap. I and 80–82, 131–132 and 400.

traditional policy of avoiding entanglements and, by permitting the United States to be manipulated for the benefit
of other nations, to have espoused the very course against
which Washington and the other Founding Fathers had
warned. The provisions of the Treaty of Versailles and the
course of world events after 1918 could be used to discredit
Wilson's apparent breach of tradition.

American intervention had neither ended the threat of
war nor made the world safe for democracy. The world-wide
economic crisis could be blamed on the dislocation produced
by the war, and America's involvement in the Depression
on its participation in the conflict. Thus, by removing the
onus of war-guilt from Germany, the revisionists started a
sequence of historical analysis that ultimately strengthened
isolationist sentiment and offered documentation for the
utterances of isolationist spokesmen.[40]

The claim that departure from unilateralism led to participation in a general war, and the fact that participation
in this war very nearly resulted in permanent entanglement
in world affairs through the League of Nations, did much
to encourage the idea that involvement in any future war
would lead to permanent international commitments and the
end of an independent foreign policy. This association promoted the combination of unilateralism and pseudo pacifism
characteristic of the isolationism of the thirties. The American revisionist view of the First World War was expanded by
the isolationists into a general doctrine regarding all wars. As
a result, they saw in the events of the thirties merely a "deadly
parallel" to what had happened before and failed to appreciate the differences that existed.

The spread of revisionist thinking, combined with the
effects of the Depression and the threat of war in Europe and

[40]Adler reaches substantially the same conclusion in *op. cit.*, 27–28.

Asia, produced a climate of opinion in America that made all dealings with foreign nations suspect. An isolationist policy appealed not only to those who had always questioned the wisdom of increased American participation in world affairs, but also to the disappointed idealists who had earlier supported internationalism. Isolationism was supported by those who saw the need for immediate attention to domestic problems in order to save the nation from socialism or communism, as well as by those who believed a break with capitalism necessary to reestablish prosperity. Above all, it won the almost unanimous approval of the politically apathetic who did not want the affairs of the world to intrude into lives already complicated by the economic crisis in the United States.

Isolationism declined only as domestic difficulties became less acute while the threat posed by Germany, Italy, and Japan appeared, by comparison, to gain immediacy. The outbreak of war in September, 1939, caused most Americans to question the adequacy of a policy of unilateralism for the defense of American interests. Axis successes led many to conclude there were greater threats to the future of this country than involvement in war.

Those who continued to support isolationism after 1939, however, held firm in the belief that the United States was once more being tricked into an unjustified departure from its traditional policies. They still maintained that the true interests of this country would best be served by remaining aloof from what they regarded as the affairs of other nations.

II

VARIETIES OF ISOLATIONISM

DURING the period before America's entry into the Second World War, the isolationists neither held to a homogeneous ideology nor were members of an organized movement. They followed varied, sometimes contradictory paths and seldom agreed on common policies. Although a number of isolationist organizations, such as the National Council for the Prevention of War and the Women's International League for Peace and Freedom, were active throughout the thirties, and others, including the American Peace Mobilization and the Keep America Out of War Congress, were formed during the decade, no serious effort to speak with a single voice was made until the formation of the America First Committee in 1940. Even then, there was no real unity. Many isolationist organizations were continuously at odds with America First, and some of the existing divisions were even apparent in the Committee's leadership. Such disparate figures as Charles A. Lindbergh and Alice Roosevelt Longworth, Chester Bowles and John T. Flynn, served at one time or another on its national committee.[1]

[1]Wayne S. Cole, *America First* (Madison, Wisconsin, 1953), 21–23, 75–79.

The disagreement in isolationist ranks over specific policies becomes particularly apparent in two 1937 magazine surveys. From February through April, *Living Age* conducted a symposium of over a thousand "distinguished American men and women" on the steps to be taken by Congress or the Secretary of State to preserve neutrality in the event of a general European war. Only 15.1 per cent of those participating believed America should not be neutral, while 19.5 per cent felt that it could not remain so. Of the sixteen suggestions most often made by those who believed neutrality to be both possible and desirable, imposing a strict embargo on trade and credit was favored by 50.4 per cent. No other proposal appealed to more than a quarter of those responding.

Neutrality

Only 4.9 per cent advocated complete isolation, 5.7 per cent favored the Ludlow Amendment for a national referendum to precede any declaration of war, 8.3 per cent were for the suppression of foreign war propaganda, and 9.1 per cent wanted the confiscation of war profits; 25.9 per cent, clearly nonisolationist, believed that American neutrality could best be preserved through support of an international system of collective security, and 7.5 per cent favored giving the President a free hand in the conduct of foreign affairs.[2]

Collective security wanted by 25%

At the same time, *Forum* reported the results from a questionnaire sent, with the cooperation of the Foreign Policy Association, to "outstanding observers of foreign affairs." On the subject of the policies the United States should pursue in order to avoid being drawn into a future European war, the responding isolationists displayed markedly divergent opinions.

"My program of action for the perils of the Far East and of Europe," wrote Charles A. Beard, "is to preserve neutrality

[2] "American Neutrality," *The Living Age,* CCCLI (February, 1937), 555–556.

and to preserve it by drastic limitations on selling munitions and lending money to all belligerents." Publisher Frank E. Gannett saw the necessity for "complete isolation from belligerent nations and nations doing business with belligerents." Harry W. Colmery, National Commander of the American Legion, advocated a universal military service plan and an impregnable national defense. All three apparently placed their faith in some sort of Congressional action. Yet the liberal journalist Oswald Garrison Villard of the *Nation* felt that the "greatest safeguard would be having a man in the White House firmly and immovably resolved not to let the country get into war under any conditions whatsoever," and W. W. Waymack, editor of the Des Moines *Register and Tribune*, proposed, among other things, setting up a "board of eminent historians, as emotionless as could be got, to issue periodical statements emphasizing the cost, the futility, and the horrors of war."[3]

Only when world events defined foreign-policy issues more sharply, and the realities of domestic politics came to limit the number of practical alternatives, did various areas of agreement finally develop. On the basis of this crystallization of attitudes, the isolationists of the period can be roughly divided into five groups. The divisions are not always sharp and there is significant overlapping. Many isolationists shifted their positions and have to be included in several groups. Others who at some time appeared as isolationist spokesmen came to support the foreign policy of President Roosevelt even before Pearl Harbor. Nevertheless, foreign-oriented isolationists can be distinguished from other types and the rest can be divided into the belligerent, the timid, the radical, and the conservative.

Foreign-oriented isolationists were those whose views were

[3]"How to Stay Out of War," *Forum*, XCVII (February 1937), 90–95.

determined primarily by sympathy for the Axis Powers or the Soviet Union. Belligerent isolationists believed in vigorous defense of American rights, reliance on international law, and strict adherence to the unilateral foreign policy of the nineteenth century. Timid isolationists were prepared to surrender some traditional rights in order to minimize direct contact with foreign nations at war and thus avoid entanglements. Radical isolationists sought to keep out of war at all costs in order to facilitate the establishment of a new social order in America. Conservative isolationists saw war as the final blow to the old order whose institutions and traditions they were desperately attempting to save. Acting from different motives and advocating varying methods, all but the foreign-oriented shared certain ideas and assumptions. This common ground was the basis for American isolationism in the years before the Second World War.

Throughout the 1930's, persons whose primary motive was to further the best interests of one or more foreign powers, rather than of the United States, were active in the isolationist movement. Since it was likely that a future war would pit Germany, Italy, and Japan against Great Britain and France, and that the only possibility for American intervention was on the side of the latter, those favoring fascism, national socialism, or establishment of the Greater East Asia Co-Prosperity Sphere campaigned against American intervention. Some may even be classed as foreign agents.

Poet-propagandist George Sylvester Viereck, for example, had acted on behalf of the German Empire during the First World War. A naturalized citizen who had been brought to the United States at the age of four, he had graduated from the College of the City of New York in 1906 as class poet. During the First World War, he had interrupted his literary career to engage in propaganda for the land of his birth. During the thirties, he served as "public relations man" for the German Consul in New York and as correspondent for the *Münchener Neueste Nachrichten*. Slim, blond, young-looking, with grey eyes set off by horn-rimmed glasses, Viereck enjoyed a not wholly undeserved literary reputation and was regarded by his acquaintances more as an eccentric than as a man with primary allegiance to a foreign power. He encouraged this estimate by offsetting his services to Germany with the fact that his novel, *My First 2000 Years,* was burned by the Nazis in 1934, and by exhibiting in his luxurious New York apartment pictures not only of Wilhelm II, Hitler, and Goebbels, but also of Sigmund Freud and Albert Einstein.[4]

In 1937 Viereck published *The Kaiser on Trial,* a fictionalized but documented account of a hypothetical trial of Wilhelm II by the Allies. The verdict was left to the reader. The evidence presented, however, clearly suggested that the Kaiser might have been somewhat remiss in his duties as a ruler, but bore little or no responsibility for the outbreak of war. Viereck's intention to produce a revisionist work warning the United States against repetition of its involvement in the First World War was made clear in his preface, entitled "It Can Happen Again."

"The complete abstention of America from the quarrels of Europe and Asia," he wrote in the preface, "is the only policy that can still prevent a world conflagration." A year later, he excused the *Anschluss* as something forced by an anxious Austria on a reluctant Germany and expressed the hope that no rift would develop in the Rome-Berlin Axis, which guarded peace and order in Europe.[5]

During the same period, Ralph Townsend, a former member of the United States Consular Service in China, was acting

[4]A convenient summary of Viereck's career up to that date may be found in *Current Biography,* I (1940), 829–830.

[5]George Sylvester Viereck, *The Kaiser on Trial* (Richmond, Virginia, 1937), xv and *passim;* "Mussolini Knew—Twelve Years Ago," *Social Justice,* 1A (May 9, 1938), 7.

as publicity agent and public relations counsel for the Japanese Committee on Trade and Information, a propaganda organization financed by the Japanese Government. In *Asia Answers,* a book published in 1936, Townsend advanced the opinion that "in results, Japan's advance is a boon to the majority of Chinese" and that "in Asia today, Japan, staunch opponent of Moscow, is fighting the white man's battle." When such arguments evoked little agreement and failed to diminish American sympathy for China, Townsend began publishing and distributing a series of pro-Japanese tracts. In a progressively more strident tone, he urged strict neutrality in Asia, aiming his words at those who, in his view, sought "to make Americanism mean support for Chiang-Kai-shek."

"There has been nothing in Japan's relation with us to deserve our hatred of Japan," he insisted, "nor has there been anything in China's relation with us to deserve our support of China." At a time when Japanese-American relations were becoming strained and war between the two powers seemed possible, Townsend's place was clearly in the isolationist camp. In 1941 he was an editor of the strongly isolationist *Scribner's Commentator.*[6]

More difficult to classify as foreign-oriented was the brand of isolationism purveyed by Father Charles E. Coughlin of the Shrine of the Little Flower in Royal Oak, Michigan, in his radio addresses and in his weekly magazine, *Social Justice.* Father Coughlin began his radio career in 1926 as part of an effort to counteract the anti-Catholicism of the Ku Klux Klan and comparable groups by explaining the principles of

[6]Ralph Townsend, *Asia Answers* (New York, 1936), 267, 271; *Seeking Foreign Trouble* (New York, 1940), 104; *America Has No Enemies in Asia* (San Francisco, 1938), 48; see also his *There Is No Halfway Neutrality* (San Francisco, 1938) and *The High Cost of Hate* (San Francisco, 1939), *passim*.

Catholicism to his listeners. His attention soon shifted from
religion to politics. He began using his rolling brogue and
vivid rhetoric to purvey his own form of Christian socialism,
damning with equal vigor both communism and capitalism.
An early supporter of President Roosevelt, he was still equat-
ing the New Deal with "Christ's deal" in April, 1934.

In view of his opposition to bankers and "plutocrats,"
Father Coughlin could not long remain approving of the
President's desire to save capitalism in America. Nor was he
content to follow like a cockboat in the wake of Roosevelt's
man-of-war. His efforts to establish himself as an independent
political power led to the founding, in 1934, of the National
Union for Social Justice, a political pressure group whose
program ultimately contained substantial elements of racism
and fascism. Slowly, but inevitably, he tied his chances of
political success to those of Hitler and Mussolini, increasingly
so after his Union party's dismal failure in the 1936 election.[7]

Father Coughlin expressed some criticism of Germany,
particularly of its attitude toward the Catholic Church, and
saw a Nazi victory in Europe as not wholly an unmixed
blessing. Nevertheless, he sympathized with Hitler's attack on
"international plutocracy" in general and on the British and
the Jews in particular. He published Viereck's strongly pro-
German articles and supplemented them with anti-British
diatribes and only slightly altered versions of the anti-Semitic
press releases of Nazi Propaganda Minister Dr. Joseph Paul
Goebbels.[8]

[7]For a summary of Coughlin's activities to 1935, see Schlesinger,
Upheaval, 16–28, *Current Biography,* I (1940), 198–201, and Charles J.
Tull, *Father Coughlin and the New Deal* (Syracuse, 1965), 1–103; an
almost wholly laudatory account of his early career (ironically, with a
foreword by Alfred E. Smith) may be found in Ruth Mugglebee, *Father
Coughlin* (Garden City, 1935).

[8]Selig Adler, *The Isolationist Impulse* (London and New York, 1957),
292; see also n. 5, above.

Viewed together with his enthusiasm for the "corporate state," his virulent Anglophobia, and the blatant anti-Semitism he exhibited after 1938, Father Coughlin's ideas on foreign policy seem motivated not so much by the fear of involving the United States in war as by a desire to do nothing to prevent the triumph of the Axis Powers. When Germany concluded its alliance with the Soviet Union in August, 1939, he curbed his own anticommunism and noted approvingly that Hitler had won a world war by his treaty with Russia.[9] Father Coughlin's isolationism was foreign-oriented in much the same way as that of the American Fellowship Forum, George Deatherage's American Nationalist Confederation, or even the German-American Bund, organizations partly subsidized by agents of the Third Reich and supplied with arguments by the German Library of Information in New York.[10]

The Communists, at the other end of the conventional political spectrum, were in the isolationist camp from 1939 to 1941. For them this represented a reversal of their earlier position. With the Comintern meeting of August, 1935, the Soviet Union had begun seeking the cooperation of other European nations in balancing off the growing power of Nazi Germany. This aim was reflected in the policies of the American Communist party.

In 1936, Earl Browder, the small-town bookkeeper from Kansas and tenth-generation American whom the Comintern had made leader of the party in 1929, denounced isolationists

[9]*Social Justice* 4A (September 4, 1939), 1.
[10]Adler, *op. cit.*, 293–294. Whether Coughlin was, in any precise sense, a fascist, or merely, as Tull would have it, "a frustrated disgruntled demagogue lashing out at the world around him" is irrelevant. His brand of isolationism bore a striking resemblance to that of the avowedly fascist groups. See, however, Tull, *op. cit.*, 244, 246, and James Shenton, "Fascism and Father Coughlin," *Wisconsin Magazine of History*, XLIV (Autumn, 1960), 6–11.

as Fascists and secret supporters of Hitler. He urged the United States to "unite with the peace forces of the world to restrain the warmakers, to keep America out of war by keeping war out of the world!" Two years later he was still attacking Charles A. Beard and others, and imploring the United States to come to the aid of the Spanish and Chinese peoples by ending "once and for all the farce of non-intervention." As late as May 1939, in a report to the National Committee of the Communist party, Browder called for vigorous action against the aggressors, repeal of the Neutrality Act, and opposition to the "Hoover-Garner coalition of Right-wing Democrats and Republicans" who through their isolationist policies were, in his view, aligning the United States with the Axis powers.[11]

Nazi-Soviet
Pact

On August 22, 1939, German Foreign Minister Joachim von Ribbentrop and his Russian counterpart, Vyacheslav Molotov, signed the nonaggression pact that doomed Poland and entirely changed the world situation. The Communist party responded immediately to this turn of events. An open letter to President Roosevelt, dated September 11, 1939, and signed by Browder and a second influential member of the party's National Committee, William Z. Foster, indicated the organization's firm opposition to "American involvement in the war, or in the rivalries and antagonisms which have led much of Europe into chaos." By December, Browder was telling the Peace Federation at the Massachusetts Institute of Technology that "to take sides in this war, even if only morally and emotionally, leads inevitably to deeper and deeper economic and political involvement," and "if our country

[11]Earl Browder, *Democracy or Fascism* (New York, 1936), 9–10; "Concerted Action or Isolation?" *New Masses* (March 1, 1938), reprinted in Earl Browder, *Fighting for Peace* (New York, 1939), 31–38; "The World Anti-Fascist Front," in Earl Browder, *The Second Imperialist War* (New York, 1940), 48.

allows itself to become economically involved in this war. . .
we are surrendering ourselves to the same forces that dragged
us into the last war, with inevitably the same results."[12]

For the next year and a half, the Communists urged the
country to remain on "the people's road to peace" by "resisting and defeating all those who want to help one side against
the other." They attempted to win sympathy for the attitude
proclaimed by Elizabeth Gurley Flynn's pamphlet, *I Didn't
Raise My Boy to Be a Soldier—for Wall Street.* Within a few
hours of the German invasion of Russia on June 22, 1941,
however, the party's slogan changed from "The Yanks Are
Not Coming" to "The Yanks Are Not Coming—Too Late,"[13]
thus demonstrating that the only consistent factor in Communist attitudes about American foreign policy was steadfast
adherence to the interests of the Soviet Union.

Although both Communist and pro-Fascist organizations
gave vigorous support to the isolationist cause and received
in turn at least tacit acceptance, if not outright help, from
such men as Hamilton Fish and Senator Ernest Lundeen of
Minnesota, foreign-oriented isolationism was outside the
mainstream of isolationist tradition. Tying American foreign
policy to decisions made in Russia represented an entanglement substantially similar to coordinating it with the actions
of Great Britain or of the League of Nations, as advocated
by the interventionists. It could not, therefore, meet with
wide approval among isolationists. Urging American neutrali-

[12]"Open Letter from the National Committee," and "The Communists on the War," in Browder, *Imperialist War,* 103, 199.

[13]Earl Browder, *The People's Road to Peace* (New York, 1940), 25;
Elizabeth Gurley Flynn, *I Didn't Raise My Boy to Be a Soldier—for
Wall Street* (New York, 1940), *passim;* Adler, *op. cit.,* 296. A number of
clearly communist-inspired "The Yanks Are Not Coming" petitions sent
to Roosevelt by various left-wing labor organizations between February
and August 1940 are in House Records (Committee on Military Affairs),
Files 76A-H 16.4 and 76A-H 16.5.

ty to enable Germany and Japan to achieve their goals has little relation to traditional unilateralism, based on a concept of American self-interest. Foreign-oriented isolationism may therefore be regarded as a peripheral aspect of the entire subject of isolationism and will not be further considered. The results of the 1936 election, held at a time when most Americans shared the isolationist position, do not support the thesis that many Americans actively subscribed to the opinions of Union party candidate William Lemke, or of his chief backer, Father Coughlin. And the Communists, whether as interventionists in 1936 or as isolationists in 1940, received only negligible popular support.

The key figures in the isolationist movement were not foreign-oriented. They believed America must be free to pursue an independent course, that to enter any war would be a national disaster, and that the United States had no more than a small stake in, or influence upon, the outcome of struggles in other parts of the world. In the course proposed by these persons and in the rationale behind their arguments may be found the real bases of American isolationism. Yet here, too, we find significant divergencies.

Before 1935, the best known and most influential isolationist spokesmen in Washington were Senators William E. Borah of Idaho and Hiram W. Johnson of California. Both men were nearing seventy, had served in the Senate for many years, and had acquired a reputation for independence and vigor. Their association with numerous progressive causes and the isolationism they had in common made them appear an influential Senatorial team. Yet, though they often reached identical conclusions, there were fundamental differences between them.

Hiram Johnson was a native Californian. His father had been school commissioner in Syracuse, New York, moved to the West during the Civil War, and served as army quartermaster clerk there. After the war he settled in Sacramento and became a successful corporation lawyer, championing the politically powerful Southern Pacific Railroad. The elder Johnson served four years in the California legislature and one term in Congress. Altogether, he played an important, if not wholly creditable, role in the politics of his adopted state. Young Hiram, therefore, had his career, though not his political views, laid out for him from the beginning. He studied for a few years at the University of California and, though he obtained no degree, was admitted to the bar in 1888 and joined his father's law firm. He became a respected, if unspectacular, trial lawyer and supported the cause of civic reform.

Not until he moved to San Francisco in 1902, did Hiram Johnson's rise to prominence begin. He won a reputation as a top trial lawyer before juries and took part in a campaign against corruption involving many city officials and virtually all of the local public utility companies. When the prosecuting attorney in a bribery trial was shot in open court in 1908, Johnson was selected to succeed him. He thus reached the conventional springboard for the progressive politician of his time and was not slow in putting it to use. In 1910, at the age of forty-four, he made his first bid for elective office. As candidate for governor he toured the state in a little red automobile, announcing his intention to speak by ringing a cowbell. His main campaign target was the Southern Pacific Railroad, for which his father was then corporation counsel. In this era of trust busters and muckrakers, he won handily.

His election and the reforms he instituted in California brought him national prominence. His espousal of the nonpartisan primary, the short ballot, prison reform, and workmen's compensation aligned him with such other progressive governors as Charles Evans Hughes of New York, Robert M. La Follette of Wisconsin, Woodrow Wilson of New Jersey, and James M. Cox of Ohio. He joined enthusiastically in the formation of the Progressive party in 1912 and emerged from its national convention as candidate for vice-president. The campaign left him with his first and only election defeat. Although losing did not diminish his reputation and he retained the unqualified endorsement of Theodore Roosevelt, his running mate, the defeat was the first of a series of incidents that hurt Johnson's pride and dimmed both his optimism and his progressivism.

The second incident followed four years later. Johnson had been re-elected governor in 1914 and ran for the Senate in 1916. In the course of this campaign, he was slighted by the touring Republican presidential candidate, Charles Evans Hughes. Although Johnson won, he neither forgot nor forgave the insult. The dramatic outcome of the presidential race, which Hughes appeared to have won until late returns from California gave the presidency to Woodrow Wilson, created the impression that the new California Senator had been responsible for the seeming turnabout.

If there was truth in this, Johnson had little time to enjoy his revenge. Two weeks after he belatedly took his seat in the Senate, he heard Wilson, the man with whose re-election he was being credited, deliver the war message to Congress. The message violated some of Johnson's most cherished convictions and he attacked it with vigor. Yet, ultimately, he yielded to the promptings of patriotic sentiment and the dictates of political expediency, and voted for war. He was soon to regret this decision.

If Wilson's course disappointed Johnson deeply, so did the direction in which the Republican party was moving. As a man with Progressive antecedents, he stood in the way of "normalcy" and had no chance for the presidential nomination in 1920. He turned down the opportunity to run for vice-president. In doing so, he indicated an admirable adherence to principle—he had no use for Harding and disagreed with the conservatism of the platform—but he also denied himself the succession to the presidency upon Harding's death. An effort to compensate for this by seeking the nomination in 1924 failed utterly.

Johnson remained in the Senate. Re-elected by ever increasing majorities, he devoted his energies to building for himself a position of lonely, though splendid, isolation. He refused Harold Ickes' offer to head a revived Progressive party in the election of 1932 and turned down the chance to become Roosevelt's Secretary of the Interior, though he approved of the new president's policies. He even declined to serve as delegate to the London Economic Conference. The man whom Franklin D. Roosevelt had once referred to as the greatest liberal of our time—which he surely never was—was getting set in his ways, conservative, and increasingly dour. It was symptomatic of his attitude, perhaps, that he insisted on keeping his old office in the Capitol long after all of his colleagues had moved to the newly erected Senate Office Building. Always dressed in a baggy blue serge suit with white piping on the vest, he was a familiar and respected figure on the floor of the Senate, a man of stubbornly independent mind whose support was worth having and whose opposition was much to be feared.[14]

Unlike Johnson, who was virtually born into a political career and reached the Senate rapidly and without much difficulty, William Edgar Borah followed a more circuitous path. Tenth child of a prosperous, hard-working Illinois farmer, Borah attended school in tiny Tom's Prairie, followed this with a stint at Enfield Academy, and then ran away to join a

[14]No useful biography of Johnson exists. For a general summary of his life and career see *Current Biography*, II (1941), 439–441 and John Gunther, *Inside U.S.A.* (New York and London, 1947), 13–15, 16.

run-down Shakespearean company, with which he played
Mark Antony. Although he retained a lifelong interest in the
theater, Borah soon gave up the thought of becoming an
actor and enrolled at the University of Kansas in Lawrence
to study law. He was admitted to the bar in 1889 and opened
an office in nearby Lyons, but with scant success. Deciding to
move on to Seattle, he stopped off in Boise, Idaho, and never
went further.

As attorney for several lumber and mining companies,
Borah accumulated a modest fortune and developed an
interest in politics. He failed in a campaign to win election to
Congress as a Silver Republican in 1896, and lost the Republican senatorial nomination in 1903 through the last-minute
desertion of several local bosses. Two years later, his opportunity came. Selected as prosecuting attorney in the trial of
"Big Bill" Haywood and other leaders of the Western Federation of Miners for the murder of Idaho's Governor Steunen-
berg, he lost the case but attracted national attention. In
1907 he was elected to the Senate.

From the day of his arrival in the Capitol, he showed
ability and independence. The nickname of "Big Patate"
given him by his colleagues alluded not merely to the best-
known product of his home state, but also to the role in the
Senate that Borah quickly assumed. He was a leading figure
in the fight against Nelson W. Aldrich and the Republican
"Old Guard" and championed an eight-hour-day law and
the income tax. Although he was an insurgent Republican
and worked for the nomination of Theodore Roosevelt in
1912, he took pride in both his insurgency and his Republicanism. Thus, while Johnson was accepting a place on the
Bull Moose ticket, Borah sat in the convention that re-
nominated William Howard Taft.

Although his belief in trust busting and his general anti-
business bias kept him opposed to every Republican president

during the twenties, the dreams of an effective third party that periodically motivated men like Johnson, La Follette, and George W. Norris of Nebraska did not appeal to the Senator from Idaho. He fought bitterly against Attorney General Harry M. Daugherty, helped expose the corruption of the Harding Administration, and refused the offered vice-presidential nomination in 1924 because he deemed it beneath his dignity to run with a man he regarded as a nonentity. But he supported neither the Progressive candidate La Follette nor the Democrat Davis. Although he had quarreled frequently with the policies of Commerce Secretary Hoover, he surprised almost everyone by stumping the Midwest for presidential candidate Hoover in 1928. Even in 1932, Borah did not join his insurgent colleagues who deserted their party to help elect Franklin D. Roosevelt.

The result was that by the early thirties, Borah, though a vigorous critic of the Republican party, had become one of its acknowledged leaders. Crusty, shaggy, and to those who failed to understand his motives increasingly unpredictable, he was unquestionably one of the most influential members of the Senate. He had often shown that he placed principle above popularity and he now fought the antilynching bill because he deemed it unconstitutional and the Townsend Plan because he thought it foolish. When he rose to speak in Congress or in public, his dark, loosely cut clothes unpressed and often threadbare, his small feet encased in beautifully polished, expensive shoes, few of his listeners remained unaffected by his oratory.

In 1936, Borah was one of four men seriously considered for the Republican presidential nomination. Though he was over seventy, he became an active candidate and entered several primaries. Even his failure at the convention and his distrust of Alfred M. Landon—ironically, the most liberal Republican candidate since Theodore Roosevelt—did not lead him to forswear his party loyalty entirely. He supported much of the New Deal, but rejected measures like the National Industrial Recovery Act which clashed with his somewhat old-fashioned liberalism. Despite twenty-five years of disappointment, he continued to hope that, after the expectations of the ultraconservative Liberty League had turned out to be delusions, the Republicans might yet be won over to Borah principles. Calmer than Johnson, less personal in his attacks and less emotional in the presentation of his views, Borah had many opponents but few enemies. His hopes were therefore not wholly without foundation.[15]

Johnson and Borah thus had different backgrounds and personalities and occupied dissimilar positions in the Senate and the country. Beneath the surface, the attitudes toward foreign policy of these two leading isolationist legislators were equally unalike. Johnson's approach to world problems was a curious compound of pride and prejudice. He thought of America not merely first but exclusively, devoted his energies to the solution of its problems and the defense of its interests, and distrusted and disliked foreign nations and their inhabitants.

As governor of California, he had acquiesced in the denial of landholding rights to aliens ineligible for citizenship and in the Senate he was a vigorous proponent of immigration restriction. His record on foreign policy consisted almost entirely of "nay" votes. He opposed American entry into the First World War, though he reluctantly voted for the declaration of war, and cast his ballot against joining the League of Nations. He rejected the treaties coming out of the Washington Conference on Naval Limitations in 1922 as entangling,

[15]Marian C. McKenna, *Borah* (Ann Arbor, 1961), *passim; Current Biography,* I (1940), 99–102. Borah's voluminous papers in the Library of Congress contain considerable biographical data.

looked with disfavor upon increased American participation
in the nonpolitical work of the League, and fought to keep
the United States out of the World Court. The only foreign
policy legislation he sponsored was the Johnson Act of 1934,
which prohibited loans to nations that had defaulted on their
debts. In practice this law barred further loans to any of the
major powers likely to become involved in future wars.

Borah, on the other hand, was seriously interested in foreign policy. He sought membership on the Foreign Relations
Committee, became one of its most active members, and
served as its chairman from 1925 to 1933. No less America-
conscious than Johnson, he nevertheless welcomed dealings
with other nations because he believed that the interests of
the United States could be advanced thereby. He applauded
the landing of Marines at Vera Cruz in 1914 as a step to
strengthen the American position in the Caribbean. He voted
for war with Germany in 1917 because he believed American
maritime rights had been violated. He was instrumental in
convening the Washington Conference of 1921–22 and did
more than any other man to bring about approval of the
Kellogg-Briand Pact by the Senate in 1929. His many constructive suggestions in regard to disarmament included the
additional "five-year naval holiday" adopted by the Hoover
Administration in 1931. He urged resumption of normal
relations with Russia in order to stimulate American trade
and facilitate the collection of debts, and he applauded President Roosevelt's decision to take this step in 1933.

To be sure, Borah was also the leader of the irreconcilables
who formed a "Battalion of Death" to prevent ratification
of the Treaty of Versailles and the Covenant of the League
of Nations. And he opposed the Nine-Power Treaty of 1922
because it committed the United States to the maintenance
of the *status quo* in the Pacific in concert with the other
signatories. He vigorously opposed "entanglements," but,

unlike Johnson, he also favored, at least in theory, an active foreign policy.

The world situation in the thirties, however, tended to emphasize the similarities in the views of Borah and Johnson rather than the differences. Since no active foreign policy was conceivable without cooperation with other nations and assumption of long-term commitments, Borah's proposals became as negative as Johnson's. Moreover, the almost belligerent nationalism of both men set them somewhat apart from other isolationists and thus identified them with each other. Unlike more timid spirits, they were fully prepared to defend American rights and interests. But they were unwilling to pursue policies that might prevent the United States from taking unilateral steps or force it into some action in the interest of other nations.[16] Although they remained convinced throughout the thirties that America's direct interests were not threatened by world events and therefore strenuously opposed intervention, they did not make a principle of rejecting recourse to war. "People who are not wholly free at any particular juncture of their foreign affairs to remain neutral or to take up arms," Borah told a national radio audience in 1935, "have already succumbed in practice, if not in principle, to the doctrines upon which all arbitrary government rests."[17]

When Congress passed the first neutrality act in 1935, providing for an embargo on arms and ammunition shipments to all belligerents, Senator Johnson hailed this as a "justification of the men, very few, who stood firmly years ago and through all the long period since have stood firmly for maintaining America in America's security and in Ameri-

Key factor

---

[16]See Adler, *op. cit.*, esp. 170–174 and 290–291.

[17]William E. Borah, "Our Foreign Policy," Press Release by the Columbia Broadcasting System of a speech delivered on September 22, 1935, in FDRL, PPF 2358.

ca's pristine glory and keeping out of every foreign entanglement and every European war." But to the proposal, made
the following year, for a general embargo on trade with
belligerents and a surrender of America's right to freedom
of the seas, he indignantly objected. Trade with foreign
nations was in the interest of this country and to relinquish
it was to permit foreign governments and foreign problems
to dictate the course which the United States must follow.
As he explained:

You can pass a bill that will take your commerce from the
seas and will make your citizens stay within the borders of this
country entirely. You may thus have peace with the rest of the
world, perhaps; and there are a great many people in this Nation
today who are advocating just that thing. Then, when you have
earned the contempt of the world by the attitude that you take,
and when you have come to a situation where you are flabby
and no longer a nation worth a rap, your nation itself is gone.[18]

Senator Borah agreed with this view. "I advocate it [neu-
trality legislation] on the theory that it has a tendency and
contributes to keeping us out of the war more than anything
else we can do," he told the Foreign Relations Committee,
"but I would not say to Great Britain and France that the
United States is not going to protect its citizens engaging in
legitimate trade upon the high seas...I would not hesitate
a moment to go to war if they invaded a vital right which this
country had established as its policy."[19]

The belligerent isolationism for which Borah and Johnson
remained the chief spokesmen was supported by other legislators. Republican Representative Edith Nourse Rogers of
Massachusetts was convinced by 1936 that "our own troubles

[18]*Congressional Record,* 74th Cong., 1st sess., 14430 (August 24, 1935),
Senate Foreign Relations Committee, *Neutrality; Hearings,* 74th Cong.,
2nd sess. (1936), 31.
[19]Senate, *Neutrality; Hearings* (1936), 29.

are so numerous and so difficult that we have neither the
time or inclination to meddle in the affairs of others," and
that we would never again "pull the chestnuts out of the fire
for some other nation." She supported the Borah-Johnson
position on neutrality in 1937. Similar sentiments were voiced
by Republican Representatives Hamilton Fish of New York
and John M. Robsion of Kentucky. Robsion championed
what he called the "Borah-Johnson-Rogers-Fish position,"
insisting that "we crave peace, but at the same time we have
billions to defend our own shores and our own people" and,
presumably, our own interests.[20]

The one other legislator in this group who could be ranked
with Borah and Johnson was Fish. Representing another
generation—he was born in 1888, the year Johnson began to
practice law—he shared many of the same attitudes and sentiments. This was unexpected since he was the son of neither a
Midwestern farmer nor a California railroad lawyer, but of
an Eastern landed aristocrat who, following family tradition,
had left the ancestral estate in Garrison, New York, to devote
himself to politics. Fish's grandfather had been a distinguished Secretary of State and his aunt, Mrs. Stuyvesant Fish,
had ruled New York and Newport society for many years.
Young Hamilton's path led naturally, like that of his Hudson
Valley neighbor, Franklin D. Roosevelt, to Harvard. He
completed his studies in three years, finding time to play football well enough to be named to Walter Camp's "All-
America" team as a tackle.

In 1914, he was elected to the New York State Assembly
as a follower of Theodore Roosevelt, and supported the direct
presidential primary and preparedness. As his personal contri-

[20]*Congressional Record,* 74th Cong., 2nd sess., 1139 (January 28,
1936); 75th Cong., 1st sess., 2275–2276, 2277, 2280 (March 16, 1937),
App. 260–261 (February 12, 1937).

bution to the war effort he organized a National Guard regi-
ment of Negroes, taking it overseas soon after the declaration
of war. Although the fame of the "Rough Riders" was denied
him in this less romantic war, he returned with a *Croix de
Guerre,* the rank of major, and a veteran's complex. He
helped organize the American Legion, went back into politics, and was elected to Congress in 1919.

Fish left a curious record in the House of Representatives.
Due to his long, uninterrupted service, he became a ranking
member of both the Rules and Foreign Affairs committees.
Yet he achieved very little, aside from special pleading for
veterans' groups and the introduction of bills to pay bonuses
and erect monuments. The bill to make the *Star-Spangled
Banner* our national anthem and his proposal to compel the
resumption of the Army-Navy football game by law typify
the causes to which he lent his support. Even his Fish Committee to Investigate Communism in 1930 was strangely
ineffectual.

He was a man of many contrasts, of prepossessing appearance but with a nasal voice and a perpetually worried
look. He was a man who could advocate the policies of the
Liberty League yet support social security and a minimum
wage law, a man who could consort with known anti-Semites,
yet sponsor the resolution in favor of creating a Jewish
national homeland in Palestine.

Perhaps Fish was first and foremost a politician. He was
adept at securing publicity for himself and at keeping the
voters at home satisfied. These skills kept him in Congress
long after his fellow Republicans came to look upon him as
something of a party handicap. The disfavor into which he
fell was not due to his behavior in the House, where he
generally voted on domestic issues with his party or, at worst,
with the more conservative Democrats. Nor did the attacks
on him by President Roosevelt, whose home district he repre-

sented, make him unpopular. The gibe about "Martin, Barton, and Fish" did not hurt his standing in the party any more than it did that of Representative Joseph W. Martin, Jr., of Massachusetts, who was subsequently chosen Speaker of the House of Representatives. Not even Fish's isolationism was to blame for his fall from favor. His views in this regard were similar to those of Borah and Johnson and of a number of his House colleagues. They, however, unlike Fish, did not count George Sylvester Viereck among their friends, nor abuse their franking privileges by mailing Nazi-inspired speeches and the pamphlets of notoriously anti-Semitic organizations, nor speak at rallies of the German-American Bund.

Although such activities made Fish a liability for his party at a time when the United States was engaged in an ideological struggle against fascism and, later, in a war against Germany, it is not likely that the man who had fought courageously against Germany in the First World War, who had supported legislation for the protection of racial minorities, and who wore his patriotism like a badge was consciously acting in a subversive manner. He hated communism and the Soviet Union and was against Roosevelt and against war. These views he expounded to all who would listen, and if they led him to questionable associations and activities, he did not seem to mind.[21]

Significantly, Fish was not among those isolationists prepared to yield American rights or curtail American trade in order to avoid involvement in world affairs. When the time came to vote on the Neutrality Act of 1937, which included a provision giving the President the right to prevent the

[21]Richard N. Current, "Hamilton Fish: 'Crusading Isolationist,' " in J. T. Salter, ed., *Public Men In and Out of Office* (Chapel Hill, 1946), 210–224; *Current Biography*, II (1941), 278–280.

export of certain commodities to belligerents in American ships, Fish did not support it. Robsion and Mrs. Rogers voted nay. Borah and Johnson were among the six Senators who opposed the measure. The four others were not isolationists.[22]

A major basis of the "Borah-Johnson-Rogers-Fish-position" was the firm belief in international law fostered by such authorities in the field as John Bassett Moore and Edwin M. Borchard. The seventy-five-year-old Moore and his former student, Borchard, had not only had distinguished teaching careers at Columbia and Yale, but had also acquired considerable practical experience in international affairs. Moore had served in the State Department at the turn of the century, rising to the position of assistant secretary. He had returned to the State Department as counsel in 1913, when he was already a member of the Permanent Court of Arbitration at The Hague. Subsequently, he also became a judge on the Permanent Court of International Justice and was, by the 1930's, unquestionably the leading American authority on international law. Borchard had represented the United States in the North Atlantic Fisheries arbitration in 1910 and Peru in the Tacna-Arica dispute, which was not settled until 1929. He had served for many years as law librarian of Congress and briefly, under Moore, in the State Department. His numerous books on international law had won him honorary degrees from the universities of Berlin and Budapest, among others.

Moore was firmly convinced that the United States should remain neutral because it had no real stake in the quarrel dividing the world in the thirties and had, in any case, "no more power to prevent other countries from going to war

[22]*Congressional Record,* 75th Cong., 1st sess., 1807, 2404 (March 3, and March 18, 1937).

than other countries have had or now have to prevent the
United States from going to war." To him, neutrality meant
pursuing normal peacetime trade and vigorously defending
international rights. "If you stop trade," he told a Senate
committee, "you are committing an unneutral act on the face
of it. You in fact 'blockade' countries, naturally with varying
effects."[23] Such arguments lent force to the Borah-Johnson
position, and Moore's public utterances were regularly introduced into the *Congressional Record* by them and by Hamilton Fish.

Borchard was even more vigorously isolationist and, at the
same time, even more insistent that freedom of the seas
should not be relinquished. "Neither tragic Europe nor Asia
can be saved by anything the United States can do," he
wrote in the *Southern Review* in 1936. "We can by intervention make it worse, but not better. To read into the perpetual
quarrels of Europe a moral issue is to succumb to romance.... An honest neutrality remains our only chance of
dignified survival."[24]

Washington's Farewell Address again

The meaning of "honest neutrality" was clarified at length
in *Neutrality for the United States,* on which Borchard collaborated with William Potter Lage. The authors argued that
unneutrality had brought the United States into the First
World War and that a vigorous defense of American rights
against both the Allies and the Central Powers would have
averted what they regarded as a calamity. The naval conferences of the twenties and the Kellogg-Briand Pact were
cited as other instances of reprehensible and dangerous conduct. As to neutrality legislation, the lesson was clear. Hope
for American survival lay neither in "peace enforcement" nor

[23]Senate, *Neutrality; Hearings* (1936), 187, 184.
[24]Edwin M. Borchard, "Neutrality," *Southern Review,* II (Autumn,
1936), 258.

in "a timorous retreat from legitimate relations with belligerents." Embargoes of any sort were by their nature discriminatory and could only lead to the involvement they were intended to prevent. The United States was to be neutral in spirit and depend on international law for the defense of its rights.[25]

The American way was to assert forthrightly and independently this country's own rights and interests, to ask for no favors and to grant none, and to rely ultimately on the righteousness of the cause and the deterrent strength of the navy. To the contention that international law was a dead letter and that dependence on it spelled disaster, Senator Johnson had a ready answer:

There is an international law just as there has always been a law against theft, but because the thief gets away with his booty at times is no reason why we should say that the law against theft has been abrogated.[26]

Reliance on international law to preserve the United States from the danger of involvement in war seemed unsafe, however, to another, increasingly influential group of isolationists. By 1935, the National Council for the Prevention of War was proclaiming that "neutral 'rights' have led us into three wars." Admiral William S. Sims, who had been in command of American naval operations in European waters during the First World War and served as president of the Naval War College until his retirement from the service in 1922, was advancing the proposition that we "cannot keep out of a

[25]Edwin M. Borchard and William Potter Lage, *Neutrality for the United States* (New Haven, 1937), vi–vii, 279, 286, 289–298, 313–350. Borchard's considerable correspondence with Borah indicates a very wide area of agreement between the two. See Borah Papers, Boxes 362, 377, 393, 405, and 426.

[26]Senate Foreign Relations Committee, *Neutrality, Peace Legislation and Our Foreign Policy; Hearings,* 76th Cong., 1st sess. (1939), 66.

war and at the same time enforce freedom of the seas—that is, the freedom to make profits out of countries in a death struggle."[27] In July, the National Council for the Prevention of War sent a letter to Marvin H. McIntyre, Secretary to the President, asserting that the maintenance of neutral rights "has become, under modern conditions of warfare and international relationships, incompatible with the preservation of real neutrality and honorable peace." The letter was endorsed by the Women's International League for Peace and Freedom, the National Council of Jewish Women, the Women's Christian Temperance Union, the People's Lobby, the Washington Foreign Policy Committee, and the American Civil Liberties Union.[28]

Acting on the same premises, Republican Senator Gerald P. Nye of North Dakota introduced a series of bills in August, 1935, that would have withheld passports from Americans wishing to travel in war zones, forbidden citizens to sail on vessels owned by belligerents, embargoed loans, credits, and munitions, prevented contraband of any sort from leaving this country under the United States flag, and in other ways would have voluntarily relinquished traditional neutral rights. Democratic Representatives Maury Maverick of Texas and Frank L. Kloeb of Ohio made similar proposals in the House.[29]

Senator Nye became identified in the public mind with timid isolationism, especially after the publicity generated by

[27] "Peace and Neutrality," Handbill of the National Council for the Prevention of War (1935), FDRL OF 1561; William S. Sims, "Neutrality," quoted in *Congressional Record*, 74th Cong., 1st sess., 7452 (May 14, 1935).

[28] Copy in FDRL OF 1561.

[29] *Congressional Record*, 74th Cong., 1st sess., 14535 (August 24, 1935); the bills introduced were SJR 99, 100, and 120 (all by Nye), HJR 259 (Maverick) and HR 7125 (Kloeb).

his investigation of the munitions industry. Although the Senator from North Dakota was an insurgent Republican like Johnson and Borah, his insurgency was of different origin. Johnson's progressivism was inspired by civic corruption and the baleful effect of the Southern Pacific Railroad on the government of California. Borah had been influenced by the company politics and labor struggles of his home state. Nye was principally a spokesman for the discontented farmer.

Born in Hortonville, Wisconsin, in 1892, he absorbed from his father, a small-town editor and early La Follette supporter, much of the political radicalism inherent in the "Wisconsin idea." He inherited little of the personality of his uncle "Bill" Nye who, as a popular humorist, competed on the lecture circuit with Mark Twain. At an early age, Nye began editing a country weekly in his home town and he continued his journalistic activities in one form or another until he came to the Senate. A brief stint on the Des Moines *Register* confirmed his instinctive dislike of cities and he moved to North Dakota to escape the conservatism of the Iowa capital. In May, 1916, he bought the *Pioneer* of Fryburg, a town of perhaps sixty inhabitants in Billings County, the heart of the Badlands.

The young editor devoted his newspaper largely to local matters, but he supported Wilson for re-election, lauded the break in diplomatic relations with Germany in February, 1917, and urged farmers to support the war effort two months later. When Senator La Follette criticized America's entry into the war in a speech in St. Paul, Nye attacked him for being unpatriotic and anti-American. He continued to support President Wilson and to denounce his critics throughout the war and the peace negotiations that followed, and wrote editorials favorable to American entry into the League of Nations.

In the meantime, Nye began to endorse the activities of

the Nonpartisan League in local politics, and the *Pioneer* became the League's voice in Billings County. By the time he sold this newspaper to assume the editorial management of the *Griggs County Sentinel-Courier* in Cooperstown, he had gained such a reputation for radicalism that he was blackballed by both the Masons and the Knights of Pythias. It was Nye's association with the Nonpartisan League and his support of agrarian radicalism in general that led to the change in his foreign policy views. When the postwar depression hit North Dakota in 1920–21, editorials in the *Sentinel-Courier* blamed big business and "Wall Street" for many of the farmer's difficulties. Once these "special interests" had been found guilty of causing domestic troubles, it became easy to blame them for international difficulties and a desire for war.

The Nonpartisan League showed its gratitude for Nye's support by helping him secure nomination for Congress in 1924. Defeat in this campaign gave him his big chance the following year, when the death of Edwin F. Ladd created a vacancy in the Senate. Governor A. G. Sorlie wanted to run for that seat in 1926 and looked for an interim appointee with little claim to the position who would retire gracefully at the end of the year. His choice was Gerald P. Nye.

There was some doubt about the Governor's right, under North Dakota law, to fill such a vacancy by appointment. When Sorlie picked Nye, who as a former La Follette supporter and potential insurgent was *persona non grata* to the Republican Senate majority, the appointment was challenged. Nye was ultimately confirmed by only two votes. But Sorlie's death in 1926 enabled the interim Senator to win renomination, and he was elected for a full term.

Although the new Senator from North Dakota was cordially disliked by the Senate leadership and President Coolidge, he was able to win the fight for his share of patronage and to make something favorable out of his poor committee assignments. The investigation of the Continental Trading Company, which he undertook as member of the Public Lands Committee, uncovered large-scale corruption unpleasantly reminiscent of the Teapot Dome oil scandals. As a result, his name became linked with that of Montana Senator Thomas J. Walsh as a vigorous and honest defender of the public interest. The hearings also established Nye's reputation as a successful investigator and confirmed him in his insurgency. He was a consistent critic of the Coolidge-Mellon tax policy and supported the McNary-Haugen farm bills despite Administration objections to them. Yet, like Borah, he was enough of a believer in party regularity to support, reluctantly, Hoover's candidacy in 1928.

He soon split with the Hoover Administration over the issue of farm relief and turned his attention once more to investigating. This time he looked into irregularities in the 1930 primaries and election campaign. His principal achievement was foiling an attempt to defeat Senator George W. Norris in the Nebraska primary through the introduction of a candidate of the same name. He also helped check the political ambitions of Ruth Hanna McCormick in Illinois by exposing the size of her primary campaign expenditures.

By 1932, Nye's name was well known, although his influence in the Senate had not risen markedly. His seven years in Washington had brought an improvement in his dress and the style of his haircuts, but he had remained essentially the small-town editor made ill at ease by social life in the big city. Nor had his political ideas matured. Always emotional rather than analytical, Nye had none of the earmarks of the constructive legislator though many of the carping critic. Yet his support of much of the early New Deal legislation and his record of opposition to Coolidge and Hoover had given him something of a liberal reputation. The attacks on bankers and businessmen that formed the substance of the

Nye Committee's revelations enhanced that reputation. So did his opposition to the National Industrial Recovery Act on the grounds it encouraged monopoly and his characterization of the Blue Eagle as a bird of prey on the masses. He drew praise from Oswald Garrison Villard of the *Nation* and was supported in his campaign for re-election in 1938 not only by Senators Borah and Norris, but also by William Green of the American Federation of Labor and by the National Non-Partisan Committee for the Re-election of Senator Nye, headed by Charles A. Beard and the *New Republic*'s Bruce Bliven.[30]

Strangely enough, Nye's reputation at the time was not greatly different from that of the liberal Democrat from Texas, Maury Maverick, who introduced legislation in the House of Representatives similar to that advocated by the Senator from North Dakota. Short, stout, bespectacled, dynamic Maury Maverick had lived up to the family name. A man of intellectual bent who wrote for the *Nation* and the *New Republic,* he published the autobiographical *A Maverick American,* and introduced the practice of inserting book reviews into the *Congressional Record.* Yet he had not been graduated from high school, college, or law school, though he had attended all three. A proud Texan who pointed out frequently that his grandfather had signed the Texas Declaration of Independence in 1836, his articles and speeches rarely contained even a trace of sectionalism.

Maverick's family had been well-to-do and he had made his own fortune by selling jerry-built houses at an exorbitant profit. Yet, in 1932, he spent months tramping the roads and

[30]The most complete biographical information on Nye is contained in Cole's *Nye.* See esp. 17–59; see also J. L. Sayre, "Gerald P. Nye: 'Essentially Negative,'" in Salter, *Public Men,* 127–146 and *Current Biography,* II (1941), 618–621.

living in hobo jungles to study the plight of the unemployed, and he was a consistent supporter of social legislation and an advocate of public housing.

Maverick was first elected to Congress in 1934 and managed to establish a national reputation in his first year there. This was partly due to the forcefulness of his personality and his facility in dealing with the press. It owed something as well to the fact that he soon became one of the principal spokesmen for a group of younger Congressmen that included Jerry Voorhis of California, John A. Martin of Colorado, John Lueckc of Michigan, Herbert S. Bigelow of Ohio, Fred H. Hildebrandt of South Dakota, John Coffee and Knute Hill of Washington, George J. Schneider of Wisconsin, and, later, Lyndon B. Johnson of Texas.

The sixteen-point program this group worked out in March of 1935 called for sweeping liberal reforms. Its content was more constructive and consistent than anything Senator Nye would have been capable of advancing, but there was little in it which he could not have supported. In its strong stand against war and for rigid neutrality legislation, the program hewed closely to the line laid down by the Nye Committee. To be sure, Nye's isolationism was largely the product of his distrust of allegedly prowar business and banking interests and an oversimplified view of foreign trade and world problems, while Maverick and many of his colleagues were principally motivated by a horror of war and the desire to keep their program of domestic reform from being pushed aside by foreign adventures. Still, the conclusions they all reached and the policies they advocated were much the same.[31]

[31]Robert C. Brooks, "One of the Four Hundred and Thirty-Five: Maury Maverick, of Texas," in J. T. Salter, ed., *The American Politician* (Chapel Hill, 1938), 150–174; Maury Maverick, *A Maverick American* (New York, 1937), *passim*.

Of the measures proposed by Nye in 1935, only the mandatory embargo on arms and ammunition was immediately adopted. The others were revived in each subsequent session of Congress by a group of Senators which, in addition to Nye, included Homer T. Bone of Washington, Bennett C. Clark of Missouri, and Arthur H. Vandenberg of Michigan. The presence of Clark and Vandenberg adds two further shadings to the spectrum of timid isolationism.

Bennett C. Clark virtually grew up on the floor of Congress. His father had come to Washington when "Young Champ" was only three years old and remained in the House of Representatives, with one brief interruption, until his death twenty-eight years later. The son campaigned for his father while still a child and was a precinct captain at fourteen. Politics and the Democratic party were his life blood. He never forgot nor forgave the Convention of 1912, when the two-thirds rule and the defection of William Jennings Bryan cost Champ Clark the presidential nomination and made possible the election of Woodrow Wilson. The rejection of his father by the party's progressive wing drove young Clark to the conservative side. Unlike Maverick or Nye, he opposed virtually all of the New Deal, with the exception of Roosevelt's monetary policies. He came into the isolationist camp not primarily because he distrusted bankers or favored reforms, but because his hatred of communism and war and his desire to protect the decisive influence of the Senate on foreign policy against presidential encroachment led him to advocate strict, mandatory neutrality legislation.[32]

[32]For a brief sketch of Clark's life and career, see *Current Biography,* II (1941), 153–155. There is some indication that Clark was also influenced in his stand by strong neutrality sentiment in backwoods Missouri. See Jack Alexander, "Missouri Dark Mule," *Saturday Evening Post,* October 8, 1938 (copy in Key Pittman Papers, Box 148).

Vandenberg gave the timid isolationists their Republican conservative. The long-time editor of the Grand Rapids *Herald* and protégé of Michigan Senator William Alden Smith came to Washington in 1928. His friendship with Senator Borah brought him good committee assignments at once. Within ten years he was actual, though not titular, leader of the Republican minority in the Senate, was twice nominated by the party caucus for the post of president *pro tem*, and was a leading contender for the presidential nomination.

He rose so rapidly because of his capacity for work, his ability to impress and influence his colleagues, his flexibility, and his talent for working out compromises on difficult questions. A man who had grown in stature during his years in office, Vandenberg was no reactionary. He could be described, in Elihu Root's phrase, as an "animated conservative" who was prepared to move with the times—but slowly.

Foreign policy was not the area to which he devoted most of his attention, though he had commented editorially on the subject in the pages of the Grand Rapids *Herald* and devoted a book, *The Trail of a Tradition*, to it in 1926. Although a member of the Foreign Relations Committee from the time he came to the Senate, Vandenberg had not taken much of a hand in the formulation of policy prior to 1934. Yet he was clearly impressed by what he heard as a member of the Nye Committee. His isolationism became neither rabid nor particularly active. Still, he definitely arrayed himself with the supporters of strict neutrality and the opponents of all entanglements, even of trade, that might lead the United States toward war.[33]

[33]Paul M. Cuncannon, "Arthur Vandenberg," in Salter, ed., *Politician*, 47–61; *Current Biography*, I (1940), 821–823; Arthur H. Vandenberg, Jr., ed. (with Joe Alex Morris), *The Private Papers of Senator Vandenberg* (Boston, 1952), *passim*.

Many of the measures these men sponsored were ultimately adopted. The most controversial, a proposal to embargo all strategic materials in wartime, led to the compromise two-year "cash-and-carry" provision of the Neutrality Act of 1937. All involved a surrender of traditional neutral rights and most showed a willingness to restrict America's foreign commerce in order to avoid dangerous contacts with belligerents.

"It is flirting with the nether regions to talk about trade now," Senator Bone declared, "when the countries in Europe, on their backs, are almost ready, like another desperate Samson, to throw their brawny arms around the pillars of the social temple and pull it down around our ears." In the House, Louis Ludlow of Indiana agreed. "Seek as we may to compromise the issue," he insisted, "there is but one way the neutrality of America may be guaranteed, and that is to break off trade and commercial relations entirely with foreign countries at war."

"There is the old doctrine of freedom of the seas and we all revere it," explained Representative Arthur H. Greenwood of Indiana, "but if the experience of that freedom is to carry our people or products into a war zone that will involve us in controversy, may it not be better that we set some example to the world and make some sacrifice of that ancient doctrine or right in order to promote a better doctrine and a higher civilization than the world has yet known?"

Representative A. Leonard Allen of Louisiana answered in the affirmative. So did Jerry Voorhis, the tall, pipe-smoking Kansan who had earned his *Phi Beta Kappa* key at Yale, traveled abroad in the service of the Y.M.C.A., been a cowboy, a freight handler, an auto assembler, a teacher of underprivileged boys, and a registered Socialist before coming to Congress as a Democrat from California in 1936.[34]

---

[34]*Congressional Record,* 75th Cong., 1st sess., 2686 (March 24, 1937);

Additional support for timid isolationism came from outside Congress. Donald W. Stewart, past commander of the Kansas Department of the American Legion, expressed the view of his organization that we "must steel ourselves to forego the unholy profit that comes from dealing in blood traffic. We must treat war as a contagious disease. We must isolate those who have it and refrain from all intercourse with them." And the Jesuit periodical, *America,* agreed that "if we wish to keep ourselves from the entanglement of war we must first keep ourselves from the entanglements created by commerce and business with nations engaged in war.... Safety can be found only in isolation." As for international law? Senator Bone spoke for many isolationists when he insisted: "Why talk of it? Why invoke it? It is as dead as Tophet."[35]

The differences between belligerent and timid isolationists involved more than a disagreement over methods. They indicated opposing conceptions of the world situation and of the role of the United States. Reliance on international law, the established rules of conduct among nations, reflected a desire by the belligerent isolationists to maintain the complete independence of action, both in the political and economic spheres, that marked American policy in the nineteenth century. World order, they argued, had collapsed in

[handwritten margin note: Opposing views - timid vs. belligerent ↓]

74th Cong., 2nd sess., 164 (January 8, 1936); 75th Cong., 1st sess., 2153, 2297–2298 (March 16, 1937); House Foreign Affairs Committee, *American Neutrality Policy; Hearings,* 75th Cong., 1st sess. (1937), 90–100; on Voorhis, see Claudius O. Johnson, "Jerry Voorhis: What is Right rather than what is Expedient," in Salter, ed., *Public Men,* 322–343, and *Current Biography,* II (1941), 888–889.

[35]Donald W. Stewart, "Planned Peace," in *Congressional Record,* 75th Cong., 1st sess., App. 397 (March 3, 1937); "Neutrality and Embargo," *America,* LVIII (April, 1938), 613; *Congressional Record,* 75th Cong., 1st sess., 1788 (March 3, 1937).

1914 not because basic international power relationships had
been altered by technological progress and the rise of militant nationalism, but rather because the nations of the world,
including the United States, had abandoned the ground rules
for international conduct developed since the days of Grotius.
Re-establishment of order in the world depended on the
revitalization of these rules and it was the mission of this
country to provide leadership toward that end. "A strong
neutral," wrote Borchard in 1937, "is the trustee for civilization in a shell-shocked world."[36]

The timid isolationists, on the other hand, regretfully
admitted that all nations had become more interdependent
in the twentieth century. They were aware that the development of the United States into a major agricultural and industrial power involved it—economically, at least—in the
general affairs of the world. But they did not think foreign
trade was essential to America's well-being, and they were
prepared to sacrifice at least some of it in order to preserve
independence of political action. In view of the sharply
decreased volume of foreign trade in the depression years, the
required sacrifice did not seem to be too great.

They were not concerned with the rehabilitation of rules
that appeared to have outlived their usefulness. Instead, they
hoped to develop new principles that could prevent nations
from being drawn, through their commercial relationships,
into wars that otherwise did not concern them. In this way,
a unilateralism stripped of what they regarded as nonessen-
tials could continue to serve the United States well. It
could not only keep America at peace and permit concentration on domestic problems. It could also demonstrate to
all nations that, even in an interdependent world, not all

[36]Borchard and Lage, *op. cit.,* 346.

conflicts had to assume global proportions. As Senator Clark told a nationwide radio audience in 1937, the United States would win "the greatest moral victory in the history of civilization if it actually keeps out of war."[37]

[37]Bennett Champ Clark, "Neutrality—What Kind?" *Vital Speeches of the Day,* III (February, 1937), 252.

III

THE LEFT AND THE RIGHT

THE division of isolationists into the belligerent and the timid cuts across party lines and has little relation to attitudes on domestic reform. Among the leading spokesmen for timid isolationism, Maverick, Bone, and Clark were Democrats; Nye and Vandenberg were Republicans. The most prominent of the belligerent isolationists were Republicans whose stand was an outgrowth of the Lodge-Roosevelt-Beveridge school of nationalist-imperialists dating from Spanish-American War days, but the Democratic chairman of the Foreign Relations Committee, Senator Key Pittman of Nevada, held basically similar views. Moreover, Nye and the entire Progressive contingent from Wisconsin belonged to one faction, while such old-line progressives as Borah and Johnson were in the other.[1] Economic conservatives such

[1] In February, 1936, for example, the entire Progressive delegation in the House protested in a letter to Speaker Byrns against the proposed limit on debate of the Neutrality Act. The signers wished to introduce and to discuss provisions for a general embargo on trade to belligerents, a move of which Borah and Johnson strongly disapproved; see *Congressional Record*, 74th Cong., 2nd sess., 2244 (February 17, 1936).

as Everett Dirksen of Illinois, then principally known as a
protégé of Colonel Robert R. McCormick and the Chicago
Tribune, and Hamilton Fish likewise had opposing alle-
giances.

[Despite this blurring of party lines and economic doctrines, *Domestic*
an informative distinction can be made between different *attitudes*
kinds of isolationists on the basis of their attitudes toward
conditions within the United States.] This is particularly true
for isolationists who did not hold public office and were not
directly concerned with the legislative process or the specific
steps necessary to implement American neutrality. Such
persons disagreed less on questions of neutral rights or foreign
trade than on the effects of international involvement and
war on the internal organization of the United States. The
essential difference was between the liberals and radicals,
who believed the New Deal offered a chance for domestic
reform but would be sidetracked by what they regarded as
foreign adventures, and the conservatives, who feared that
involvement in world affairs would lead to the complete
elimination of the American free enterprise system.

Both groups saw involvement in war as a prelude to dictatorship. Those liberals who were inclined to regard modern
war as the by-product of advanced capitalist competition,
believed the elimination of both war and unrestricted capitalism was essential to prevent the rise of fascism. Many conservatives, on the other hand, saw in what they considered
the deliberate creation of war hysteria a means for distracting
attention from the shortcomings of the New Deal, and consequently believed that involvement in war, with the governmental planning that would be required and accepted under
wartime conditions, would lead to Socialist or Communist
totalitarianism in America. [Concern for the internal problems of the United States thus led individuals whose political
beliefs were opposed on most issues to pursue identical

aims in foreign policy and to join forces in the isolationist camp.

By 1935, many who regarded themselves as liberals agreed with the *New Republic* that "the isolationist sentiment that is so strong in the Middle and Far West particularly, and that dominates Congress today, while it is partly irrational and deluded, is also in part founded on an understanding of realities that is entitled to the respect of the radicals."[2] To Charles A. Beard, for example, one of the realities was the need for dedication "to the making in the United States of a civilization, as distinguished from a combination of aggregated wealth, economic distresses, almshouses, work relief and public doles. . . . Surely such a policy is as defensible. . . ," he continued "as, let us say, one that leads to the killing of American boys in a struggle over the bean crop in Manchuria." Beard considered the task of this country to be the fashioning of a continental policy looking toward the establishment of a democratic, cooperative commonwealth. He expounded this theory in his three-volume *The Rise of American Civilization* and in a number of books written between 1936 and 1940.[3]

Charles A. Beard personified, in significant ways, the academic and intellectual element in isolationism, even though he was by no means alone in this category. Not only Moore of Columbia and Borchard of Yale, but also Phillips Bradley of Amherst, Harry Elmer Barnes of Smith and the New School for Social Research, Robert M. Hutchins of Chicago,

²Bruce Bliven, "They Cry 'Peace, Peace'," *New Republic*, LXXXIV (November, 1935), 354.

³Charles A. Beard, "Peace Loads the Guns," *Today*, IV (June, 1935), 23; for Beard's general views on American goals see Beard and Mary R. Beard, *The Rise of American Civilization* (3 vols., New York, 1928 and 1939); Beard and George H. E. Smith, *The Old Deal and the New* (New York, 1940); Beard, *A Foreign Policy for America* (New York, 1940).

and Henry Noble MacCracken of Vassar were prominent isolationists. The group of nonacademic intellectuals included Voorhis, Villard, Stuart Chase, and Norman Thomas. But Beard occupied a different niche in American life and letters. The man whose *An Economic Interpretation of the Constitution* opened new paths for the investigators of America's past, who was one of the guiding spirits of the "New History," who, as teacher and friend, became the idol of two generations of American historians, whose books were serialized in *Harper's* and distributed by the Book-of-the-Month Club, and who, in *The Rise of American Civilization*, created what is still one of the outstanding reinterpretations of the American past written in the twentieth century, brought into the fight against foreign involvement a towering reputation with his colleagues and with the public.

Beard was sixty years old when the worsening world situations brought him into the battle against American entanglement. He was born into a wealthy and staunchly Republican family near Knightstown, Indiana, and reared in an environment that emphasized the importance of business and the sanctity of private property. Yet the most vivid impressions the maturing Beard absorbed came from the raw industrialism of Chicago in the nineties. There he drifted into contact with Populists and Socialists and with the dedicated social workers of Hull House. Upon graduation from DePauw University, he went to Europe and remained there for four years, principally in Germany and in England.

From Germany, Beard brought back a distaste for professorial pretensions and a hatred of militarism. But he also found much to admire in German social legislation and became convinced that the United States lagged far behind in this field. In England, he became actively involved in the various streams of dissidence then combining to form the Labour party. He was influenced by John Ruskin's economic theories, helped set up the workingmen's Ruskin Hall at Oxford University, and lectured tirelessly on social problems and their solution. He became so prominent in British reform circles that Ramsay MacDonald, who believed the formation of a Labour government to be imminent, was prepared to consider Beard for a post in it.

Beard returned to the United States in 1899 to continue his studies, and earned his doctorate at Columbia in 1904. By 1915, he had published ten books, including *An Economic Interpretation of the Constitution, The Economic Origins of Jeffersonian Democracy,* and a half-dozen widely used textbooks on European and American history, and had been appointed professor of politics at Columbia University. He sought to exorcise the conservative, Anglo-Saxonist spirit of John W. Burgess, which hung heavily over Columbia, by offering challenging reinterpretations of the American past. His published works were cosmopolitan in outlook and showed few isolationist tendencies.

Beard's doctoral dissertation had dealt with English history and he continued to write voluminously about the European states. Moreover, his early books on the United States were attempts to apply general principles of historical development to the American past. By rejecting the traditional view of America's uniqueness and emphasizing the principle of economic causation, he was, at least by implication, pointing to the universality of the American experience and to its close relationship to European ideas and events.

The First World War changed Beard's career and, to some extent, his outlook as well. He supported America's entry into the war because his personal experience left him no doubt about the proper choice to be made between Germany and England. Yet he was appalled by the hysteria and intolerance the war produced in the United States. When

Columbia fired a pacifist faculty member in 1917, Beard protested against this infringement on academic freedom by resigning. He had little sympathy for the views of his dismissed colleague, but regarded the action of the trustees as undermining American war aims. "I am convinced," he wrote to President Nicholas Murray Butler of Columbia, "that while I remain in the pay of the trustees of Columbia University I cannot do effectively my humble part in sustaining public opinion in support of the just war on the German Empire or take a position of independence in the days of reconstruction that are to follow."[4]

The war and its aftereffects caused Beard to concentrate on America's internal problems, though he did not lose his interest in world affairs. His *Cross Currents in Europe Today* appeared in 1922, the year he served as adviser to the Institute for Municipal Research in Tokyo. Subsequently he was an adviser to the Japanese Minister for Home Affairs, Viscount Goto, worked with the governments of several Balkan nations, and published, with George Radin, *The Balkan Pivot—Yugoslavia*. But postwar developments disillusioned Beard about the prospect of reforming the world. When, after he had worked out an administrative arrangement for Yugoslavia that met the demands of both the Slovenes and the Croats, the Croat leader rose to his feet in the Yugoslav Parliament and shot his Slovene counterpart, the author of *The Development of Modern Europe* turned his back decisively on the Old World. "Let Dorothy Thompson settle the problems of Europe," snapped Beard, "I can't."[5] In *The Rise of American Civilization,* first published in 1927, the doctrine of American "continentalism," with its deliberate

---

[4]Quoted in Eric F. Goldman, *Rendezvous with Destiny* (New York, 1953), 260.

[5]Interview with Beard, in *ibid.,* 283. Goldman inadvertently refers to "Slovaks."

disregard for events elsewhere and its implied recommendation to "till our own garden," indicated the line of thought
that would determine his future activities.[6]

Liberal

Beard, like many others of a liberal and progressive bent,
welcomed the New Deal. Roosevelt's pragmatism and his
willingness to experiment appealed particularly to a man
who had always sought reforms yet eschewed the formal and
the dogmatic. Even the National Industrial Recovery Act of
1933, a stumbling block for many opponents of business
domination, was accepted by Beard as something worth trying. Yet doubts about Roosevelt's foreign policy intentions
came early. They became apparent in *The Open Door at
Home,* published in 1934, and were made explicit in an
article in *Scribner's Magazine* in February, 1935. "Confronted by the difficulties of a deepening domestic crisis and
by the comparative ease of a foreign war, what will President
Roosevelt do? Judging by the past history of American politicians," thought Beard, "he will choose the latter."[7]

Discerning what he took to be the handwriting on the
wall, Beard became an active isolationist. His nationalism and
his vigorous Americanism brought him, in some respects,
near the position of Borah and other belligerent isolationists.
However, his belief in economic causation led him to see
trade and commerce as particularly entangling factors. Since

---

[6] The literature on Beard is already very extensive. The most useful
comprehensive commentary on his life and work remains Howard K.
Beale, ed., *Charles A. Beard* (Lexington, Kentucky, 1954), esp. the
following essays: Eric F. Goldman, "Charles A. Beard: An Impression,"
1–7; Max Lerner, "Charles Beard's Political Theory," 25–45; Howard K.
Beale, "Charles Beard: Historian," 115–159; and, with some reservations,
George R. Leighton, "Beard and Foreign Policy," 161–184. See also
Goldman, *op. cit.,* 149–151, 235–236 and 283–284.

[7] Charles A. Beard and George H. E. Smith, *The Open Door at Home*
(New York, 1934), *passim;* Beard, "National Politics and War," *Scribner's Magazine,* XCVII (February, 1935), 70.

he also regarded foreign trade as a minor factor in the internal development of the United States and, in any case, believed in its regulation, he championed the methods urged by more timid spirits and lobbied for ever more stringent neutrality legislation.

Others saw the problems facing the United States in more doctrinaire terms but reached substantially the same conclusions. Norman Thomas was certain that "a declaration of war in capitalist America would not initiate a new struggle to make the world safe for democracy," but would simply show a desire, "intelligent or futile, to further national economic interests. . . . It is preposterous to think," he added, "that the workers in the United States, in the supreme emergency of war, can maneuver the capitalist state and its military organization to gain their own ends."[8]

Norman Thomas was the political left's gadfly during the thirties. A prolific, effective writer and a fiery, dynamic speaker, he purveyed a mixture of emotion and idealism whose appeal transcended the Socialist party and its circle of admirers. As an opponent of nationalism, capitalism, communism, and fascism, Thomas gained a large following among intellectuals. As a champion of the impoverished and neglected, he found sympathizers even among persons who had little use for Karl Marx. He had no political power, for his admirers were willing to give him everything but their votes. But the tireless presentation of his ideas to all who would listen was not without effect. His correspondence with President Roosevelt and other national leaders reveals the respect with which his views were considered even when, as was usually the case, their wider implications were dismissed.

Thomas had grown up in a thoroughly middle-class en-

[8]Norman Thomas, "The Pacifist's Dilemma," *Nation*, CXLIV (January, 1937), 67, 68.

vironment. His father was a Presbyterian minister in Marion, Ohio. Both of his grandfathers had also been active in church work. Young Norman had a normal Midwestern small-town boyhood, which included a stint as delivery boy for Warren G. Harding's *Daily Star*. He compiled a brilliant high school record before going on to Bucknell University and then to Princeton, where he graduated in 1905. After working for two years in a settlement house in New York City's slums and traveling around the world, he became assistant pastor at Christ Church Settlement and then assistant at Brick Presbyterian Church on Fifth Avenue in New York. Still far from being a Socialist, Thomas voted for William Howard Taft in the election of 1908. He continued studying for the ministry at Union Theological Seminary and was ordained in 1911, becoming pastor of the East Harlem Presbyterian Church, located in a poverty-stricken area inhabited largely by immigrants.

By the First World War, Norman Thomas had seen a great deal of wretchedness and misery. His experiences in East Harlem had led him to believe that churches and settlement houses were ineffectual in dealing with the conditions he had encountered. His reading of Socialist writers had convinced him that these ills were inherent in America's social institutions. The entry of the United States into the war crystallized these views. As a convinced pacifist, Thomas saw the churches' approval of the war as an admission of impotence and a betrayal of their trust and mission. He supported Socialist Morris Hillquit for the mayoralty of New York City in 1917. When, as a result, a number of belligerent church elders succeeded in cutting off the funds necessary for his social service work, he resigned his pastorate. Thomas did not formally leave the ministry until 1931, but he had already joined the Socialist party in 1917, at a time when the party was under heavy attack for its opposition to the war and was losing members steadily. His action was greatly appreciated and he soon rose to a position of leadership.

Norman Thomas also became active in the antiwar Fellowship of Reconciliation, and founded its publication, *The New World* (later *The World Tomorrow*). He edited this magazine until 1921, when he resigned to become associate editor of the *Nation*. With lawyer Roger Baldwin, he founded the National Civil Liberties Bureau, the forerunner of the American Civil Liberties Union; with labor unionist Harry Laidler, he reorganized the old Intercollegiate Socialist Society into the League for Industrial Democracy.

Liberty and economic justice were the principal aims for which he fought. He defended minority rights, attacked corruption, and supported strikes in all parts of the country. This brought him into frequent trouble with the police, as in Passaic, New Jersey, in 1926, but it also made him a well-publicized national figure. His Emergency Committee for Strikers' Relief was able to raise large sums of money, and he did more than any other man to alert America to the plight of the southern sharecropper.[9]

From 1924 on, he was repeatedly a candidate for public offices ranging from alderman to the presidency of the United States. He never had the remotest possibility of victory, yet gladly accepted the opportunity the campaigns offered to carry his views to his fellow citizens. Increasingly, these views had isolationist overtones. With the onset of the world crisis in the thirties, Thomas became one of the chief spokesmen for the isolationism of the left.

As a Socialist, he was an internationalist by definition. But he was first and foremost an American who sought to

[9]Don D. Lescohier, "Norman Thomas," in Salter, ed., *Politician,* 247–260; *Current Biography,* V (1944), 688–691; Murray B. Seidler, *Norman Thomas: Respectable Rebel* (Syracuse, 1962), *passim.*

reorganize the economic system of the United States, and a
pacifist who saw war as the greatest enemy of progress everywhere. The United States, he believed, might yet be saved
for socialism. As part of a wartime capitalist coalition, even
against the fascism Thomas hated and feared, America would
lose that chance.

A similar approach to America's problems found strong
support in the pages of *Common Sense*. Until the fall of
France, this magazine combined vigorous isolationism with
espousal of a third-party movement designed to reorganize
the American economic system. Editor Alfred M. Bingham
came from a wealthy Connecticut family and was a graduate
of Groton and Yale. His father, Hiram, had been a noted
amateur archeologist and a very conservative member of the
United States Senate. Young Bingham found no satisfaction
with his father's world and was favorably impressed by what
he saw on a trip to Italy and the Soviet Union in 1931. In
Common Sense, which he founded in 1932, and in his book,
Insurgent America, published three years later, Bingham
spoke up for a new America, which would acquire the
dynamism he detected in the Communist and Fascist states
without having to pay the same price in lives and terror. Such
views brought him into association with the League for
Independent Political Action, which Paul H. Douglas of the
University of Chicago and John Dewey had organized in 1929;
with Floyd Olson and the Minnesota Farmer-Labor party;
and with the American Commonwealth Political Federation,
founded in 1935 in the hope that it would become the party
of rational radicalism in the United States.[10]

[10]Schlesinger, *Upheaval,* 147–150; Alfred M. Bingham, *Insurgent
America* (New York, 1935) and *Man's Estate* (New York, 1939). The
Common Sense Papers in the Yale University Library contain little
biographical information.

Bingham's dreams of a new political alignment were never fulfilled, but he made *Common Sense* the liveliest radical journal in the United States. Along with his ideas of an insurgent America, he propagated isolationist doctrine. Like Norman Thomas, he believed all hope of rational reorganization of the American economic and political system would be destroyed if the United States participated in another war. In 1937, he stated his case clearly:

For the last four years America has taken the first awkward but nevertheless giant strides toward a new social order. If the march continues as it has begun . . . we may see a gradual but nonetheless swift elimination of our capitalist past. If we have peace, if we keep our hands to our own task, if we set our own house in order, we may be able to show a mad world the way to sanity. . . . If we are drawn into a war of the democracies against Fascism, it will simply mean that the last of the democracies has vanished, and we shall become, like the Fascist powers, a military dictatorship. . . . To support capitalism against Fascism is like supporting earlier laissez-faire capitalism of the Jeffersonian agrarian ideal, against the devouring encroachments of monopoly capitalism. The clock cannot be turned back. The past cannot be perpetuated. Capitalist democracy cannot be made the bulwark against Fascism. The only positive alternative to Fascism is a Socialist democracy.[11]

"You cannot defeat fascism by defeating fascist nations in war," editorialized the *New Republic,* taking up the same theme. "You cannot end war by waging war. On the contrary, nothing is more likely than that the United States would go fascist through the very process of organizing to defeat the fascist nations." And Representative Herbert S. Bigelow of Ohio told a radio audience: "Social and industrial justice is the only hope of democracy and the only guaranty

[11]Alfred M. Bingham, "War Mongering on the Left," *Common Sense,* VI (May, 1937), 10, (June, 1937), 15.

against war. While we know this, while we know that the
seeds of war are embedded in the very type of social order
that we have, changing this social order is a long evolutionary
process, and in the meantime we are wise to resort to any
expedient that promises any protection whatever against the
probabilities of war."[12]

Underlying such arguments was confidence that something
like social democracy could be achieved in the United States,
a confidence largely undimmed throughout the thirties. "If
the democracies can keep out of war," Bingham wrote in
1938, "the chance of carrying through this peaceful transition
to democratic planning is good. . . . The movement in America
is particularly hopeful because of the courage and good
will and occasional intelligence of the New Deal."[13]

Also in 1938, Jerome Frank, a New Deal lawyer who had
been counsel for the Agricultural Adjustment Administration
and the Reconstruction Finance Corporation, was then a
member of the Securities and Exchange Commission, and
later became a judge of the United States Circuit Court of
Appeals for the Second District, offered in *Save America
First* a blueprint for the remaking of the United States. It
included a strong and lengthy warning against putting the
project in jeopardy through needless involvement in war. In
the following year, Norman Thomas and his fellow Socialist,
Bertram D. Wolfe, admitted that "here in the 'healthiest' and

[12]"Positive Neutrality," *New Republic*, LXXXXII (October, 1937),
327; Herbert S. Bigelow, "A Referendum on War," in *Congressional
Record*, 75th Cong., 1st sess., App. 1633 (June 30, 1937). The fear that
this country might go Fascist had been expressed in liberal circles as
early as 1935. The pacifist minister of New York's Community Church,
John Haynes Holmes, for example, believed that "Fascism is definitely
on the way." See Holmes to Amos Pinchot, dtd April 19, 1935, in
Pinchot Papers, Box 56.
[13]"Why Commit Suicide?" *Common Sense*, VII (March 1938), 5.

'wealthiest' land of the modern world, there is an unsolved crisis of ten years' duration, and forces driving toward state capitalism, fascism, and war." Yet they remained optimistic about the results that would be obtained by enlisting the "heroism, loyalty and energies of all men and women of understanding and good will" in "this war against poverty, yes, and war against war."[14]

By the end of 1940, even though Hitler was triumphant in Europe and the United States was already partially committed to underwriting an Allied victory, labor economist Stuart Chase still believed this country possessed "a workable pattern for community survival and well-being" independent of the rest of the world. A New Englander who had been educated at Harvard, Chase saw "clearly visible" the "abolition of poverty, unprecedented improvements in health and energy, a towering renaissance in the arts, an architecture and an engineering to challenge the gods"—if only participation in war could be avoided. But if war comes, Oswald Garrison Villard assured Congresswoman Jeanette Rankin of Montana, who had voted against war in 1917 and returned to Washington after a twenty-year absence just in time to cast the only vote against war in 1941, we shall "watch the destruction of everything we hold dear in American life and the loss of all our great gains under Roosevelt."[15]

Villard typified yet another element in left-wing isolationism. Neither an academic iconoclast like Beard, nor a dogmatic Socialist like Thomas, nor, like Bingham, a young

[14] Jerome Frank, *Save America First* (New York, 1938), *passim,* esp. 150 ff; Norman Thomas and Bertram D. Wolfe, *Keep America Out of War* (New York, 1939), 160–161, 183; see also John T. Flynn in "If War Comes," *Common Sense,* VIII (March 1939), 12.

[15] Stuart Chase, "Four Assumptions About the War," *Uncensored,* Suppl. to no. 65 (December 28, 1940), 1–2; Villard to Rankin, dtd December 17, 1940, Villard Papers, File 3162.

man in revolt against the world of his father, Villard was
basically an old-fashioned democratic liberal with both the
virtues and shortcomings implied by the epithet "do-gooder."
A catalogue of the causes he supported is virtually a complete
list of the American reform movements of the twentieth
century. He was active in the struggle for women's rights,
helped found the National Association for the Advancement
of Colored People, uncovered insurance scandals and corruption in the New York legislature, attacked the Espionage
Act of 1917 and the Palmer Raids that followed as violations
of civil liberties, and regarded himself as an enemy of trusts,
tariffs, and "Wall Street." As a pacifist, he opposed the Spanish-American War and American entry into the First World
War. He attacked the Treaty of Versailles as an inadequate
basis for world peace.

His German-born father, Henry Hilgard, had been a
protégé of Horace Greeley who abandoned journalism and
went on to become president of the Northern Pacific Railroad
and the Edison General Electric Company. His mother was
a daughter of that fieriest of Abolitionists, William Lloyd
Garrison. From this home environment, young Villard inherited the crusading moralism of New England, the ideals
of the German Revolution of 1848, and sufficient shares of
railroad stock to make him financially independent.

After earning a master's degree at Harvard in 1896, he
served briefly as an assistant in the History Department there
and then went into journalism. He worked for the Philadelphia *Press,* for his father's New York *Evening Post,* and
for the *Nation,* which at that time was a literary supplement
to the *Post.* As editorial writer, and later as president of the
Post, he built an effective crusading newspaper. He strongly
supported Wilson in 1912, but was bitterly disillusioned by
American entry into the war. His outspoken pacifism brought
him under heavy attack. In 1918, he sold the *Post* but retained

the *Nation,* which he turned into a fighting, muckraking magazine during the twenties.

As the worsening world crisis of the thirties brought America closer to war, Villard increasingly devoted himself to promoting isolationism. In numerous articles in the *Nation* and in a series of books and pamphlets, he sought to awaken the public to what he believed were the lessons of the First World War and urged strict neutrality for the United States. Because the New Deal fitted in with his undogmatic liberalism, he was anxious that the benefits he believed could accrue from the Roosevelt policies should not be frittered away in pointless foreign quarrels. Although he had no sympathy for German expansionism and attacked it in print, he never came to regard the war in Europe as of vital concern to the United States.

On June 29, 1940, he resigned from the *Nation* to protest its decision to support all-out aid to the Allies. He had sold the magazine some years earlier. He became embittered toward the New Deal and Roosevelt, and did not keep himself entirely free of a peripheral form of anti-Semitism. In his own way, however, he continued what he had always regarded as the fight for a better America, free of poverty and injustice, and free of war.[16]

In 1941, Norman Thomas was still convinced "we have totalitarianism because of the apparent failure of what men call democracy to provide national security and private security in a woefully disorganized condition in Europe." He still maintained that "if we show that it is possible to improve and keep democracy and settle better than the dictatorships have ever settled the problem of jobs and the cries of

[16]D. Joy Humes, *Oswald Garrison Villard, Liberal of the 1920's* (Syracuse, 1960), Chap. I and *passim;* Oswald Garrison Villard, *Fighting Years* (New York, 1939); *Current Biography,* I (1940), 830–832.

poverty, no dictator could ever keep Europe under his thumb." To go to war would halt such progress in the United States and do nothing to resolve the basic problems of the world, which he saw in economic terms. In the end, it would bring fascist dictatorship to America.[17]

Fear that involvement in war would turn the United States into a dictatorship was not confined to the liberals and radicals. Conservative critics had been claiming from the New Deal's inception that economic regimentation and centralization of power in the executive were its chief evils. As early as 1934, Herbert Hoover had pointed out that "its very spirit is governmental direction, management and dictation of social and economic life. It is a vast shift from the American concept of human rights which even the government may not infringe to those social philosophies where men are wholly subjective to the state. It is a vast casualty to Liberty if it shall be continued."[18] Such pronouncements were the substance of the materials published by the American Liberty League in the years that followed.

While the Roosevelt Administration refrained from actively participating in world affairs such arguments did not seem to apply to foreign policy. Conservative isolationists usually identified themselves, therefore, with either the international-law or economic-isolationist schools. By 1937, however, conservatives began associating the President's new interest in the troubles of Asia and Europe with his domestic policies. They began to express fears that involvement in war would mean the culmination of the trend toward dictatorship they had so long described and opposed. Albert Shaw, editor of the *Review of Reviews,* now foresaw the possibility that "a

[17]House Foreign Affairs Committee, *Lend-Lease Bill; Hearings,* 77th Cong., 1st sess. (1941), 348.

[18]Herbert Hoover, "Challenge to Liberty," in Edwin C. Rozwenc, ed., *The New Deal—Revolution or Evolution?* (Boston, 1949), 61, 70.

population as easily hypnotized as ours by the appealing tones of a radio voice" might once again be convinced of the necessity for American participation in war. "What a chance," he exclaimed, "to perpetuate the one-man rule under which we have lived of late, with ever increasing demands for more power."[19] Roosevelt's Quarantine Speech of October 5, 1937, added to these apprehensions.

Speaking before the Council on Foreign Relations in March, 1938, Hoover pointed out that both communism and fascism "are the aftermath of the gradual infection of democracy.... And let me again repeat," he continued, "that democracies are first infected by the plausible motives of 'cure the business slump' through so-called economic planning. Every step in this direction requires another. Every step further demoralizes the economy. And step by step more force and coercion must be applied until all liberty—economic and personal and political—is lost." Involvement in war would merely create further emergencies, further excuses for regimentation, additional denials of liberty, and the ultimate triumph of dictatorship at home.[20]

By January, 1939, Senator Robert A. Taft of Ohio was spelling out the issues even more clearly on the American Forum of the Air. He was convinced that "a war to preserve democracy or otherwise would almost certainly destroy democracy in the United States. We have moved far towards totalitarian government already. The additional powers sought by the President in case of war, the nationalization of all industry and all capital and all labor, already proposed in bills before Congress, would create a socialist dictatorship

---

[19]Albert Shaw, "The Progress of the World," *Review of Reviews*, XCV (June 1937), 7.

[20]Herbert Hoover, "The Greatest Service the Nation Can Give," *Vital Speeches of the Day*, IV (April, 1938), 411, 407–412.

which it would be impossible to dissolve when the war ended." Five months later, he reiterated this position in an editorial in *Current History*. And Hoover agreed that "the lowered vitality of free enterprise. . .together with the ideas of economic power which impregnate our government, all drive to the improbability of after-war demobilization of centralized power."[21]

Hoover and Taft were unquestionably the key figures among the conservative isolationists. Although both belonged to the right wing of the Republican party and shared many political views, the former President and the freshman Senator from Ohio came from completely different backgrounds. The rise of Herbert Hoover, son of an Iowa Quaker blacksmith, first to wealth and fame as a mining engineer and then to the Presidency, embodied the American dream, even though it had occurred on a world-wide stage. Before the First World War, Hoover had resided for many years in Europe and the Orient. During the war, he spent considerable time in Belgium and was instrumental in organizing relief work there. As head of the United States Food Administration, as Secretary of Commerce, and as President, he was constantly concerned with the international scene for fifteen years. Although his economic policies were consistent with his later isolationism, his general views on foreign policy were not militantly isolationist prior to 1933.

To be sure, in 1919 Hoover told Woodrow Wilson that the United States could not afford to be "dragged into European entanglements," because he had come to believe that the rivalries among the Continental powers were malign, en-

[21]Robert A. Taft, "Let Us Stay Out of War," *Vital Speeches of the Day*, V (February, 1939), 255; "Let Us Mind Our Own Business," *Current History*, L (June, 1939), 32–33; Herbert Hoover, "Our New Foreign Policy," *Vital Speeches of the Day*, V (February, 1939), 260.

demic, and eternal.[22] But he was sufficiently favorable to the League of Nations to be briefly considered as a Democratic presidential possibility in 1920. He did not oppose adherence to the World Court and supported, though with considerable reluctance, the active foreign policy of his Secretary of State, Henry L. Stimson, which included reliance on international conferences to settle world problems. He even agreed to some cooperation with the League of Nations after the Mukden incident of 1931, which led the Japanese to set up the puppet state of Manchukuo, and sent Prentiss Gilbert, and later Charles G. Dawes, to sit in on the meetings in Geneva.

After his defeat in 1932, however, Hoover's efforts at political rehabilitation turned him increasingly in an isolationist direction. Blaming the American economic crisis on international developments, he ultimately concluded that less contact with foreign nations would have spared the United States the Depression. When Roosevelt began following an internationalist course, Hoover suspected a plot to increase presidential power he already regarded as dictatorial and charged the President with attempting to cover up failure at home by embarking on foreign adventures.[23]

These views were shared by <u>Robert A. Taft</u>, who regarded the refurbishing of Hoover's reputation as a prerequisite for the fulfillment of his own ambitions. He had shown himself, in his Uncle Horace's Taft School in Connecticut, at Yale, and at Harvard Law School, to be a solemn and diffident

(margin handwritten notes:) Conservative views of Hoover + Taft

Conservative isolationist

---

[22]Hoover to Wilson, dtd April 11, 1919, quoted in William Starr Myers, *The Foreign Policies of Herbert Hoover: 1929–1933* (New York, 1940), 17.

[23]For a convenient summary of Hoover's career, see Harris Gaylord Warren, *Herbert Hoover and the Great Depression* (New York, 1959), 19–38. See also Robert H. Ferrell, *American Diplomacy in the Great Depression* (Yale Historical Publications, David Horne, ed., Studies 17, New Haven, 1957), esp. 17–18, 39–43 and 140–143. Hoover's own extensive writings contain very little information on his foreign policy views.

young man, and a brilliant and hard-working student. After
obtaining his law degree, he had returned to his native
Cincinnati to practice, and had married the daughter of his
father's Solicitor General, Lloyd Bowers.

Taft was no provincial Midwesterner. He had been educated entirely in the East, had accompanied his father to the
Philippines at the turn of the century, and had served during
the First World War as Assistant Counsel for Hoover's
United States Food Administration. For his latter services as
American Relief Administrator in Europe he was decorated
by the governments of Poland, Finland, and Belgium. Once
more following the lead of his father, he supported the
League of Nations, though with some reservations, in 1919
and 1920.

In 1922 he entered politics and was elected to the Ohio
legislature. During his four-year tenure, he acquired the unspectacular reputation of being a silk-stocking politician
with an interest in tax reform. He retired from public office
in 1926, but became a power in the politics of his native state
and was a favorite-son candidate for the Republican presidential nomination in 1936. Two years later, after a campaign during which he traveled more than 30,000 miles,
spent money lavishly, and was ably supported by his wife,
Taft was elected to the Senate.

He began at once to make his presence felt. Taft's name
and undoubted ability, the smallness of the Republican contingent in the Senate, and the sparseness of Republican election victories, all combined to allow him to become a leading
figure among the opponents of Roosevelt's domestic and
foreign policies almost at once. His isolationism, like most of
the policies he advocated, bore a distinctive Taft stamp. He
parted company with almost all of the other isolationists, for
example, on the question of arms embargo repeal in 1939,

and was less reluctant than most of them to aid Great Britain in its struggle against Hitler's Germany. But, like Hoover, he vigorously opposed all entanglements and was convinced that the President's warnings of danger from abroad were merely part of an attempt to distract the American public from the shortcomings of the New Deal and to provide an excuse for enlarging presidential powers.[24]

The idea that there was a relationship between the New Deal's failure and the shift in Administration foreign policy after 1937 was also propounded in a series of *Saturday Evening Post* editorials appearing in 1939. At the same time, William J. Goodwin, Democratic leader of New York's Queens County, went even further, declaring that the "attempt of the administration to line up on the side of Stalin in the European war which now seems to be threatening, throws a startling light upon some of the past actions of the present administration." The increased public debt, the Works Progress Administration, and the concentration of power in the executive seemed to Goodwin to have paved the way for a Communist dictatorship. Conservationist Amos Pinchot, a self-styled "anti-New Deal Progressive" who, in fact, was moving in very conservative circles by 1936, had expressed his fear of a Socialist Roosevelt dictatorship even earlier, and eventually became a member of the national committee of America First, was certain that:

Roosevelt, having shot his bolt and missed the bull's eye, which is recovery, is a desperate man as well as a reckless one. And if it suits his book to gain support by the tom-tom and war dance method, he will act without sitting down and asking himself: Am I being a patriot or just a common or garden S.O.B.?

[24]William S. White, *The Taft Story* (New York, 1954), *passim; Current Biography,* I (1940), 787–789. For Taft's view on the arms embargo, see his letter to F. J. Libby, dtd May 1, 1939, in Pinchot Papers, Box 66.

A year later he was to express the same sentiments to the President himself, albeit in somewhat more genteel tones.[25]

Pinchot and those who shared his views were equally certain that involvement in war would destroy America's free institutions and the foundations of its economy. Former Secretary of State Bainbridge Colby made this clear to the Foreign Relations Committee and Representative Roy C. Woodruff of Michigan explained it to a nation-wide radio audience. The Most Reverend Francis J. Beckman, Archbishop of Dubuque, saw the fine hand of "Communist anti-Christs" behind the movement to involve the United States, and freely predicted a Communist America, if this nation exhausted itself in war.[26]

Such arguments were the mainstay of the America First Committee after its formation in 1940. By October, 1939, General Robert E. Wood, chairman of the board of Sears, Roebuck and Company and soon to be head of the Committee, was urging in a letter to President Roosevelt that the "only possible way of preserving our own institutions is to stay out of the conflict at any cost." Although Wood voiced his approval of the social gains of the past six years, he clearly did not favor their extension, especially not through further centralization of executive power justified by a war emergency. Similar sentiments were expressed or implied in

[25]See, for example, "Who Cultivates War," *Saturday Evening Post,* CCXI (April 8, 1939), 24, 109; Senate, *Neutrality, Peace Legislation, etc.; Hearings,* 436; Pinchot to Frank Gannett, dtd April 27, 1939, in Pinchot Papers, Box 66; Open Letter to Franklin D. Roosevelt, dtd March 13, 1940, in Pinchot Papers, Box 67.

[26]Open Letter to the President, dtd September 19, 1939, and Roy C. Woodruff, "What War Means," speech delivered over the facilities of the National Broadcasting Company on April 15, 1939, in Pinchot Papers, Box 66; a copy of Archbishop Beckman's radio speech of October 29, 1939 is in the Borah Papers, Box 426; for Colby's remarks, see Senate, *Neutrality, Peace Legislation, etc.; Hearings,* 512.

America First literature following the formation of the group.[27]

General Wood was probably the best example of a responsible member of the business community who was an active isolationist. His father had fought with John Brown's raiders, been a captain in the Union Army, homesteaded in Kansas, and prospected for gold in Colorado. Young Wood went to West Point, probably because it gave him a free education, and was graduated in 1900. He served in the Philippines and Montana, then taught Spanish and French at West Point. Later, he was transferred to Panama, where he became chief quartermaster and director of the Panama Railroad Company. For ten years, he was in charge of both personnel and supply for the construction of the Panama Canal.

His experience made him valuable to private industry. He resigned his commission in 1915 to accept executive positions with DuPont and, later, with the General Asphalt Company. Soon after America's entry into the war he returned to the Army and served until 1919 as Acting Quartermaster-General with the rank of brigadier general. His job was keeping four million men supplied with food, clothing, and other items, and the experience he gained served him in good stead when he became vice-president of Montgomery Ward in 1924. He later transferred to Sears, Roebuck and Company, where he was made president in 1928 and chairman of the board of directors in 1939.

Wood was a respected and successful businessman who held directorships in numerous corporations, was one of the "public" governors of the New York Stock Exchange, and chair-

[27]Wood to Roosevelt, dtd October 6, 1939, FDRL PPF 1365; America First Committee pamphlets and handbills in FDRL OF 4330, America First Papers of the Swarthmore College Peace Collection, and Pinchot Papers, esp. Box 88.

man of the Economic Policy Committee of the National
Association of Manufacturers. He was neither narrow-minded
nor reactionary, did not move in Liberty League circles, and
was not a Roosevelt-hater. Though nominally a Republican,
he had, in fact, supported the Roosevelt candidacy in 1932
and 1936. He disagreed with various aspects of the New Deal,
but favored its agricultural policy, its regulation of the stock
exchanges, and Social Security.

On foreign policy questions, he came to differ widely with
the Administration. He finally agreed, though reluctantly, to
lead the America First Committee when R. Douglas Stuart,
Jr., the Yale law student and son of a Quaker Oats Company
vice-president who was the group's chief organizer, suggested
it to him. His reluctance was not feigned. Wood was only a
moderate isolationist, who eventually supported some form
of aid to the Allies. His concept of America First, unlike that
of many of his associates, included the realization that it
would be senseless to divide the United States into bitterly
warring factions, even over the question of intervention in
war.[28]

Other members of the Committee were far less moderate.
By 1941, Colonel Charles A. Lindbergh was convinced that
if "our American ideals are to survive, it will not be through
the narcotic of a foreign war, but through a reawakening of
the spirit that brought this nation into existence. . . . The
future of America, of our way of life and of western civilization itself lies not so much in the outcome of these wars
abroad as in the action *we* take *now* in our own country."
And over the signature of Amos Pinchot, the New York
Chapter of the America First Committee urged everyone to
oppose the twin evils of "involvement in the bloody conflicts

[28]*Current Biography,* II (1940), 933–935; Cole, *America First,* 12–14,
17–19 and *passim.*

of Europe, Africa and Asia" and "political and economic
dictatorship—that is to say ONE MAN GOVERNMENT—
right here in the United States."[29]

By enlisting Charles Augustus Lindbergh in their ranks,
the isolationists acquired the services of a genuine popular
idol. The elder Charles Lindbergh, a radical politician of
Swedish descent who had been elected to Congress in 1906 as
an opponent of "the money trust" and "the House of Morgan," had bitterly opposed American entry into the First
World War. His book, *Why Is Your Country at War?* had
been suppressed by government agents, and he had failed of
election to the governorship of Minnesota in 1918 at least
in part because of the charges of "Bolshevism" leveled against
him. His son was no radical and no politician, but he was
probably the most effective proponent of isolationism in the
years immediately preceding Pearl Harbor.

Young Lindbergh had begun to study engineering at the
University of Wisconsin in 1920 but soon left for Lincoln,
Nebraska, to enroll as a flying student with the Nebraska
Aircraft Corporation. By 1925, he had made his mark as a
barnstorming stunt flier, received training in the United
States Air Reserve, and been commissioned a first lieutenant
in the Missouri National Guard. Two years later, he re-
ceived the necessary financial backing from a group of St.
Louis businessmen to order the construction of an airplane,
the *Spirit of St. Louis,* in San Diego. He flew it across the
continent in record time and, on May 20, 1927, took off from
New York on the first solo nonstop flight across the Atlantic
to Paris. Thirty-three and a half hours later, he landed at
Le Bourget Airfield.

[29]Charles A. Lindbergh, "A Letter to Americans," in Schoonmaker
and Reid, eds., *op. cit.,* 81; form letter from New York Chapter,
America First Committee, in Widener Library, Harvard University.
Italics and capitalization in the originals.

The blond, boyish American's feat of skill and courage caught the imagination of the world like no other single event of the hectic twenties. Lindbergh was entertained by the heads of many European governments, and received medals from the President of France, the King of the Belgians, and the King of England. The United States awarded him the Distinguished Flying Cross and the Congressional Medal of Honor, and promoted him to a colonelcy in the Army Air Corps. President Coolidge even sent a cruiser to France to bring him home. In 1930, he married Anne Spencer Morrow, a daughter of former Morgan partner Dwight Morrow. His father-in-law was serving as American ambassador to Mexico at the time. In the three years between his flight and his marriage, Lindbergh amassed a fortune estimated at one and one-half million dollars.

Life in the limelight soon became burdensome to the shy, reticent Midwesterner. The constant hounding by reporters, who even followed his honeymoon yacht in a motor launch, made him skeptical of the value of freedom of the press long before the tragic kidnap-murder of his infant son in 1932 made the most intimate details of his private life public property. In 1934, a Senate committee headed by Hugo L. Black of Alabama, investigating graft in connection with the awarding of airmail contracts, accused Lindbergh, then an executive of Transcontinental and Western Air, Inc., "The Lindbergh Line," of illegally accepting money from various airlines, and the flyer's regard for democratic institutions declined further. In 1935, the arrest and trial of Bruno Richard Hauptmann for the 1932 kidnapping once more projected the Lindberghs into the headlines. After Hauptmann's conviction they left the United States.

They sought safety and privacy in England, where they moved in the fashionable Cliveden set. A trip to Germany in July, 1936, at the invitation of Reich Minister of Aviation

Hermann Goering and with the blessing of the United States Government, convinced Lindbergh of Germany's military strength, a conviction strengthened further by visits in October, 1937, and October, 1938. In contrast, a journey to the Soviet Union in August, 1938, led him to conclude that Russia's military potential was greatly overrated. He passed such information on to Prime Minister Neville Chamberlain, whose actions at the Munich Conference may have been affected by this news.

In April, 1939, the Lindberghs returned to the United States for a visit that became a permanent stay. Soon after, the Colonel made his first isolationist speech at the invitation of Fulton Lewis, Jr., Washington correspondent for the Mutual Broadcasting System. Many similar speeches followed. By 1940, Lindbergh was boomed by Father Coughlin's *Social Justice* for the vice-presidential spot on a ticket headed by Wendell Willkie. The following year, he joined the national committee of America First.

Lindbergh's isolationism had many roots. It may have owed something to his home environment and the antiwar stand of his father. If so, the connection was purely emotional, for he shared none of the radicalism which had supported the pacifism of the elder Lindbergh. Moreover, he was in no way moved by sympathy for the Soviet Union, whose social system he despised, but was attracted by Nazi Germany, whose efficiency and military prowess he admired. He justified the Third Reich's expansion toward the East and placed responsibility for the outbreak of the Second World War on the shoulders of Great Britain and France.

Lindbergh cannot simply be dismissed as foreign-oriented, because his conduct after Pearl Harbor attests to his patriotism. But his personal experiences led him to distrust democracy and to doubt both the virtue and the strength of Great Britain. He also feared and distrusted President Roosevelt

and went so far as to propose countermeasures for the event—
which he regarded as likely—that Roosevelt should curb the
freedom of speech of his opponents and cancel the 1944
elections.[30] There can be little doubt that a general lack of
political judgment was an ingredient of Lindbergh's isolationism. General Wood, whose organization benefited from
the Colonel's popularity but suffered criticism because of
some of the views he expressed, thought Lindbergh was absolutely sincere—but politically blind.[31] It is likely that Wood
was right in his judgment. Nevertheless, no speaker in the
isolationist camp enjoyed greater popularity than Lindbergh
or received a more enthusiastic response to the oft-repeated
assertion that America's true interests would best be served
by noninvolvement in the troubles of the world.

Summary   Avoidance of war and rejection of international entanglements thus were considered desirable both by those who
feared the New Deal and by those who regarded it as the only
hope for America's salvation. The left-wing isolationists
sought to insulate America against the historical forces they
associated with monopoly capitalism and its internal contra-
dictions. By so doing, they expected to assure this country of
the independent opportunity to work out a just and democratic Socialist solution. If the United States became closely
aligned with Great Britain and France, they argued, it could
not escape the downfall that would be the inevitable fate of
those nations.

No Europe   The conservatives' motives were much the same, although
ties   the result they desired was different. To Hoover and Taft,
as well as to Beard and Thomas, the tying of America's
fortunes to Europe's meant common disaster. But while the
liberals and radicals hoped to remake the economy in order to

[30]*Current Biography,* II (1941), 513–518; Cole, *America First, passim;*
Charles A. Lindbergh, *"We"* (New York, 1927).
[31]Interview with Wood, in Cole, *America First,* 252, n. 121.

forestall this eventuality, the conservatives hoped to restore *Conserv.* it to its pre-Depression vigor and thus to save democracy by *save* *capitalism* saving capitalism.

To both groups, the essential consideration was the necessity for the United States to operate freely and independently. What set isolationists apart from other Americans was not fear of war per se—since that was to some degree a universal fear—nor unwillingness to tackle the major political and economic problems that were troublesome here and abroad. Isolationists were merely distinguished by the conviction that it would be far better, even in a contracting world, to attempt to work out these problems independently in the one nation that still seemed to have the strength and the will to do so, rather than to risk an unnecessary war whose strains even this country would not likely survive.

IV

BASES OF ISOLATIONISM

FEAR that involvement in war would breed dictatorship at home and jealous concern for the preservation of America's independence in foreign affairs did not wholly justify the isolationists' position. If the malady besetting the United States, whether the inevitable result of monopoly capitalism or of creeping socialism and the failure of economic planning, was a world-wide disease, it probably could be cured only through concerted international action. If nineteenth-century individualism in international relations was to be restored, this could be done best by supporting Great Britain and France, powers that had shown some respect for international law in the past and had no territorial ambitions likely to keep the world in turmoil. Isolationists dismissed these alternatives because they held an additional set of beliefs that remains to be examined.

The rejection of international cooperation in the face of the crisis of the thirties required the assumption that a war in Europe or Asia, regardless of its outcome, would not threaten the most vital interests of the United States. Such was the case, the isolationists maintained, because all the countries likely to be involved in conflict were following selfish aims unrelated to American objectives and antithetical to American principles. Tactical considerations of trade or defense might indeed produce a preference for one or another of the potential belligerents. But none of these countries, the isolationists insisted, were closely linked to the essential interests of the United States, and American gains or losses in a war among them would thus be of only marginal importance.

To some extent, this attitude sprang from the application of what were widely regarded as the lessons of the First World War. Then, it was argued, the United States entered the conflict in the mistaken belief that Great Britain and France shared its moral and idealistic aspirations, but had discovered that the Allies were merely interested in altering the map of the world in order to satisfy their own narrow political and economic ambitions. If the repetition of this mistake was to be avoided, it was essential to show that the crises of the thirties were simply new manifestations of the traditional mania for redrawing boundary lines, were wholly devoid of moral content, and thus of relatively little interest to this country.

The insistence that Europe's wars were endemic and bore little relation to the aims, interests, and principles of the United States also reflected a much older point of view. In 1776, Thomas Paine favored a declaration of independence because, among other things, "Europe is too thickly planted with kingdoms to be long at peace." By breaking the connection with Great Britain, he insisted, the new nation could steer clear of wars that were unavoidable for the European nations but senseless from the American standpoint. Washington maintained in his Farewell Address that "Europe has a set of primary interests, which to us have none, or a very remote relation." Jefferson wrote to his friend, the German naturalist Alexander von Humboldt, that the "European

nations constitute a separate division of the globe; their locali-
ties make them part of a distinct system; they have a set of
interests of their own in which it is our business never to
engage ourselves."[1]

Under those conditions, European wars might be wholly
irrelevant to American principles and, in fact, wholly devoid
of principles of any kind. Alexander J. Dallas opposed Jay's
Treaty in 1795 because of the attendant danger of *"wantonly
involving ourselves in the political intrigues and squabbles
of the European nations."* John Quincy Adams warned his
listeners in 1821 that "by once enlisting under banners other
than her own" the United States would become party to "all
the wars of interest and intrigue, of individual avarice, envy
and ambition."[2]

These assertions did not rule out the possibility that there
might be European wars in whose outcome the United States
was vitally interested and in which it ought to intervene. But
this fact was largely ignored at a later time, when a belief in
the uniqueness of the position and destiny of the new nation
became an important ingredient of American nationalism. It
was then argued that an essential difference existed only
between America and Europe and not, from the cisatlantic
viewpoint, between one European power and another. If
such was the case, it could not matter to the United States

[1]Thomas Paine, *Common Sense and Other Political Writings*, Nelson
F. Adkins, ed., The American Heritage Series, No. 5, Oskar Piest, gen.
ed. (New York, 1953), 23; James D. Richardson, ed., *A Compilation of
the Messages and Papers of the Presidents, 1789–1897* (8 vols., Washington, 1899), I, 222. A. A. Lipscomb and A. E. Bergh, eds., *The Writings
of Thomas Jefferson* (Washington, 1903–04), IX, 431.

[2]George M. Dallas, ed., *Life and Writings of Alexander James Dallas*
(Philadelphia, 1871), 188 (italics in the original); John Quincy Adams,
"July 4th Address," *Niles Weekly Register,* XX (July, 1821), 331 (on
microfilm in John F. Kennedy–Institut Library, Free University of
Berlin).

which nations won and which lost a foreign conflict. Henry Clay's American System supported such assumptions. So did the Monroe Doctrine with its insistence on mutual noninterference between Europe and America.

Indifference to the affairs of Europe turned the course of Manifest Destiny away from the populous centers of civiliza tion into the wilderness. It became the basis for an isolationist foreign policy whose obligatory character was, in the words of President Martin Van Buren, "regarded by its constituents with a degree of reverence and submission but little, if anything, short of that which is entertained for the Constitution itself."[3] The belief that no other nation fully accepted American principles and that none was worthy of American support was implicit in this policy.

Although the United States occasionally deviated from this course even during the nineteenth century, its underlying theory was eloquently restated just before the outbreak of the First World War. Washington had urged the avoidance of entangling alliances, Woodrow Wilson explained in May, 1914, "because he saw that no country had yet set its face in the same direction in which America had set her face. We can not form alliances with those who are not going our way; and in our might and majesty and in the confidence and definiteness of our own purpose we need not and we should not form alliances with any nation in the world."[4]

The isolationists who were called upon to justify their position during the thirties could thus base their argument on the traditional view of the relationship of the United States to conflicts among foreign nations. They had only to

[3]Francis Wharton, *A Digest of the International Law of the United States,* 2nd ed. (Washington, 1887), 175–176.
[4]Ray S. Baker and William E. Dodd, eds., *The Public Papers of Woodrow Wilson* (6 vols., New York and London, 1925–1927) III, 109.

prove, or at least to assert vigorously, that the propositions laid down in the early years of the Republic still held true and that a new war in Europe would deviate in no way from the established pattern.

For the Far Eastern crisis, genuine precedents were lacking. Before the twentieth century, no country of Asia had been strong enough to raise through its actions the possibility of a war involving the United States. In the First World War, the United States and Japan had fought on the same side against Germany, but there had been no real American involvement in the Pacific. Now the situation had changed, and American sympathies lay generally on the side of China. But the likelihood of America's going to war in Asia still seemed remote. Even if this country were actively to espouse the cause of China at some future date, it would certainly be as the senior partner in an alliance in which the United States would be free to determine the nature and extent of its commitments in a manner which would do little violence to the principle of unilateralism. The isolationists, therefore, did not regard a war in Asia as the prelude to the kind of entanglement they feared from a war in Europe. They consequently saw less reason to discuss the Far Eastern crisis. When they did so, however, they insistently proclaimed the absence of overriding American interests in this area of the world as well, and included Japan's conflict with China in the general category of wars over boundaries and trade, with which the United States ought not to concern itself.

In 1935, when the subject of neutrality legislation was first broached, Professor Phillips Bradley of Amherst College told the Foreign Affairs Committee that Allied victory in the First World War had been unimportant and that the outcome of the next war was also likely to be of little consequence to the United States. Hitler and Mussolini, he admitted, were aggressive, unscrupulous, and unethical, but there was also little of "the milk of human kindness flowing from any of the foreign offices at Paris, London, Belgrade, or the other Entente countries." The people of Europe, Senator Bone informed his colleagues a short time later, were not drawn into the First World War by their differences on matters of principle but "through the stupidity and ineptitude of old men in the chancellories of Europe, and there are still a lot of doddering old men over there in positions of power, along with a sorry lot of confirmed megalomaniacs, egomaniacs, and psychopaths, who are literally preparing to dip their hands in blood and drag the whole world into the frightful mess they are creating for themselves." Early the following year, Hamilton Fish urged the United States to remain uninvolved in the "European boundary disputes and ancient blood feuds" that would bring on a general war.[5]

These themes were repeated in endless variations throughout the thirties. Democratic Representative B. Frank Whelchel of Georgia protested in 1936 against the spilling of American blood in the "ever-existing strifes and wars that are now existing in Europe" and in "this ever-raging conflict between the foreign nations." Former Republican Senator George Wharton Pepper of Pennsylvania found Europe once again playing its age-old game. The American Legion's conservative Donald W. Stewart saw the new tension as merely an outbreak of "periodical conflicts." Among the liberals, Charles A. Beard observed that "the Great Powers of Europe and Asia, whether in or out of the League, are pursuing their 'national interests' in the good old way. . . . My trouble," he continued, "lies in the fact that greed, lust and ambition in Europe and Asia do not seem to be confined to Italy,

[5]House Foreign Affairs Committee, *American Neutrality; Hearings,* 74th Cong., 1st sess. (1935), 21–22; *Congressional Record,* 74th Cong., 1st sess., 13778 (August 20, 1935); 74th Cong., 2nd sess., 3586 (March 11, 1936).

Germany and Japan; nor does good seem to be monopolized by Great Britain, France and Russia." And Oswald Garrison Villard saw so little difference between the opposing powers that he believed any attempt to take sides meant no more than aiding "those, whom at the hysterical moment of the explosion we believe to be aggrieved. Who can be sure under such circumstances?"[6]

Since most Americans disliked dictatorships and distrusted Hitler and Mussolini, the isolationists could substantiate their claim that the impending war involved no principles of concern to the United States only by partially justifying German, Italian, and Japanese policies and criticizing the actions of Great Britain and France. They therefore insisted that the "have-not" nations had legitimate grievances which ought to be recognized. "As long as Japan, Germany, and Italy feel (with reason) that they are underprivileged, as long as Great Britain, the United States, Russia and France hold in an iron grasp a virtual monopoly of many essential raw materials," Father Laurence K. Patterson wrote in *America*, "war is ever menacing."[7]

The same view was expressed by the isolationist journalist Frank H. Simonds in a series of books and *Saturday Evening Post* articles. Germany and Italy, Simonds argued, were justified in their demands because Great Britain and France had committed "an act of pure plunder" in depriving them of their colonies. Population pressures and lack of raw materials

---

[6]*Congressional Record,* 74th Cong., 2nd sess., 2256 (January 17, 1936); Senate, *Neutrality, Peace Legislation, etc.; Hearings,* 568; *Congressional Record,* 75th Cong., 1st sess., App. 397 (March 3, 1937); Charles A. Beard, "Peace for America—In Time of Peace Prepare for Peace," *New Republic,* LXXXVI (March, 1936), 157–158; Oswald Garrison Villard, "Issues and Men," *Nation,* CXLIV (January, 1937), 19.

[7]Laurence K. Patterson, "Drifting Toward Armageddon," *America,* LIII (June, 1935), 270.

were forcing the Axis nations to expand; and the League of Nations, like the Holy Alliance and the Concert of Europe before it, was simply a device for preserving for the "have" powers "their pleasant but precarious possession of the fruits of past conflicts." The League, he was certain, would fail. "Peoples moving toward war as the German and Italian peoples are visibly moving, as the Japanese have already marched, because of the pressure of material privation are equally beyond the reach of moral suasion and of military coercion."[8] This was an excellent argument against American intervention, since it made cooperation with the League powers appear both morally wrong and practically useless.

The Executive Secretary of the Women's International League for Peace and Freedom, Dorothy Detzer, used substantially the same reasoning in an article written for the *Nation*. Miss Detzer, a Hull House alumna who had been a relief worker for the American Friends Service Committee in Austria and Russia and proudly wore the Liberian Order of African Redemption, urged the United States to abstain from interference in the Italo-Ethiopian War and warned against cooperation with other powers in the imposition of sanctions against Italy. The existing world order, she insisted, was unjust, and Americans should await "basic corrections" before rushing to uphold it. A short time later, Senator Nye, who had favored the Versailles settlement in 1919, noted with satisfaction that the United States had not been a party to the treaty ending the First World War. In view of the injustice then done to the "have-not" nations, he doubted that "the people of the United States would today consciously endorse a war which had no other object than to maintain

[8]Frank H. Simonds, "Shall We Join the Next War?" *Saturday Evening Post*, CCVIII (August 17, 1935), 72–73; "John Bull's Holy War," *ibid.* (December 21, 1935), 16–17, 58; See also his *America Faces the Next War* (New York and London, 1933), *passim*.

that particular status quo which was established at Versailles."[9]

Many other isolationists took up these arguments. "Germany and Italy, among the Great Powers, and most of the new states of the second grade in Europe," explained Professor Bradley, "are so seriously undersupplied at home and so effectively cut off (by the preemption of the other Great Powers) from expansion in territories or markets abroad that their deficiencies are measurable in the health and vitality of their peoples as well as in the indices of wealth and production. Is it any wonder that war seems to countless thousands the lesser of two evils?" The same ideas were expressed by Representative John P. Higgins of Massachusetts in a speech urging strict American neutrality. They were repeated by C. P. Carroll, Jr., "a student of and speaker on international relations in Yale University," whose address favoring the economic isolation of the United States was introduced into the *Congressional Record* by Hamilton Fish. Even elder statesman Bernard Baruch, surely no admirer of Nazi Germany, cautioned in 1936 that we "must not be too quick in judging other nations in more straitened and dangerous circumstances than our own."[10]

If Germany, Italy, and Japan had legitimate grievances, then the developing world crisis could not be resolved by the simple expedient of trying to dissuade potential aggressors from taking violent action. On the contrary, nothing was more likely to provoke war than a refusal by Great Britain, France, and the United States to admit the legitimacy of the Axis Powers' claims and thus to close off all channels for the

[9]Dorothy Detzer, "What Neutrality Means," *Nation,* CXLI (December, 1935), 642–643; Senate, *Neutrality; Hearings* (1936), 150.

[10]Phillips Bradley, *Can We Stay Out of War?* (New York, 1936), 28; *Congressional Record,* 74th Cong., 2nd sess., 2271–2272 (February 12, 1936); *ibid.,* 4646–4647 (March 31, 1936); Bernard Baruch, "Neutrality," *Current History,* XLIV (June, 1936), 37.

peaceful resolution of difficulties. If, on the other hand, the United States declared its intention to be neutral in any future conflict, it might be hoped that Britain and France would hesitate to go to war in defense of their ill-gotten gains and be more ready to make meaningful concessions that would prevent a world conflagration.[11] The isolationists who subscribed to this view in effect supported a policy of appeasement based on the assumption that the totalitarian states would be satisfied if their more reasonable demands were met, and that the threat of war could be averted by an attempt to promote a more equitable balance of economic and political power in Europe and Asia. Even Edward Price Bell, whose early career as a foreign correspondent for the Chicago *News* had made him an ardent champion of collective security and an outspoken Anglophile, returned from a world tour for the *Literary Digest* in 1937 convinced that "Japan, Italy, and Germany have cases and standpoints which must be understood and justly met if this world is to escape utter disaster." By 1941, Bell was an active member of the America First Committee.[12]

Justifying the actions of Germany and the other "have-not" nations was not the only way ambivalence on the outcome of a future war could be established. The effort to show that Great Britain and France were concerned primarily with defending their unfair position as the world's leading imperialist powers was equally important. Norman Thomas

[11]This view was most clearly stated by Florence Brewer Boeckel of the National Council for the Prevention of War and by Representative Herman P. Koppleman of Connecticut in testimony before the Foreign Affairs Committee in 1937; see House, *American Neutrality Policy; Hearings* (1937), 55, 406.

[12]Bell sent a telegram to this effect to President Roosevelt in response to the Quarantine Speech; copy in FDRL PPF 200. An America First press release, dtd March 28, 1941, carrying Bell's name is in Pinchot Papers, File 87.

admitted in 1934 that anti-Semitic fascism was a monstrous evil. Nevertheless, he urged Americans to remember "that French imperialism is actually and potentially a curse to mankind and that the anti-German phobia of the French did much to create the Nazi movement."[13]

After Mussolini had launched his invasion of Ethiopia in 1935, Dorothy Detzer pointed out to readers of the *Nation* that the Duce's action did not differ from the course pursued by the British in Afghanistan or the French in Morocco. Democratic Representative Emanuel Celler of New York, speaking over the radio station whose call letters are the initials of Eugene V. Debs, concluded that "Italy, in dismembering Ethiopia, may be no more guilty than England in dismembering the Boer Republic and India." Edwin M. Borchard reminded his readers at the same time that Great Britain, as well as Germany, had violated America's rights as a neutral during the First World War and asked how the British could presume to "lecture others, like Italy, on the observance of law and morality?"[14]

Such arguments struck a responsive chord in the minds of men who believed the United States to have a specific grievance against the European democracies. Senator Borah had never forgiven Great Britain and France for defaulting on their financial obligations stemming from the First World War. "It is claimed," he now informed his colleagues,

that Germany has ignored the obligations of the Versailles Treaty and that Italy has ignored the obligations of the Covenant of the League of Nations, and that by reason of these actions Europe has been placed again in a state of chaos and turmoil. There is no

[13]Norman Thomas, *The Choice Before Us* (New York, 1934), 179.
[14]Dorothy Detzer, "What Neutrality Means," *Nation,* CXLI (December, 1935), *passim; Congressional Record,* 74th Cong., 2nd sess., 125 (January 7, 1936); Edwin M. Borchard, "Neutrality," *Southern Review,* II (Autumn, 1936), 240–241.

difference in law or morals, in international obligations, between the act of Germany and the act of Italy, and the acts of those nations in repudiating these debts which they contracted to pay.

Representative Joseph W. Martin, Jr., of Massachusetts took up the same theme in the House. He indicated that "with the European governments in a mood to appreciate the solemnity of contracts" he regarded it "an opportune moment for the United States Government to remind nations with whom we have debt agreements that those are just as binding as the Locarno or any other agreement."[15]

The isolationists' failure to see a fundamental moral issue in the European struggle led them to regard the conflict as a jockeying for power among nations who did not deserve the sympathy or support of the United States. Bruce Bliven, editor of the *New Republic,* saw the efforts of the League of Nations essentially as a battle of "the members of the old European Alliance against the remnants of the old Entente." Republican Representative George Holden Tinkham of Massachusetts, of whom Columbia University President Nicholas Murray Butler subsequently wrote that "he faces backward more consistently than any other man in public life except Congressman Fish," believed he was watching a contest between Great Britain and Italy over control of the Mediterranean. To Democratic Congressman Maury Maverick of Texas, the League's actions were simply part of an attempt to uphold the *status quo* by preserving the boundaries set up by the Treaty of Versailles and were thus wholly unrelated to questions of right and wrong.[16]

[15]*Congressional Record,* 74th Cong., 2nd sess., 4478 (March 27, 1936), 5423 (April 13, 1936).

[16]Bruce Bliven, "They Cry 'Peace, Peace'," *New Republic,* LXXXVI (January, 1936), 40; House Foreign Affairs Committee, *American Neutrality Policy; Hearings,* 74th Cong., 2nd sess. (1936), 17; Butler to Sol Bloom, dtd February 12, 1940, House Records (Committee on Foreign

In 1937, Phillips Bradley still saw the coming war as originating "in a dispute over the distribution of spoils, chiefly economic and secondarily psychological, of military victory." Journalist Quincy Howe regarded a policy of support for England and the League of Nations as nothing more than an agreement that "the greatest Empire on earth and the world's strongest nation will be putting their combined support behind the *status quo* everywhere." The Director of the National Council for the Prevention of War, Frederick J. Libby, spoke disparagingly of the "game of international poker now going on in Europe." "All of this talk about lining up with England and France to stop Fascism, by some radicals as well as conservatives," Senator Wheeler wrote to Oswald Garrison Villard, ". . . might possibly indicate that we were fighting over the control over the colonies in Africa."[17]

In the process of developing these arguments, isolationists pointed out repeatedly that no identity of interest existed between the United States and the European democracies. America might favor their form of government but, it was argued, had no valid reason for aiding them in the preservation of their imperial domains. To the extent that isolationists emphasized the economic and territorial bases for the world crisis while minimizing its ideological aspects, this argument could be used to deny the desirability of American support for the World War I Allies. Occasionally it was even suggested that Great Britain and France were the most formidable business competitors of the United States and

Affairs), File 76A-F 17.1; *Congressional Record,* 74th Cong., 2nd sess., 1403 (February 3, 1936), 1404 (February 3, 1936), 1738 (February 10, 1936).

[17]Phillips Bradley, "Neutrality and War," *Amerasia,* (April, 1937), 79; Quincy Howe, *England Expects Every American to Do His Duty* (Garden City, New York, 1937), 75; Libby to L. B. Thacher, dtd September 17, 1938, NCPW Papers, Drawer 82; Wheeler to Villard, dtd December 16, 1937, Villard Papers, File 4151.

that it was, therefore, absurd for this country to uphold and defend the interests of these nations.[18]

Less widely used, but significant in the light of subsequent events, was the argument that the European crisis was merely the prelude to a struggle between communism and fascism. Governor George H. Earle of Pennsylvania made this point in a speech to the Philadelphia meeting of the United Businessmen of Pennsylvania in April, 1937, and asserted that "American democracy has nothing in common with either of these doctrines." Three months later, Representative Voorhis of California told the Institute of Public Opinion of the University of Virginia that the coming war would see Russia on one side and the Axis Powers on the other and that none of the dictatorships deserved the support of the United States.[19]

significant till Hitler-Stalin Pact 1939 (handwritten marginal note)

Some Catholic isolationists were particularly fearful of involving the United States in a war on the side of the Soviet Union. If this should happen, Professor M. J. Hillenbrand of the University of Dayton informed the readers of *America,* "we will be aiding the very state which, in basic political and social philosophy, in violation of all human rights, in advocacy of atheism, looms as the foremost menace to civilization and Catholicism in the modern world." Donald W. Stewart told the Junior Chamber of Commerce at Coffeyville, Kansas, that the coming war was likely to be a contest between the

[18]See Hubert Herring, *And So to War* (New Haven, 1938), 117 ff. Herring was a Congregational minister who headed he Committee on Cultural Relations with Latin America, Inc., and subsequently became Professor of Latin American Civilization at Claremont Graduate School and Pomona College. The "business competitor" argument was stated most cogently by the former executive secretary of the Nye Committee, Stephen Raushenbush, in *The Final Choice* (New York, 1937), 76.

[19]*Congressional Record,* 75th Cong., 1st sess., App. 854 (April 9, 1937); App. 1735–1736 (July 9, 1937).

advocates of communism and those of fascism and offered his opinion that the cause of democracy and the cause of the United States could best be advanced by their unhindered mutual extermination.[20]

These sentiments were not shared initially by the isolationists of the left. The *New Republic,* in fact, argued for American neutrality in 1935 on the grounds that neither the Axis Powers nor Great Britain and France sufficiently resembled the Soviet Union in aims and policies. "Except for Soviet Russia," the magazine editorialized, "there is no great European power that is not pursuing policies leading to war, or that could be counted on to make a wise and enduring peace."[21] Not until the full extent of Stalin's purges became apparent did the views of many liberal isolationists begin to change, and not until the signing of the Russo-German Treaty of August, 1939, did sympathy for the Soviet Union cease to be a significant factor in the thinking of isolationists of the left. Many conservative isolationists, on the other hand, found it difficult to portray Great Britain as engaging in a war to establish communism or fascism in Europe, whatever its other sins may have been. Since no conflict to which England was not a party would threaten to involve the United States, the concept of a battle between rival totalitarianisms was not frequently used even by right-wing isolationists.

The overwhelming majority of all isolationists had no desire to see the Axis Powers gain their ends. Their arguments justifying the "have-not" position and attacking the activities of the great colonial powers cannot be dismissed as mere rationalizations of pro-German or anti-British senti-

[20]M. J. Hillenbrand, "If War Comes Will Moscow Be Our Ally?" *America,* LVII (July, 1937), 294; *Congressional Record,* 75th Cong., 1st sess., App. 396 (March 3, 1937).

[21]"Dress Rehearsal for Neutrality," *New Republic,* LXXXV (November, 1935), 5.

ment, since they contained substantial elements of truth. The isolationists magnified these elements in their pronouncements primarily in order to convince their fellow-citizens that any future war would be devoid of moral or ideological content of concern to the United States. Their statements were not intended to favor one side or the other, but rather to express American indifference to the results of foreign conflicts.

The United States was generally conceded to have no territorial ambitions or desires for economic expansion that required military intervention in Europe or Asia. The isolationists sought to demonstrate that this country also had no idealistic interests in overseas developments by pointing to the absence of clearly defined moral issues in the European rivalries. By vindicating the foreign policy of the dictatorships while denigrating the aims of the democracies they hoped to make certain that, as Ernest Hemingway wrote in 1935, "never again should this country be put into a European war through mistaken idealism."[22] Theirs was an attempt to apply what they regarded as the primary lesson of the First World War, a lesson that had been repeated again and again by revisionist historians.

The isolationists' conclusions about the First World War were admirably summed up in 1935 in Walter Millis' *Road to War*. Millis, an editorial writer for the New York *Herald-Tribune* and author of a debunking history of the Spanish-American War, was not a confirmed isolationist. He began his book with a disclaimer. "If this book gives an appearance of relative hostility toward the Entente," he wrote in the introduction, "that is simply an unavoidable consequence of the subject itself and implies no verdict whatever as between the European belligerents."

[22]Ernest Hemingway, "Notes on the Next War," *Scholastic*, XXVII (November 9, 1935), 7.

The absence of any moral judgment was itself a verdict. It made the First World War appear an inevitable result of "the ceaseless, intricate, and insane game of European diplomacy" and deprived it of moral content. By dispassionately setting forth the history of British propaganda efforts, the activities of American banking and financial interests, and the pro-Allies maneuvers of Colonel House and Secretary of State Lansing, Millis created the impression that specific American interests had had little to do with this country's declaration of war and that the United States had been duped into seeing a "cause" where none existed. *Road to War,* containing no new information but written in a popular and readable style, became a Book-of-the-Month Club selection and a best seller. It exerted considerable influence on public opinion.[23]

The effects of Millis' book were ably seconded by the writings of more dedicated isolationists. Oswald Garrison Villard asserted in his weekly column for the *Nation* that in 1917 "the excuse made by many pro-Ally Americans was that there was a higher law; that conscience and moral indignation overruled patriotism and loyalty to their government. The world was on fire; they must take sides. It was Evil against Good; who could hesitate?" Yet, he was certain, "morally there was not one thing to choose between the Allies and the Central Powers in the last war," nor was there between the Axis Powers and the democracies in the thirties.[24]

[23]Walter Millis, *Road to War* (Boston and New York, 1935), vii, 21 and *passim;* a later, more scholarly work, Charles C. Tansill's *America Goes to War* (Boston, 1938), while also not specifically substantiating the isolationist viewpoint, went even further in challenging the ethical nature of Allied activities.

[24]Oswald Garrison Villard, "Issues and Men—Neutrality and the House of Morgan," *Nation* CXLI (November, 1935), 555; "Issues and Men—Another Word on Neutrality," *ibid.,* CXLIV (May, 1937), 508.

Edwin H. Borchard insisted that "to read into the perpetual quarrels of Europe a moral issue is to succumb to romance," and the *New Republic* laid down this challenge to interventionists:

Behind most advocates of collective security there is something resembling the parable of the Good Samaritan. Consciously or unconsciously, they seek to put those who believe in strict neutrality in the position of urging that the United States play the part of the Pharisee who looked the other way and passed by. For centuries this Pharisee has been a highly despicable character.... The question that advocates of collective security need to answer, however, is whether the parable of the Good Samaritan has any relation to modern international power politics.[25]

For the isolationists of the thirties the answer was clearly no. A potential Good Samaritan would not only have difficulty in deciding whom to aid, but his ministrations, if offered, were not likely to be effective.

The contention that the United States could do nothing to help solve the problems of the world or to avert war, even were it to intervene, was not altogether novel. It had had obvious validity in the early years of independence when the United States possessed neither the economic nor the military means to determine the course of world events to a significant extent. Alexander Hamilton, in his "Americanus" articles of 1794, attacked the idea of going to war in defense of France and the principles of the French Revolution on the grounds that if France really faced defeat "our intervention is not likely to alter the case;... it would only serve prematurely to exhaust our strength."[26] In later years, however, when America grew stronger in fact and yet more powerful in the imagination of its citizens, such modesty became un-

[25]Borchard, "Neutrality," 258; "Dress Rehearsal for Neutrality," 4.
[26]Henry Cabot Lodge, ed., *The Works of Alexander Hamilton* (Constitutional Edition, New York and London, n.d.), V, 88–89.

fashionable. By 1917, the United States believed it to lie within its power to end war for all time and to make the world safe for democracy.

The evident failure of this attempt revived doubts concerning America's ability to intervene effectively in world affairs and provided another of the lessons isolationists professed to have learned from the First World War. American intervention in 1917 neither brought peace nor insured the survival of democracy. The isolationists were certain this country was equally impotent in the crisis of the thirties. In a battle between good and evil the United States might be able to throw its weight into the balance with some hope of producing desirable results. In a struggle between competing evils there was no such hope.

"We should feel some obligation to humanity, of course," Maury Maverick told the House of Representatives in 1937, "but I think the best way to discharge that obligation to humanity at this state of history is by staying out of wars; it seems perfectly apparent that we cannot stop that war." "We have had one costly experience in becoming involved in other nations' quarrels," Ray Murphy, National Commander of the American Legion, wrote at the same time, "we want no more of it. America has had an abundance of lessons to convince us that we cannot prevent other nations from going to war." The Foreign Relations Committee heard Judge Frank Leverone of Boston, a member of the executive committee of the League for American Neutrality, express the same sentiments. Representative John B. McClellan of Arkansas repeated them on the floor of Congress.[27]

[27]House, *American Neutrality Policy; Hearings* (1935), 51; Ray Murphy, "Let's Mind Our Own Business," *Scholastic*, XXVII (November 9, 1935), 15; House, *American Neutrality Policy; Hearings* (1936), 183; *Congressional Record*, 74th Cong., 2nd sess., 2247 (February 17, 1936).

The assertion that America was powerless to help solve world problems was made with ever greater frequency as international tensions increased and the danger of American involvement became greater. In 1937, Borchard pointed out that "by intervention in European quarrels we can make the situation worse, but never better. . . . Europe must work out its own problems; it understands them better than we ever can." The following year, Jerome Frank based his entire book on the conviction that, though the troubles of other peoples "cannot but cause deep sorrow to any decent American," we "can do nothing of substance to solve the basic problems of Europe—except to insure a sane and flourishing civilization in America." Borchard now found it necessary to remind a wavering Senator George W. Norris of Nebraska that "we did a most effective job of bringing chaos to Europe in 1917" and could do nothing better at this time.[28]

George Cless, a forestry expert who had spent most of his life in the lumber business but who now devoted much of his time to writing and lecturing on international politico-economic questions, was certain the whole world was "too heavy for America to lift; so the only end to the internationalists' program will be that the rest of the world drags us down to their level." Norman Thomas referred to "those of us who believe that America's entry into a new war means fascism at home without corresponding benefit anywhere." Major George Fielding Eliot concluded his optimistic appraisal of the defensive capabilities of the United States with the assertion: "We cannot bring peace to a warring world; but we can keep the peace of our own part of the world. We cannot settle the troubles of distant continents;

[28]Edwin M. Borchard and William Potter Lage, *Neutrality for the United States* (New Haven, 1937), 349–350; Jerome Frank, *Save America First* (New York, 1938), xii; Borchard to Norris, dtd January 3, 1938, Norris Papers, Tray 104, Box 4.

but we can prevent the peoples of these continents from transporting their wars to the Western Hemisphere."[29]

Early in 1939, the Foreign Affairs Committee heard Norman Thomas declare he was "convinced that the disorganization of Europe and the problems of Asia can no more be solved by new American participation in Europe's or Asia's wars than did we solve [sic] them by our participation in the first World War." At the same time, the Foreign Relations Committee listened to similar arguments from a distinguished group, including Bainbridge Colby, Bernard Baruch, and Professor Charles C. Tansill of Fordham University. "Now for this nation to take a positive role, to attempt to put out those sparks which are everywhere breaking out in Europe," thought Tansill, "is a large order. I do not know whether this particular fire engine or this particular fireman is capable of doing that."[30]

The most colorful witness before the Committee was the former head of the National Recovery Administration, retired Brigadier General Hugh S. Johnson, who told the members:

It is, of course, true that if we make economic war with a threat of military war in an alliance in advance we might possibly stop a European war. . . . But if it does not stop war, one thing is certain—we shall have bought a war. Nobody can deny that. It is a gamble—and a magnificent gamble on a hair-line chance.

Well, this is a magnificently gambling Government. It has shot craps with destiny with three to five billion a year—at least five

[29]George H. Cless, Jr., *The Eleventh Commandment* (New York, 1938), 11–12; Thomas to Villard, dtd January 21, 1937, Villard Papers, File 3830; George Fielding Eliot, *The Ramparts We Watch* (New York, 1938), 355.

[30]House Foreign Affairs Committee, *American Neutrality Policy; Hearings*, 76th Cong., 1st sess. (1939), 134; Senate, *Neutrality, Peace Legislation, etc.; Hearings*, 512, 55, 368.

times—on a bet that it could restore our prosperity, and it has lost every single pass.

But all the 20 billions or so that have been gambled and lost throughout these years would be as nothing compared to this gamble. . . . I think it is too much to risk.[31]

The belief that, in all likelihood, the United States could make no effective contribution to the solution of European problems was an important facet of isolationism. It negated a secondary moral factor that might have required America to play an active role in world affairs. If the United States possessed the power to aid materially in the solution of the world's ills, then a duty to humanity—unrelated to any specific interest and unaffected by the relative moral worth of other nations—might impel this country to take up arms. If such an effort was certain to be nothing more than a useless sacrifice, however, it was all the more important for America to eschew entanglements and continue to till its own garden.

The isolationists were thus convinced the United States had no direct reason for fighting a war on foreign soil. Yet, the possibility remained that failure to fight a foreign war might permit a would-be world conqueror to acquire the necessary strength to carry war to America. The isolationists denied this possibility. They were certain the Western Hemisphere was impregnable and they believed the Axis Powers would be unwilling and unable to attack this country even if they were successful in other parts of the world.

The thesis of America's safety from attack was, like that of the moral turpitude of the European powers, a traditional, widely accepted concept. It was so generally believed throughout American history that it rarely found expression outside the more platitudinous Fourth of July orations. But Alexander Hamilton had stated it in 1794 in words that, virtually

[31]Senate, *Neutrality, Peace Legislation, etc.; Hearings,* 280–281.

unchanged, might have been uttered by any one of the isolationists of the thirties. Answering the assertion that the defeat of France by the First Coalition would result in an attack on the United States, Hamilton declared:

The war against France requires, on the part of her enemies, efforts unusually violent. They are obliged to strain every nerve, to exert every resource. However it may terminate, they must find themselves spent in an extreme degree; . . .

To subvert by force republican liberty in this country, nothing short of entire conquest would suffice. This conquest, with our present increased population, greatly distant as we are from Europe, would either be impractical, or would demand such exertions as, following immediately upon those which have been requisite to the subversion of the French Revolution, would be absolutely ruinous to the undertakers.

It is against all probability that an undertaking, pernicious as this would be even in the event of success, would be attempted.[32]

The subject of America's invulnerability moved the youthful Abraham Lincoln to soaring flights of rhetoric. "All the armies of Europe, Asia and Africa combined," he told the Young Men's Lyceum of Springfield, Illinois, in 1838, "with all the treasure of the earth (our own excepted) in their military chest, with a Buonaparte for a commander, could not by force take a drink from the Ohio, or make a track on the Blue Ridge, in the trial of a thousand years." Carl Schurz was less lyrical but quite as definite. He informed the readers of *Harper's Magazine* in 1893 that

no European enemy could invade our soil without bringing from a great distance a strong land force; and no force that could possibly be brought from such a distance, were it ever so well prepared, could hope to strike a crippling blow by a sudden dash, and thus force us to peace, or to affect a lodgment within our boundaries without the certainty of being soon overwhelmed

[32]Lodge, ed., *op. cit.*, V, 88–89.

by an easy concentration of immensely superior numbers....In other words, in our compact continental stronghold we are substantially unassailable.

He repeated these thoughts in 1896 in speeches before the Arbitration Conference in Washington and the New York Chamber of Commerce. The Venezuela Crisis of 1895 provided the occasion.[33]

Hamilton was not an isolationist in any meaningful sense of the term, nor was Lincoln, though the latter's determined opposition to the Mexican War, to filibustering expeditions in Central America, and to the first section of the proposed Crittenden Compromise of 1860 stamp him as an antiexpansionist. Only Schurz, an ardent anti-imperialist, can properly be regarded as a forerunner of the isolationists of the thirties. But the traditional view expressed by all three men served the opponents of entanglement in the period preceding Pearl Harbor. As early as 1935, the isolationism of the American Legion was coupled with an insistence on adequate defense to assure the impossibility of invasion and the unlikelihood of attack. Isolationism and impregnability were combined in the remarks Representatives John B. McClellan of Arkansas and Eugene B. Crowe of Indiana addressed to the House of Representatives. Crowe warned against being dragged into war by "the greed of the DuPonts and their coterie," and urged the United States to attend strictly to its own affairs. But, he continued, "let us build up our national defense in fleet, troops, and air. Fortify our coasts so that they may be made impregnable. Fortify our outlying possessions, particularly the Panama Canal Zone,

[33]Roy P. Basler, ed., *The Collected Works of Abraham Lincoln* (9 vols., New Brunswick, New Jersey, 1953–55), I, 109; Frederic Bancroft, ed., *Speeches, Correspondence and Political Papers of Carl Schurz* (6 vols., New York and London, 1913), V, 207, 258–259, 264–265.

and make of the territory of Hawaii a veritable Gibraltar."[34]

In October, 1936, the *Saturday Evening Post* spread retired Major General Johnson Hagood's views on national
defense before a large and general audience for the first time.
"The people of the United States," wrote Hagood, "stand
for the principle of Europe for Europeans, Asia for Asiatics
and America for Americans." He urged the building of a
high-seas navy second to none, strong harbor and coast
defenses, a good air force, and a defensive army of the militia
type to insure the triumph of such principles. The United
States, he was certain, could "build a fence around our
property and warn everybody to keep out." These theories
were offered in expanded form in *We Can Defend America*,
published in 1937. In this book, Hagood reiterated both his
basic isolationism and his conviction that this country was
safe from attack provided proper defensive measures were
taken early enough.[35]

Other isolationists accepted Hagood's theories of American
impregnability without emphasizing the need for adequate
defensive measures. Congressman Martin Dies of Texas,
subsequently notorious for his belief in the vulnerability of
the United States to the "un-American" activities of some
of its inhabitants, was certain in 1937 that this country was
safe from war merely because it was separated "by thousands
of miles of ocean and natural barriers" from the centers of
contagion. The same opinion was expressed by Vienna-born
Representative Henry Ellenbogen of Pennsylvania in a radio
address. Phillips Bradley was sure "our geographical posi-

[34]Ray Murphy, "Let's Mind Our Own Business," *Scholastic*, XXVII
(November 9, 1939), 15; *Congressional Record*, 74th Cong., 2nd sess.,
2247, 2261 (February 17, 1936).

[35]Johnson Hagood, "Rational Defense," *Saturday Evening Post*,
CCIX (October 24, 1936), 6, 40–43; *We Can Defend America* (Garden
City, New York, 1937), *passim*, esp. 2–29.

tion, unique among the nations, makes avoidance of involvement in other people's wars possible. We are insulated by water against effective attack...from potential enemies." M. J. Hillenbrand pointed out that "all the non-lobbying military experts agree on our impregnability in case of attack, our overpowering naval superiority in home waters."[36]

Common Sense added another dimension to the argument by discounting even the intention of other nations to launch an attack against the United States. "Looked at dispassionately," the magazine editorialized, "this talk of the world conquest by Fascist powers is dream stuff, the kind of dream stuff used by propaganda agencies to whip up war fever."[37]

The doctrine of American impregnability received the support of another influential military expert in 1938. Major George Fielding Eliot's *The Ramparts We Watch* was the most thorough analysis of the military position of the United States to reach the general public up to that time. The conclusions it contained were most reassuring to the isolationists. "Providence in its infinite mercy and wisdom," wrote Eliot, "has been very good to this nation. We have been given a geographical position far removed from dangerous neighbors. The genius of man has not yet created instruments of aggressive warfare which can span the oceans which protect us on either hand, save as those instruments may move upon the surface of these oceans." In the construction of naval vessels, which were expensive, the United States had the great ad-

[36]*Congressional Record,* 75th Cong., 1st sess., App. 748 (March 29, 1937); Phillips Bradley, "Neutrality and War," *Amerasia,* I (April, 1937), 79; M. J. Hillenbrand, "The Meddlesome Muddle of Foreign Policy Makers," *America,* LIX (June, 1938), 224.

[37]"Why Commit Suicide?" *Common Sense,* VII (March, 1938), 4. Jeannette Rankin expressed similar views in a radio speech delivered on December 29, 1937, a copy of which is in the National Council for the Prevention of War Papers, Drawers 82.

vantage of being wealthy. The military expert of the New
York *Times,* Hanson Baldwin, agreed with this conclusion.
"The Army and Navy," he told readers of *Foreign Affairs* in
April, 1938, "are at present prepared to defend both coasts
of the United States against simultaneous invasion, and at the
same time protect Hawaii, Panama, Alaska and probably
South America from any attack that can be reasonably fore-
seen." "What nation would attack us at this time?" Senator
Borah asked rhetorically of the Brooklyn *Eagle's* John A.
Heffernan in December, 1938. To one of his constituents
he provided the unequivocal answer: "There is no nation
going to attack us."[38]

As Europe drew closer to the brink of war, these assertions
were more frequently heard in America. Senator Taft told
a radio audience in February, 1939, "We can defend ourselves, and the Caribbean Sea south of us, if we maintain
an adequate Navy and an attendant air force." Moreover, he
asserted, it was difficult to see what Germany and Italy could
hope to gain by an attack on the United States in the unlikely event they defeated Great Britain, France, and the
other anti-Axis nations. Harry Elmer Barnes consoled himself and his readers with the thought that "at worst it will
be decades before we lose our democracy at the hands of some
foreign dictator who overruns our shores." Were this country
to enter a foreign war, however, democracy would be lost
at once. Borah agreed. And a "People's Neutrality Resolution" prepared by the Pleasantville (N.Y.) Peace Forum and
sent to Senator Vandenberg for possible sponsorship on
March 31, 1939, contained in its first plank the assertion that
"an attack on the United States by a foreign power or by a

[38]Eliot, *op. cit.,* 351; Hanson Baldwin, "America Rearms," *Foreign
Affairs,* XVI (April, 1938), 444; Borah to Heffernan, dtd December 21,
1938, Borah Papers, Box 427; Borah to J. C. Fenton, dtd December 26,
1938, Borah Papers, Box 417.

combination of foreign powers is at the present time impossible."[39]

At the same time, the Foreign Relations Committee heard the theory of American impregnability supported by Bernard Baruch, General Hugh Johnson, and Dr. L. D. Stillwell of Dartmouth College. Baruch thought our oceans plus a strong national defense still protected us. "Our defeat here," he insisted, "can never happen if we maintain a defense adequate to prevent it." Stillwell was sure the United States was safe, since the process of defeating France and Great Britain would exhaust the Axis Powers and leave them unable to cross three thousand miles of ocean. Hanson Baldwin also had not changed his mind. "No military tidal wave could prevail against our continental and hemispherical impregnability," he wrote in the *American Mercury*. But, he warned, "if we go far beyond our borders, into distant seas, we face an end, in treasure, human life and national destiny which no man living can foresee. By frittering away our great strength in foreign theaters, we may well destroy that impregnability which today means certain security for the American castle."[40]

Just before the outbreak of the Second World War, the thesis that America was safe from attack regardless of events abroad was reaffirmed in three widely circulated books. Boake Carter was at that time one of the better known radio news commentators. Born in Russia, he had been educated at Christ College, Cambridge, and had served in the Royal

[39]Robert A. Taft, "Let Us Stay Out of War," *Vital Speeches of the Day*, V (February, 1939), 255; "If War Comes," *Common Sense*, VIII (March, 1939), 13; Borah to F. A. Moss, dtd January 9, 1939, Borah Papers, Box 427; copy of "Peace Resolution" in Senate Records (Committee on Foreign Relations), File 76A-F 9. See also, Roy O. Woodruff, "What War Means," in Pinchot Papers, Box 66.

[40]Senate, *Neutrality, Peace Legislation, etc.; Hearings*, 55, 562, 280; Hanson W. Baldwin, "Impregnable America," *American Mercury*, XLVII (July, 1939), 267.

Air Force during the First World War. In 1920, he left
England to enter the oil business in Central America. Some
years later, he settled down to a career in journalism and
broadcasting in the United States. In *Why Meddle in
Europe?*, published in 1939, Carter attempted to document
the entire isolationist position. He showed utter contempt
for those who feared—or, in Carter's opinion, pretended to
fear—the threat of invasion. "Military experts (not politicians masquerading as experts)," he postulated, "are agreed
that, even in the entirely improbable hypothesis of the destruction or capture of the British Navy, still no nation or
group of nations could successfully attack the Western
Hemisphere."[41]

At the same time, Stuart Chase, long active in left-wing
isolationist circles, devoted much of *The New Western
Front* to an explication of the glories awaiting America if it
only remained at home and tended to its own pressing problems. He also felt compelled to consider the possibility of an
attack on the United States. His conviction that fear of such
an occurrence was absurd was reflected in his concluding
statement: "I apologize for wasting your time in this discussion. It would make an admirable topic for a debate in an
insane asylum."[42]

Chase and Carter considered the problem of hemispheric
defense only in passing and failed to treat the possibility of
invasion with any degree of seriousness. Oswald Garrison
Villard, on the other hand, devoted *Our Military Chaos*
entirely to an analysis of the military position of the United
States. Citing the opinions of Baldwin, Eliot, Hagood, Major
General William C. Rivers, Rear Admiral W. W. Phelps, and
Admiral Sims, among others, Villard concluded that "of all

[41]Boake Carter, *Why Meddle in Europe?* (New York, 1939), 164.
[42]Stuart Chase, *The New Western Front* (New York, 1939), 167.

the defense impostures and delusions, the worst is that a war with Japan is physically possible, that Japan may attack us and we may fight in Japanese waters." "As for Germany," he declared, "I believe Hitler for once tells the truth when he says that Germany is not contemplating any attack on the United States." In any case, he was certain, "it is not humanly possible for Germany with a Navy one-fourth the size of ours to conquer our fleet, or produce transports enough to bring a sizable force to the United States."[43]

The isolationists' common belief in American invulnerability did not lead them to automatic agreement on questions of preparedness. On the one hand, strengthening the Army and Navy appeared to be a step toward war that had to be vigorously opposed by all isolationists. On the other hand, even those isolationists who relied most heavily on the protection afforded America by its geographical position and who were most certain no invasion would ever be attempted could not be unaware of the desirable deterrent effects of a powerful military establishment. Senator Clark of Missouri attempted to resolve this dilemma in a nationwide radio address, delivered in 1938. "We should," he told his listeners, "vote every dollar which is reasonably necessary for the defense of the United States. We should oppose every appropriation which might lead us into offensive wars and intervention in foreign quarrels."[44]

In a period in which the Administration proposed ever larger budgets for both the Army and Navy and supplementary appropriation bills became the rule, such standards proved difficult to apply. As a result, isolationists displayed no unanimity in their stand on specific defense measures.

[43]Oswald Garrison Villard, *Our Military Chaos* (New York, 1939), 69, 45, 27–44.

[44]Bennett C. Clark, "The Question of National Defense," *Vital Speeches of the Day*, V (January, 1939), 219.

They made no concerted effort to block expansion of America's armed forces, however. Many isolationists, in fact, became ardent champions of the strongest possible defense and, occasionally, outdid the Administration in their efforts to improve America's military capabilities.

"Neutrality legislation was designed to insulate America against foreign dangers," Hanson Baldwin noted, "but as the United States has sought to withdraw into its shell it has felt the urge to make that shell strong. . . . These apparently contradictory trends—the one pacifist and the other militarist—are not so incongruous as might appear on the surface; they represent in fact a reversion to that old policy enunciated earlier in the century by another Roosevelt—'speak softly and carry a big stick.' "[45] The association of the "Big Stick Policy" with isolationism is misleading. The existence of a "militarist trend" in isolationist thinking is substantially borne out, however, by the Congressional vote on military and naval appropriation bills from 1935 to 1940.

In 1935, the year Congress gave overwhelming approval to the Neutrality Act, the House of Representatives passed the measure allocating funds to the Army without a roll call. The Senate approved the same measure 68 to 15. Among the isolationists, Nye, Clark of Missouri, Lynn Frazier of South Dakota, Arthur Capper of Kansas, and Robert M. La Follette, Jr., of Wisconsin opposed the bill. Borah and Johnson supported it, however, and Bone, Wheeler, and Vandenberg did not vote. When Democratic Representative Fred J. Sisson of New York proposed cutting the Navy's budget for 1936 by 20 per cent in the interest of economy, the motion failed by 56 to 289. Although most Wisconsin Progressives, as well as Ludlow, Koppleman, and Maverick, voted for the cut, such staunch isolationists as Fish, Martin, Greenwood, Robsion,

[45]Baldwin, "America Rearms," 430.

Rogers, Kloeb, and Dirksen did not. When the bill containing the full appropriation reached the Senate, it passed by 55 to 18. Johnson and Vandenberg voted for it.[46]

The situation was substantially the same in the years that followed. In 1936, the Senate increased the Army appropriation approved by the House and then passed the bill 53 to 12 with Senators Borah, Johnson, and Vandenberg aiding the majority. Only 84 House members opposed the conference report that included the increases at a time when at least 250 Representatives could be counted on to support isolationist measures. In 1937, the conference report on a bill calling for even greater expenditures was approved by a margin of 300 to 42. Such leading isolationists as Dies, Fish, Greenwood, Ludlow, Martin, Maverick, Robsion, Tinkham, and Voorhis gave their support to the measure. The Naval Appropriations Bill of 1937 passed the Senate 64 to 11. Bone, Borah, Johnson, and Vandenberg voted for it.[47]

In 1939, the House of Representatives, for the first time in its history, passed an Army appropriation bill without a single roll-call vote and without any amendments being offered. The Senate endorsed the same measure by voice vote. Isolationist Senators Bone, Wheeler, Johnson, and Taft supported the Navy's request for increased funds in the same year. After the outbreak of war in Europe, the vote on money bills for the armed forces became virtually unanimous. The Naval Appropriations Bill of 1940, calling for expenditures of one billion dollars, passed by voice vote in the House

[46]*Congressional Record,* 74th Cong., 1st sess., 2500–2501 (February 22, 1935), 3214 (March 8, 1935), 6487 (April 26, 1935), 8161 (May 24, 1935).

[47]*Ibid.,* 74th Cong., 2nd sess., 2110 (February 14, 1936), 4172 (March 23, 1936), 6543 (May 1, 1936), 6722 (May 6, 1936), 6904 and 6906 (May 8, 1936); *ibid.,* 75th Cong., 1st sess., 6609 (June 30, 1937), 1936–1937 (March 5, 1937), 2554 (March 22, 1937).

and by 63 to 4 in the Senate. The following year, the Army's request for funds was approved 352 to 1. Only Representative Vito Marcantonio of New York, converted to isolationism by the Hitler-Stalin Pact, voted against it. There was no formal vote on the measure in the Senate.[48]

Some isolationists thus supported the expenditure of more than seventeen billion dollars for national defense in the five years preceding America's entry into the war. The others offered no substantial opposition to this buildup. Since isolationists controlled Congress until 1939, it is certain they could have made a better showing had they objected on principle to military spending or adequate defense. Yet, isolationists were frequently blamed for opposing preparedness and thereby contributing to American military setbacks in the early months of the war with Japan. Such charges arose largely from misleading publicity given by the Administration and by the press to the Congressional debate over the Vinson Naval Expansion Bill of 1938 and the Naval Construction Bill of 1939.

The Vinson Bill incorporated President Roosevelt's request for a 20 per cent increase in the size of the Navy, and was clearly a result of Roosevelt's new concern for the international situation. Since most naval experts had assured the country that the existing Navy was adequate for the task of defending the Western Hemisphere, the new proposal could easily be construed as a measure primarily concerned with preparing the United States for participation in a foreign war. The bill was bitterly attacked by many isolationists who, in their turn, were bitterly attacked by the internationalist press. Yet, the Vinson Bill passed both Houses of Congress by

[48]*Ibid.*, 76th Cong., 1st sess., 2240 (March 3, 1939), 7724 (June 22, 1939), 5262–5263 (May 8, 1939), 5702 (May 18, 1939); *ibid.*, 76th Cong., 3rd sess., 4709 (April 18, 1940), 8424 (June 17, 1940); *ibid.*, 77th Cong., 1st sess., 4912 (June 9, 1941).

large margins. The House of Representatives approved it 294 to 100 with the help of Dies, Dirksen, Greenwood, Ludlow, and Voorhis. In the Senate, Homer T. Bone belonged to the 56 to 28 majority that supported it.[49]

The Naval Construction Bill of 1939 authorized the Secretary of the Navy to proceed with improvements at various naval installations throughout the world. The House, by a vote of 205 to 168 and with the support of all isolationists, struck out a five-million-dollar appropriation for dredging the harbor of Guam and for other construction work on that island. Subsequent developments in the Pacific made the isolationists' conduct seem particularly reprehensible. In 1939, however, neither the State Department nor the War Department was anxious to have the Guam appropriation passed, for fear of antagonizing Japan. And isolationists accepted without protest the provisions of the bill calling for the improvement of military installations on Wake and Midway Islands.[50] The fate of Wake Island suggests that the money that might have been spent on Guam would not have altered the course of events.

Taken as a whole, the isolationists' voting record up to 1940 reveals a willingness, sometimes even an eagerness, to expand the American military establishment in order to provide an impregnable defense. Some went so far as to accuse President Roosevelt of negligence in the area of preparedness, in the hope, no doubt, of using this country's alleged unpreparedness as an argument to keep it out of war.[51] Only later, when the Selective Service Act and similar

[49]*Ibid.*, 75th Cong., 3rd sess., 3768 (March 21, 1938), 6135 (May 3, 1938).

[50]*Ibid.*, 76th Cong., 1st sess., 1842–1843 (February 23, 1939), 4468 (April 19, 1939); Langer and Gleason, *op. cit.*, 149–150.

[51]See, for example, Pinchot to Tinkham, dtd May 3, 1940, to Roy Howard, dtd July 2, 1940, and to Arthur Krock, dtd May 17, 1940, in

measures clearly pointed to a foreign war, did anything resembling a solid isolationist front against some forms of preparedness legislation develop.

The isolationists of the thirties built much of their position on the belief that the United States lacked a substantial
motive for going to war but had vital reasons for remaining
at peace. Like all Americans, they knew this country desired
no additional territory. They believed the world situation
offered no moral requirement for American intervention because they saw no struggle of good against evil and believed
the United States to be powerless to bring about a just solution to international problems. They were sure the United
States could not and would not be attacked and had no
need, therefore, to forestall the rise of a possible aggressor.

Moreover, they saw no urgent and immediate need to
expand or, in the case of some, to defend the foreign commerce of the United States, or any real danger that a victory
of the Axis Powers would mean the economic strangulation
of the United States. Roosevelt and Hull were clearly concerned about the latter possibility as early as 1938 and those
Americans who shared their apprehensions left the isolationist camp as soon as an Axis victory began to seem
possible. But most isolationists were convinced that the
American economy would survive even that. The economic
nationalists among them had relatively little concern for
world trade in general. The others were convinced not only
that we could do business with Hitler, but that economic
necessity would force Hitler to do business with us. As late
as 1941, Raymond Moley envisioned with equanimity a
world economy in which Germany would dominate Europe

Pinchot Papers, Box 68, and speech by Representative Henry Cabot
Lodge, Jr., dtd October 1940, in America First File, Swarthmore College Peace Collection.

and the United States the Americas. Bernard Baruch told a *Wall Street Journal* reporter at the same time that the United States could always undersell the totalitarian states in the world market, and could, in fact, wage successful economic war even against a victorious Germany.[52]

The isolationists maintained, in sum, that this country had no valid reason for deep concern about the affairs of other nations or the results of foreign wars. Despite all that had occurred in the twentieth century, the United States was, in the isolationists' eyes, still largely independent of the rest of the world and capable, if it only took proper precautions, of developing a unilateral foreign policy tailored to its own needs. Foremost among these needs was complete dedication to the solution of pressing domestic problems, and, therefore, to the avoidance of war. If we make a success of our republic, Senator Borah assured Richard L. Neuberger of the Portland *Oregonian*, "we need not be disturbed in the least about some half-baked, crazy, totalitarian theory taking possession of this country, or even attacking it. Our work is right here at home."[53]

[52]See Robert Laffan's interview of Baruch in *Wall Street Journal*, June 6, 1941, and Moley's column in *Newsweek*, June 9, 1941. The views of Baruch and Moley, as well as the similar ones of George N. Peek and others were widely circulated by the America First Committee. See America First File, Swarthmore College Peace Collection.

[53]Borah to Neuberger, dtd May 1, 1939, Borah Papers, Box 426.

V

THE DEVIL THEORY OF WAR

THE isolationist argument was coherent, logical, and self-contained: nations go to war for territorial gain or economic advantage, or in defense of their boundaries, their trade, or their principles; none of these reasons applied to the United States during the thirties; America's proper policy was, therefore, to insulate itself as well as possible against outside dangers and to attend to its own affairs in its own way. As a stratagem for keeping America out of war, this argument had one glaring weakness. It could be applied with equal logic to the years from 1914 to 1917, yet the United States had apparently entered the First World War willingly. In order to strengthen their position, the isolationists had to find an explanation for the American declaration of war of April, 1917, that would not challenge the validity of their other premises.

One possible explanation was based on the revisionists' claim that this country had been duped by British propaganda into seeing nonexistent moral issues in the conflict between the Allies and the Central Powers. Senators Norris and Borah privately supported this interpretation as early as October, 1935. In April, 1936, Representative William T.

Schulte, Democrat of Indiana, publicly warned against "the same propagandists that lit the torch that led the way for the god of war into America in 1917, 1898, in 1863 [sic], and during the Revolutionary War." Shortly thereafter, the Philadelphia *Record* urged editorially that "for the same reason that there must be an embargo on goods, the State Department must make every effort to circumvent any nation which, for propaganda purposes, tries to put an embargo on European news to the United States." Advancing the claim that American views toward Germany in the First World War had been molded by insidious forces, the paper warned that "British propaganda methods are so much more subtle and effective than those of any other nation that foreign news, almost invariably, takes on a pro-British tinge." The editorial's arguments led Representative Paul J. Kvale, Farmer-Laborite from Minnesota, to propose federal control of the means of communication and propaganda in times of emergency. The following month, Representative Harold Knutson of Minnesota warned against "the lavish use of false propaganda intended to inflame the passions" and M. J. Hillenbrand of Dayton University, looking gloomily into the future, predicted that aided "by our own predisposed press, England will again hamstring American public opinion with its propaganda machine."[1]

Acceptance of this view required belief in the diabolical cleverness of the agents of Great Britain and in the monumental gullibility of the American people. Few Americans were prepared to concede the latter point. As a result, the

[1]Norris to R. Mauthey, dtd October 14, 1935, Norris Papers, Tray 31, Box 1; Borah to G. S. Anderson, dtd January 14, 1936, Borah Papers, Box 393; *Congressional Record*, 74th Cong. 2nd sess., 5484 (April 14, 1936); *ibid.*, 75th Cong., 1st sess., 2391 (March 18, 1937) and 3200 (April 6, 1937); M. J. Hillenbrand, "If War Comes Will Moscow Be Our Ally?," *America*, LVII (July, 1937), 294.

issue of British propaganda, though occasionally raised,[2] was not very effective, and seemed inadequate even to most isolationists.

"The Debacle of 1917" could also be blamed on the folly of President Wilson and of his chief advisers, Colonel House, Secretary of State Lansing, and the Ambassador to Great Britain, Walter Hines Page. In February, 1936, Representative Tinkham of Massachusetts bitterly attacked Colonel House in a speech before Congress. He blamed House not only for America's entry into the First World War, but also for the League of Nations and the Treaty of Versailles, "which treaty has brought chaos to Europe and is now bringing war." Tinkham further charged that House had been the principal promoter of Roosevelt's candidacy in 1932 and was now one of the President's most intimate advisers. He called for a Congressional investigation "to ascertain to what extent the State Department was under the domination and control of the British Foreign Office during the administrations of President Wilson from 1914 to 1920, of President Hoover from 1928 to 1932, and of President Roosevelt from 1933 to date." Representative Dirksen of Illinois charged at the same time that Lansing had taken sides and "shaped our national policy in the direction of the Allies." Secretaries of State Henry L. Stimson and Cordell Hull, thought Dirksen, had displayed similar tendencies.[3]

Such attacks were not often repeated. Wilson was, during the 1930's, widely regarded as a great man, whose administration had been a precursor of the New Deal and whose idealism presented a sharp and welcome contrast to the dis-

[2]See, for example, Borchard to Borah, dtd March 1, 1937, Borah Papers, Box 405; Borah to J. A. Heffernan, dtd December 21, 1938, and Borah to G. L. Dean, dtd March 10, 1939, Borah Papers, Box 427.

[3]*Congressional Record,* 74th Cong., 2nd sess., 1625 and 1626 (February 6, 1936), 2249 (February 17, 1936).

credited materialism of the Harding-Coolidge-Hoover era. Moreover, many former supporters of the New Freedom and a number of Wilson's former lieutenants were still in Congress. While these men often agreed with the isolationists that American entry into the First World War had been a mistake, they were quick to defend their former chief against the charge that he had deliberately led the country into a war which did not involve its basic interests. When Senator Nye, for example, accused Wilson and Lansing of having "falsified" by claiming ignorance of the secret treaties existing among the Allies, the response stretched the bounds of Congressional propriety. It is difficult, thundered Tom Connally, Democrat of Texas, on the day after the North Dakota Senator made his accusation, "within the compass of parliamentary procedure to find language adequate to express my contempt for efforts of this kind to besmirch the memory of the man Woodrow Wilson." Seventy-eight-year-old Senator Carter Glass of Virginia, who had been Secretary of the Treasury under Wilson, answered Nye a day later: "If it were permissible in the Senate to say that any man who would asperse the integrity and veracity of Woodrow Wilson is a coward, if it were permissible to say that his charge is not only malicious but positively mendacious, that I would be glad to say here and elsewhere to any man, whether he be a United States Senator or not." The furor over Nye's remark almost ended the munitions investigation. It did not help the isolationist cause.[4]

Another explanation for America's entry into the First World War found more supporters. It was not difficult for a

[4] *Ibid.*, 501–513 (January 16, 1936), 562–570 and 572–579 (January 17, 1936); Tom Connally, *My Name is Tom Connally* (New York, 1954), 214; New York *Times*, January 17 and 18, 1936; Wayne S. Cole, *Senator Gerald P. Nye and American Foreign Relations* (Madison, 1953), 88, 90.

nation in the throes of a severe economic crisis to accept the idea that all calamities, war included, have economic causes. Nor was it hard for a people disabused of their faith in business leadership to believe that American commercial and financial interests were largely responsible for this country's involvement in the First World War.

Liberal and radical isolationists were veterans of the attack on the business community, and the heirs of the traditions of progressivism had an inborn suspicion of Eastern financial interests. When investigation of the circumstances surrounding America's declaration of war revealed the fine hand of the House of Morgan, many isolationists were quick to jump to the conclusion that the greed of some Americans had produced what they regarded as a major calamity in 1917. The United States as a whole, they insisted, had had no interest in the war. A sufficiently powerful and influential group of men did have such an interest, however, and had manipulated the entire nation for its own selfish purposes. The same thing might happen again unless positive steps were taken to prevent it. This explanation, which Charles A. Beard dubbed the devil theory of war, found widespread acceptance in isolationist circles.

The devil theory of war, in the form which it now assumed, was the only original contribution of the isolationists of the 1930's to the definition of America's relationship to conflicts in other parts of the world. To be sure, certain elements in the population had been blamed in the past for leading the country into war. In the last decade of the eighteenth century, the Federalists charged American "Jacobins" with seeking war against England. New England was certain the War of 1812 was the work of self-seeking Southern and Western "War Hawks." The machinations of the land-hungry "Slave Power" were regarded by most Free-Soilers as the cause of the Mexican War. Southerners blamed the abolitionists for the Civil War, and Northerners blamed Southern "fire-eaters." The yellow press played the devil's role with respect to the Spanish-American War.

The devil charged with involving the United States in the First World War and threatening to repeat his evil deed in the thirties was different from these others. The "Jacobins" made no secret of their intentions. The "War Hawks" loosed their militant rhetoric in the halls of Congress. The Southern planters declared their desire for Texas and New Mexico openly. "Fire-eaters" and abolitionists, while less specifically calling for war, hurled belligerent abuse at each other for years. The yellow press proclaimed its desire for war in banner headlines. The twentieth-century culprits, the isolationists claimed, were, by contrast, hidden devils who placed self-interest above patriotism and worked in secret to gain their nefarious ends. They had not misled their countrymen openly in 1917 but—and this was far worse—had manipulated them without their knowledge and against their will.

From the outset, the most obvious candidates for the role of the modern devil were the munitions makers. In 1933, William T. Stone devoted an issue of *Foreign Policy Reports* to the increasing international trade in arms and suggested that this represented a threat to world peace. In March, 1934, *Fortune* published "Arms and the Men," a widely quoted and frequently reprinted description of this trade and of the men behind it. The authors charged munitions makers with prolonging wars and disturbing peace. They accused arms dealers of trying to keep the world engaged in a continuous battle of nerves, and of a lack of national loyalties that allowed them to cooperate with each other even when their respective countries were at war. The discussion was largely confined to the activities of Krupp, Skoda, Vickers-Armstrong, Schneider-Creusot, and other European manufacturers. Du

Pont and Bethlehem Steel were mentioned, but it was pointed out that American companies played a minor role in this international game.[5]

Despite its limited applicability to American munitions manufacturers, the *Fortune* article produced a great outcry in this country. It was followed quickly by a number of books that expanded on its central theme. George Seldes' *Iron, Blood and Profits* and H. C. Engelbrecht and F. C. Hanighen's *Merchants of Death,* both published in 1934, were exposés of the munitions industry in the muckraking tradition. Though neither work blamed munitions makers for starting wars, both propounded the theory that the arms manufacturers' greed and lack of national loyalty were inimical to the cause of peace.[6]

The most significant result of this agitation was the Senate's creation of a special committee to investigate the munitions industry. Pacifist groups had been demanding such an investigation since the early days of the First World War. Their demands became more insistent after the Manchurian Crisis of 1931 raised the specter of a new war. The Women's International League for Peace and Freedom renewed its endorsement of a munitions investigation at its annual meeting in 1932, and the indefatigable Dorothy Detzer set out to make such a probe a reality. Finding no other Senator willing to undertake what seemed so thankless a task, she finally persuaded Senator Nye to introduce Senate Resolution 179, calling for an investigation of the munitions industry

[5]William T. Stone, "International Traffic in Arms and Ammunition," *Foreign Policy Reports,* IX (October, 1933), 130–140; "Arms and the Men," *Fortune,* IX (March, 1934), 53–55, 116–120.

[6]George Seldes, *Iron, Blood and Profits* (New York, 1934) and H. C. Engelbrecht and F. C. Hanighen, *Merchants of Death* (New York, 1934), *passim.*

by the Foreign Relations Committee, on February 8, 1934.[7]

Chairman Pittman of the Foreign Relations Committee wanted no part of such an investigation and had the resolution transferred to the Military Affairs Committee. In order to make that committee's approval more certain, Dorothy Detzer and other lobbyists urged Nye to combine his proposal with one sponsored by Senator Vandenberg, which was designed to take the profits out of war. Nye's resolution had pacifist support, while Vandenberg's was backed by the American Legion. The combined pressure of these groups could not long be resisted by any Congressional committee. Accordingly, Senate Resolution 206, introduced by Nye on March 12, 1934, combined the two earlier measures and also proposed that the investigation of the munitions industry be conducted by a special committee set up for that purpose. The new resolution was referred to the Military Affairs Committee which promptly reported it out favorably.[8]

The uproar produced by the *Fortune* article and the continued pressure applied by veterans' organizations and peace societies caused the Senate to approve the resolution without a dissenting vote on April 12. Congress thus authorized an initial expenditure of fifteen thousand dollars for a committee to investigate the nature of organizations engaged in the manufacture or traffic in arms, the methods used in promoting this trade, the volume of it coming in or out of the United States, the adequacy of existing legislation and treaties, the findings of the War Policies Commission, and the desirability of setting up a government monopoly for the manufacture of arms and ammunition.[9]

[7]Dorothy Detzer, *Appointment on the Hill* (New York, 1948), 150–157.

[8]*Ibid.*, 159–160; *Congressional Record*, 73rd Cong., 2nd sess., 3783–3784 (March 12, 1934); Cole, *Nye*, 69.

[9]Detzer, *op. cit.*, 162–163; *Congressional Record*, 73rd Cong., 2nd sess., 6485 (April 12, 1934).

The seven-member committee, selected by Vice-President John Nance Garner together with Nye and Vandenberg, had an isolationist majority consisting of Senators Bone, Clark, Vandenberg, and Nye. Although the Democrats controlled both the Senate and the new committee, the chairmanship was given to the Republican Nye. Secretary of State Cordell Hull subsequently blamed Key Pittman for this development, but Vice-President Garner, who permitted the committee to choose its own chairman, bears more of the responsibility. In any event, Nye had sponsored the authorizing resolution and no other Senator was anxious to head the group.[10]

The Nye Committee, as it came to be known, held hearings for nearly two years. According to Hull, it concentrated on revisionist theory by "impugning the motives and honesty of President Wilson in the First World War, by etching a sordid caricature of our former associates, Britain and France, and by whitewashing the Kaiser's Germany." But Dorothy Detzer was convinced that "no Senate committee ever rendered to the American people a more intelligent or more important service."[11]

The gist of the Nye Committee's findings was contained in testimony given before it in September, 1934, and in January and February, 1936. The first part of this testimony established in a sensational manner, to the accompaniment of reams of newspaper publicity, the substantial accuracy of the charges made by *Fortune*. It implicated American firms to a much larger extent than earlier information had indicated. The statements of the witnesses showed, for example, that an agreement existed between the Electric Boat Company, an American firm, and Vickers Ltd. to monopolize world sub-

[10]Cordell Hull, *Memoirs* (2 vols., New York, 1948), I, 398; Cole, *Nye*, 71–72.
    [11]Hull, *op. cit.*, I, 399; Detzer, *op. cit.*, 171.

marine construction, that the indiscriminate traffic in arms had brought vast fortunes to shadowy international super-salesmen such as Sir Basil Zaharoff, and that American companies had collaborated with their European counterparts in rearming Germany in violation of the Treaty of Versailles.

The Committee concluded from such evidence that the practices of munitions companies were "highly unethical" and "a discredit to American business," and carried within them "the seeds of disturbance to the peace and stability of those nations in which they take place." Nye's group also found it to be "against the peace of the world for selfishly interested organizations to be left free to goad and frighten nations into military activity." It proposed constitutional amendments to "permit the commandeering of plants, goods and industrial equipment for public use in war, without the determination of 'fair compensation' in the present way" and to allow Congress "to tax for war-profits control on such bases of investment or fixed capital as it finds to be fair and just." It also insisted on the virtually complete nationalization of the munitions industry.[12]

By 1936, the Nye Committee, in its search for devils, had shifted its attention from munitions makers to more important quarry. By assiduous rummaging in State Department files, it unearthed documents that had passed between President Wilson, Colonel House, Secretary of State Lansing, and Secretary of the Treasury William Gibbs MacAdoo. These documents seemed to show that concern for America's domestic situation had led to the lifting of the ban on credits to belligerents in 1915, to the increasing identification

[12]New York *Times*, September 5, 6, 9, 15, and 19, 1934; Senate Special Committee on Investigation of the Munitions Industry, *Munitions Industry*, 74th Cong., 1st and 2nd sess., (7 vols., 1935 and 1936), II, 3; III, 3, 4, 8, 12, 15.

of the United States with the Allied cause, and, finally, to the declaration of war itself. When collated with documents taken from the files of J. P. Morgan and Company, the Federal Reserve Banks, the Chicago First National Bank, and other financial institutions, and with the reluctant and rather vague testimony of men such as Thomas W. Lamont and J. P. Morgan, this evidence seemed to prove to Nye and the other investigators that the United States had been pushed into the First World War by the pressure of greedy bankers on vacillating politicians.

The Nye Committee delegated a special assistant, Josephine Joan Burns, who subsequently married the Committee's chief investigator and became Mrs. Stephen Raushenbush, to prepare an article entitled "A Study of the Neutrality of the United States, 1914–1917" for inclusion in the report to the Senate. Miss Burns arranged her material skillfully and concluded each chapter with a "lesson" ostensibly to be learned from the facts she presented. She claimed to have demonstrated the necessity for a fixed policy before war broke out by showing that the pressure of "vested interests" could not be resisted once the conflict was under way. She urged a ban on loans that created these vested interests, as well mandatory neutrality legislation to protect the President from pressure and shield him from temptation. The 135 documents on which this analysis was based formed the appendix to the article. Miss Burns' theories were incorporated in yet another Nye Committee report, which clearly placed the blame for American participation in the First World War on the House of Morgan and its allies.[13]

The devil theory of war developed in this manner into one of the mainstays of isolationist thinking. It provided a scapegoat for what isolationists regarded as the tragedy of 1917

[13]*Ibid.*, V, *passim*, esp. 33, 44, 58, 77, 87; VI, 1–7.

without discrediting either the intelligence or the peace-loving nature of the American people. It suggested that all wars were caused by greedy vested interests and that the United States had no valid reasons for becoming involved in such conflicts. It offered, finally, a simple method for insulating this country against foreign troubles, for exorcising war by exorcising the devils that caused it.

Even before the Nye investigation began, Harry Elmer Barnes noted in his introduction to *Merchants of Death* that "through their pressure to put the United States into the War these bankers brought about the results which have well nigh wrecked the contemporary world." After the rash of publicity accorded the Nye Committee, such sentiments were expressed with increasing frequency. "We were pulled into the World War," editorialized the Philadelphia *Record* in 1935, "because American bankers and American manufacturers tried to profit from the world holocaust." "We all know," Representative Tinkham of Massachusetts agreed, "that in the last war the reason we got into the war was largely on account of the sale of munitions, and that men in this country became so committed in such a large way that they were all for our intervention when it seemed that Germany was going to whip the Allies."[14]

"We were drawn into that war," Representative Kloeb of Ohio told his colleagues, "through the surge of economic demands that bound us to the fortunes of the nations that later became our allies. What propaganda, seeking to draw us into that conflict, was disseminated by the munitions merchants and the international bankers of this country who saw a possible loss ahead of them, we shall never know."

[14]Engelbrecht and Hanighen, *op. cit.*, viii; "How We Can Keep Out of War," reprinted in *Congressional Record*, 74th Cong., 1st sess., 4497 (March 27, 1935); House Foreign Affairs Committee, *National Munitions Act; Hearings*, 74th Cong., 1st sess. (1935), 15.

The *Nation,* noting that we had entered the First World War because of "the temptation to enrichment by the sale of munitions and needed raw materials," added philosophically: "Given a society based on profit making, war was the inevitable result."[15]

This line of argument became even more prominent after the Nye Committee published a letter Robert Lansing had written on September 6, 1915, which appeared to suggest that the United States go to war in order to preserve prosperity and to insure the repayment of money loaned to the Allies. Many isolationists were quick to point out that the letter mirrored the views of the House of Morgan, and Oswald Garrison Villard found this sufficiently damning to come perilously close to accusing both Lansing and Morgan of treason. Villard, to be sure, believed that some American officials had learned their lesson and would not act so foolishly again, but such optimism was not widespread in isolationist circles. The Jesuit periodical *America,* for example, expressed grave doubts in January, 1936, that American neutrality could be secured "against the insidious wiles of the extreme capitalist classes who with their usual folly see in war only an opportunity to revive business."[16]

In the months that followed, numerous isolationist spokesmen echoed these sentiments. Few of their speeches and writings were wholly devoid of references to small, selfish groups whose greed had plunged the nation into war and stood ready to do so again. Nor was there any reluctance to identify these groups as consisting largely of bankers, muni-

[15]*Congressional Record,* 74th Cong., 1st sess., 12661 (August 7, 1935); "Must We Fight in the Next War?" *Nation,* CXLI (August, 1935), 228.

[16]Oswald Garrison Villard, "Issues and Men—The War and the Pacifists," *Nation,* CXLI (October 1935), 455; Villard, "Lansing Self-Revealed," *ibid.,* 427; "Neutrality," *America,* LIV (January, 1936), 370.

tions makers, and other war profiteers.[17] In February, 1937, the Republican members of the Foreign Affairs Committee submitted a minority report on neutrality legislation in which they specifically warned against a new war "in defense of the war profiteers [and] munitions makers."[18]

In April of the same year, the Railway Labor Executives' Association, speaking for the twenty-one railroad brotherhoods, declared that America had been dragged into war in 1917 by propagandists, professional patriots, and munitions makers, and laid the blame for all wars on "political adventurers, military leaders, and those industrial interests which profit from wars and preparation for wars." Two months later, the Chicago Federation of Labor placed on record its conviction that "war and warfare since time immemorial have been primarily instituted by a comparatively few of the high and mighty in the political and financial structures of the countries of the world, for political aggrandizement and commercial advantage."[19]

Two corollaries to this general proposition were deemed by many isolationists to have direct bearing on America's posture towards the conflicts of Europe and Asia. If bankers and munitions makers are permitted to commit themselves

[17]Typical were the remarks of Senator Arthur Capper of Kansas and Representatives Harry Sauthoff and George J. Schneider of Wisconsin and Fred H. Hildebrandt of South Dakota. See *Congressional Record,* 74th Cong., 2nd sess., 500 (January 16, 1936), 1738 (February 10, 1936), 1902 (February 17, 1936), and 2259–2260 (February 7, 1936).

[18]House, *American Neutrality; Hearings* (1937), 177. The report was signed by Representatives Fish, Martin, Rogers, Leo E. Allen of Illinois, and George A. Dondero of Michigan.

[19]*Congressional Record,* 75th Cong., 1st sess., App. 877 (April 14, 1937), 1692 (July 2, 1937). The words used by the Chicago Federation of Labor were identical to those appearing in Joint Resolution 62,A adopted by the legislature of the State of Wisconsin and sent to Congress on May 25, 1937. Copy in House Records (Committee on the Judiciary), File 75A-H 8.7.

through their business dealings to one set of belligerents, it was argued, they and their favored belligerents will represent a combined force against which no popular government can prevail in the name of neutrality. The avoidance of war requires, therefore, that such a combination of interests be prevented by laws looking to the restriction of credit and of wartime business in general.[20] Moreover, if wars are brought on by greedy minorities, the curbing of these minorities is equivalent to the prevention of war. This second proposition was endorsed by numerous isolationists, including Senator Clark of Missouri, who was certain that war could be avoided by a simple willingness to forego "the tear-rusted, bloodstained profits of the munitions trade," and Norman Thomas, who urged "the workers and all lovers of peace to keep America out of the pursuit of profits and hence out of war."[21]

By 1938, the effects of these arguments on American policy were clearly discernible. The neutrality legislation of 1935, 1936, and 1937 was largely a device for exorcising the devil who had been so frequently and energetically described. The Act of 1935 prohibited the shipment of arms to warring nations, barred American vessels from carrying war material to belligerents, and established a National Munitions Board to bring the armament industry under federal control. In 1936 this law was extended for fourteen months and, in addition, all loans to belligerents were forbidden. The new provision clearly shows the force of the Nye Committee revela-

[20]One of the clearest statements of this position is found in Raushenbush and Raushenbush, *op. cit.,* 174–175.

[21]Clark, "Neutrality—What Kind?" 252; Thomas, "The Pacifist's Dilemma," 68. See also House, *American Neutrality; Hearings* (1937), 94. Among those writing to the White House in response to the Quarantine Speech, many shared the view of Joseph M. Mulligan of Albany, New York, who voiced his vehement refusal to go to war for "trade or munitions makers or international bankers." Copies of the letters and telegrams received are in FDRL PPF 200.

tions. The Johnson Act of 1934 already banned loans to any nation that had defaulted on its debts to the United States, and there was no great likelihood that credits would be extended to Germany. Nevertheless, Congress was so impressed by the threat ostensibly posed by the activities of international bankers that it incorporated the ban on loans specifically into American neutrality legislation.

In 1937, the provisions of all previous neutrality acts were made permanent. An effort was also made by some isolationists to obtain a complete embargo on trade with belligerents. This move failed, but the new law did contain the so-called cash-and-carry provision, a compromise which was also designed to reduce the danger of involvement in war by restricting American business contacts with warring nations. Even after these safeguards had been erected into law, the devil theory remained part of the isolationist argument. Norman Thomas still thought in 1939 that the United States might be drawn into a war to save trade, and Hamilton Fish still could not see "why we should continue to be the slaughterhouse of the world for profit or money."[22]

Not all isolationists accepted the devil theory. John Bassett Moore, for example, explained in a letter to the Foreign Relations Committee: "The theory that the United States became involved in the late war by endeavoring to protect its trade, I believe to be destitute of foundation." Other international law isolationists such as Borchard and Borah shared that belief and insisted that American participation in the First World War had been due to a largely unexplained lack of basic neutrality or to a mistaken idealism.[23] Repre-

[22]House, *American Neutrality Policy; Hearings* (1939), 137, 15.
[23]Senate, *Neutrality; Hearings* (1936), 184; see also Edwin M. Borchard and William Potter Lage, *Neutrality for the United States* (New Haven, 1937), vi–vii, 33–44, and Senator Borah in *Congressional Record*, 75th Cong., 1st sess., 1682 (March 1, 1937).

sentative Kloeb, while expressing approval of a Washington
Star article that stated the United States went to war in
1917 to save its investments, felt compelled to add that there
had also been other reasons. Lawrence Dennis rejected economic motivation altogether, claiming that in a modern
democracy "it is the moral idea about an economic situation, rather than the situation itself, which determines
whether the reaction is to be war or peace." Similarly,
General Hagood maintained that munitions makers and
bankers do not make war but merely support it, and Philip
Marshall Brown of the American Peace Society took the
identical position.[24] Many conservative isolationists were
themselves identified with the business community and, therefore, reluctant to lay all the blame there. To the extent to
which these men supported neutrality legislation, however,
they give implicit support to the theories of those who saw
in the curbing of financiers and munitions makers one of the
surest means for preserving the nation from war.

There can be little doubt, in fact, that the devil theory
profoundly influenced even those isolationists who sometimes
criticized it. The writings of Charles A. Beard clearly show
this to be the case. In a series of articles in the *New Republic*,
entitled "Peace for America," and, subsequently, in *The
Devil Theory of War*, Beard set out to show that "war is
not the work of a demon. It is our very own work, for which
we prepare wittingly or not, in ways of peace." Bankers and
munitions makers, he maintained, do not operate in a
vacuum, but respond to the prevailing forces in their society.
Historians, though they may describe the relationships exist-

[24]House, *American Neutrality Policy; Hearings* (1935), 6; Lawrence
Dennis, "The Highly Moral Causes of War," *American Mercury*,
XXXVIII (July, 1936), 299, 301; Johnson Hagood, "Rational Defense,"
Saturday Evening Post, CCIX (October 21, 1936), 5; Senate, *Neutrality,
Peace Legislation, etc.; Hearings*, 381–382.

ing within that society and show the influence exerted by some persons on particular decisions, "can reduce no total situation to an equation to make a Q.E.D." It was absurd, therefore, to regard the scheming of financial interests as *the* cause of America's declaration of war in 1917.[25]

The contents of *The Devil Theory of War* tended, within the context of the times, to reduce Beard's argument concerning causation to little more than a semantic quibble. Beard himself repeated the evidence uncovered by the Nye Committee regarding pressure exerted on the Wilson Administration by financial interests to lift the embargo on loans and to underwrite an Allied victory, by American intervention if necessary. He also went to great pains to discredit the widely accepted belief that unrestricted German submarine warfare was the basic cause of America's declaration of war. By thus eliminating a plausible alternative, Beard strengthened the case of those who placed full blame for American involvement in the First World War on bankers and businessmen.[26]

The impression left on the reader was precisely the same as that given by publications of the Nye Committee. Indeed, Beard presented the evidence with so much more skill and wrote with so much more grace and style, that there can be little doubt his book contributed greatly to fixing the onus of guilt on the already suspected parties. It thus had the effect of advertising, rather than refuting, the devil theory. Beard himself drew this conclusion:

We do not know the "cause" of American intervention. We do know something about the operations of bankers and politicians which verged in the direction of war. We know that these operations were carried on secretly, that knowledge of them was not

[25]Beard, "Peace for America," 101; Charles A. Beard, *The Devil Theory of War* (New York, 1936), 11–29, esp. 15 and 29.
[26]*Devil Theory of War*, 30–102.

then revealed to the people of the United States or to the Congress of the United States. We know that these operations helped to entangle the fate of the American economy in the fate of the Allied belligerents.[27]

Furthermore, Beard pointed out that "powerful economic and political personalities seeking to avoid one domestic crisis after another by extending credits to the Allies" finally induced President Wilson to avoid an immediate economic collapse by leading this country into war. He insisted on mandatory neutrality legislation, so that "bankers would have to go to Congress more or less openly, instead of slipping around to the State Department or the Metropolitan Club to deliver their ultimata." A stronger indictment of bankers and businessmen could scarcely be imagined.[28] Few readers were likely to take seriously the technicalities about historical causation which Beard raised. Indeed, he prescribed for the "situation" the identical remedies others ordered for the "cause."

There can be little doubt that all supporters of neutrality legislation accepted the devil theory at least implicitly. The principal provisions of the Neutrality Acts prohibited loans and the sale of munitions to belligerents. Such measures could prevent war only if munitions makers fostered wars in order to derive profits from them or if persons lending money to particular belligerents could form a pressure group of sufficient strength to force a declaration of war on the President and Congress if their investments were in jeopardy.

House Resolution 7344, introduced by Representative Usher L. Burdick of North Dakota in 1935, made the connection between neutrality legislation and the devil theory explicit. It was, according to its own text, a bill to "prohibit

[27]*Ibid.*, 102.
[28]*Ibid.*, 107, 123–124.

the private manufacture of munitions of war, defining the term 'munitions,' and designed to prevent any war except that of self-defense of the United States and the territory over which it now exercises a protectorate, adhering to the principles of the Monroe Doctrine, eliminating all possibility of war profits, and for other purposes." The bills introduced in the same year by Kloeb, Tinkham, Maverick, and Fish in the House, and by Nye, Clark, and William H. King of Utah in the Senate, had somewhat less elaborate statements of purpose, but were designed to fulfill the same functions.[29]

A curious sidelight further illustrating the connection between the devil theory and neutrality legislation is the fate of those measures specifically designed to take the profits out of war. Most isolationists strongly supported such legislation in principle. Yet they always opposed it in the form in which it reached the floor of Congress. The originators and strongest and most consistent supporters of antiprofiteering bills were the American Legion and other veterans' organizations. These groups assumed the lure of profits to be one of the basic causes of war and expressed their members' resentment of those "slackers" who remained at home to make money while young men were drafted for duty in the front lines.

The first antiprofiteering bill to receive serious consideration was the work of the chairman of the Committee on Military Affairs, Representative John J. McSwain of South Carolina. House Resolution 3, introduced in 1935, was a measure designed to "prevent profiteering in time of war and to equalize the burdens of war and thus to promote the

[29]Kloeb introduced House Resolution 7125, to prohibit loans to the governments or nationals of belligerents; all the other resolutions called primarily for arms embargoes. These were: House Resolution 8979 (Tinkham), House Joint Resolutions 339 and 259 (Maverick), House Joint Resolutions 266 and 267 (Fish), Senate Joint Resolution 20 (King), and Senate Joint Resolutions 100 and 120 (Nye and Clark).

national defense." After undergoing various changes, it was referred, as House Resolution 5529, to the Senate Committee to Investigate the Munitions Industry for further study. The Nye Committee returned it to the House with a recommendation for adoption.

The provisions of the McSwain Bill were far-reaching. A revenue section provided for a 50 per cent tax on corporate profits and a 100 per cent excess profits levy, both to become effective as soon as the United States entered a war. The bill also authorized the drafting of manpower for work in war plants and called for an Industrial Management Board with power to induct plant executives into the armed forces, where they would be paid military salaries for the duration of the war. A Commodities Control Board was to be set up for the purpose of fixing the prices suppliers of war materiel could charge the government. This measure, with only the provisions for a manpower draft stricken, passed the House by a vote of 258–71. A considerable number of isolationists opposed it. Many conservatives resented the proposed extension of federal control over business, some liberals feared for the rights of labor, and the belligerent isolationists regarded this type of legislation as both unnecessary and undesirable. The objections of the timid isolationists, who basically wanted to take the profits out of war, centered on the fact that under the measure profits would not be eliminated but merely tied to plant capitalization. Since such capitalization would increase in wartime, larger profits would flow to industry despite the higher taxes. Under such circumstances, they held it to be unwise to give the President the sweeping powers called for by the measure under consideration.[30] The bill never reached the Senate floor.

[30]Senate, *Munitions Industry,* IV; the text voted on by the House and the vote on the measure are in *Congressional Record* 74th Cong., 1st sess., 4958–4969 (April 3, 1935).

Some isolationists now began to press for more effective antiprofiteering legislation. In 1937, bills to take the profits out of war were introduced in the House by Fish, Maverick, and Lyle H. Boren of Oklahoma. In the Senate, the Nye Committee offered a measure sponsored jointly by Nye, Bone, Clark, Vandenberg, and James P. Pope of Idaho that, in addition to the usually stated aims, also sought to "promote peace."[31] Resolutions endorsing such legislation were passed by the legislatures of Nebraska, Kansas, and Ohio, as well as by the American Legion and the Jewish War Veterans of the United States. At the same time, vigorous opposition was voiced by labor organizations fearful of the effects of a manpower draft on wages and working conditions, and by some isolationist organizations, such as the Women's International League for Peace and Freedom, which viewed the proposals as an undesirable abridgement of civil liberties. The only legislation actually to reach the floor of Congress was a much diluted version of the McSwain Bill. In the report of the Military Affairs Committee, Representative Lister Hill of Alabama insisted that "this bill kills any incentive that anyone might have to do anything that might encourage, provoke or lead to war."[32] Many isolationists were not convinced of this and continued to work for more effective legislation.

The only result of their efforts was an even less satisfactory bill reported out of the Committee on Military Affairs in 1938, ironically by Representative Andrew J. May of Ken-

[31]The proposals were: House Resolution 272 (Fish), House Resolution 4014 (Boren), House Resolution 4042 (Maverick), and Senate Bill 1331 (Nye *et. al.*).

[32]*House Reports,* No. 808 (Committee on Military Affairs), 75th Cong., 1st sess. (1937), 8. Numerous resolutions and petitions both pro and con, are in House Records (Committee on Military Affairs), File 75A–H 12.2.

tucky, who was subsequently to be convicted of war profiteering. This measure was bitterly attacked by Representatives Maverick and Kvale, who were themselves members of the Military Affairs Committee, and did not come to a vote. Legislation to take the profits out of war was never adopted, though agitation for it continued until after the outbreak of war in Europe.[33] The attempt to secure such legislation indicates widespread acceptance of the devil theory, and the failure of this attempt distressed many isolationists. Said Representative Dirksen of the Neutrality Act of 1937:

In years to come this measure will furnish delicious humor and stir the funnybone of history students who may have the patience and fortitude to dig through the *Congressional Record* for light on contemporary affairs. . . . We are still attempting to eat our cake and have it too. We say we want neutrality, but along with it we want a slice of the profitable trade of belligerent nations.[34]

Widespread acceptance of the devil theory of war also led to the energetic drive conducted during the thirties to make a declaration of war by the United States subject to a national referendum. A constitutional amendment requiring such a procedure had been introduced by Senator Thomas P. Gore of Oklahoma on August 31, 1917, only four months after America entered the First World War. Similar proposals were made in every subsequent Congress, except the sixty-sixth, by Representative (later Senator) C. C. Dill of Washington, Senator Edwin F. Ladd of North Dakota, and Representatives Edward Voigt of Wisconsin, Henry R. Rathbone of Illinois, John M. Evans of Montana, Hamilton Fish of New York, and James A. Frear of Wisconsin among

[33]See, for example, Borah to G. W. Hammer, dtd October 25, 1939, Borah Papers, Box 426.

[34]*House Reports,* No. 870 (Committee on Military Affairs), 75th Cong., 3rd sess. (1938), *passim; Congressional Record,* 75th Cong., 1st sess., 2257 (March 15, 1937).

others.[35] All such resolutions were referred to the appropriate Judiciary Committee and buried there.

In 1934, Frear reintroduced a number of similar measures and Representative Denver S. Church of California presented one of his own. At the same time, Congressman George B. Terrell of Texas explicitly tied the war referendum proposal to the devil theory. House Joint Resolution 283, which Terrell sponsored, stipulated that no American declaration of war can take effect until approved by popular vote and that, if such approval is given, "the wealth of the country shall be drafted through such tax laws as Congress may enact to prosecute the war" and "no profit shall be made out of the Government by any person or corporation from the sale of munitions or other implements of war, but all munitions or other necessary war materials shall be sold at actual cost." The following year, Representative Ludlow of Indiana, who was to become the most consistent and energetic advocate of such proposals introduced House Joint Resolution 89: "Proposing an amendment to the Constitution of the United States with respect to the declaration of war and the taking of property for public use in the time of war."[36]

Louis Ludlow was virtually unknown to the general public in 1935. He had begun his professional career in 1895 as reporter for the Indianapolis *Sun* and moved to Washington in 1901 as political correspondent for the Indianapolis *Sen-*

[35]The most important of these proposals were Senate Joint Resolution 97 (Gore, 1917), House Joint Resolution 374 (Dill, 1919), Senate Joint Resolution 89 (Ladd, 1921), Senate Joint Resolution 8 (Ladd, 1924), Senate Joint Resolution 102 (Dill, 1926), House Joint Resolution 19 (Evans, 1927), House Joint Resolution 112 (Fish, 1929), and House Joint Resolution 125 (Frear, 1933).

[36]Frear introduced House Joint Resolutions 217, 218, 313, and 321; Terrell's resolution is reprinted in *Congressional Record*, 73rd Cong., 2nd sess., 3523 (March 1, 1934); House Joint Resolutions 159 and 167, two further proposals made by Ludlow in 1935, were similar in scope.

tinel. Subsequently he represented a number of Indiana and Ohio newspapers in the Congressional press gallery. In 1924, styling himself "a veteran Washington correspondent," he wrote the autobiographical *From Cornfield to Press Gallery,* and three years later he added the satirical *Senator Solomon Spiffledink* to the growing list of his publications. In 1927, Ludlow was president of the National Press Club. In this capacity, he introduced Lindbergh to an audience assembled in the Washington Auditorium upon the flyer's return from France. Ludlow often pointed to this event with pride, and it is likely he felt confirmed in his own isolationism by Lindbergh's subsequent stand.

In 1928, Ludlow ran successfully for Congress as a Democrat in Indiana's Seventh District, and thus became the first person ever to move directly from the press gallery to the floor of Congress. Although he remained in the House for twenty years, the Indiana Congressman developed into neither an outstanding legislator nor a power in party circles. But he gained national prominence as the sponsor of the Ludlow Amendment, a constitutional amendment to require a referendum prior to any declaration of war.[37]

Ludlow energetically sought approval for his measure in Congress and among organizations interested in the peace movement. He received immediate, enthusiastic support from Oswald Garrison Villard and other isolationists, and induced a subcommittee of the Committee on the Judiciary to hold hearings on House Joint Resolution 167. Retired Marine Corps Major-General Smedley D. Butler and Homer T. Rainey, President of Bucknell University, as well as Representatives Matthew A. Dunn of Pennsylvania and Harold Knutson of Minnesota, supported Ludlow's proposal in their

[37]Louis L. Ludlow, *From Cornfield to Press Gallery* (Washington, 1924) and *Senator Solomon Spiffledink* (Washington, 1927).

testimony. So did Dorothy Detzer, representing the Women's International League for Peace and Freedom, and Arthur J. Lovell of the Brotherhood of Locomotive Firemen and Engineers, who claimed to speak for all twenty-one railroad brotherhoods.[38] Nevertheless, the amendment proposal died in committee.

Two years later, Ludlow reintroduced his resolution and Nye, Fish, and Luther A. Johnson of Texas sponsored similar measures. All the proposals called for a war referendum, though without the draft-the-wealth provisions previously included. When the House Judiciary Committee failed to act, Ludlow introduced House Resolution 165, to bring the amendment proposal directly to the floor as a special order of business. The new resolution was referred to the Rules Committee, which took no further action.[39]

Many isolationists and several pacifist organizations now rallied to the support of the amendment. The Women's International League for Peace and Freedom endorsed Ludlow's stand in a letter to House Speaker William B. Bankhead of Alabama and the legislature of Wisconsin memorialized Congress in the same vein. The National Council for the Prevention of War put former Nye Committee investigator Stephen Raushenbush in charge of a major campaign which it launched in support of the war referendum proposal. In a series of radio broadcasts, entitled "Between War and Peace" and sponsored by the NCPW, Representatives Ludlow, Fish,

[38]House Subcommittee No. 2 of the Judiciary Committee, *To Amend the Constitution with Respect to the Declaration of War; Hearing,* 74th Cong., 1st sess. (1935), *passim;* for Villard's attitude see Villard to Caroline O'Day, dtd November 5, 1936 Villard Papers, File 2886, and Villard to various Congressmen, dtd April 21, 1937, Villard Papers, File 2345.

[39]The proposals were House Joint Resolution 20 (Ludlow), Senate Joint Resolution 10 (Nye), House Joint Resolution 33 (Johnson), House Joint Resolution 63 (Fish), and House Joint Resolution 199 (Ludlow).

Koppleman, Kvale, and Francis H. Case of South Dakota, as well as Senators Capper, Nye, Bone, and Lynn J. Frazier of North Dakota, spoke in favor of the Ludlow Amendment. A National Committee on the War Referendum was formed under the leadership of Ludlow, Raushenbush, General Butler, and Major-General William C. Rivers, and continued its propaganda activities for some time.[40]

In the meantime, Ludlow began collecting signatures on a discharge petition designed to pry House Resolution 165 out of the Rules Committee. "My war referendum resolution (copy enclosed)," he informed his colleagues, "will do more, I believe, to keep America out of slaughter pens in foreign countries than any other measure that could be passed." By December 4, 1937, 197 Congressmen had signed the petition.[41] The sinking of the United States river gunboat *Panay* by Japanese aircraft in Chinese waters on December 12 produced a minor war scare in America. By capitalizing on this, Ludlow was able to secure the additional 21 signatures he needed, and on January 10, he moved that his war referendum proposal be brought to the floor.

The debate on Ludlow's motion was brief but bitter. Its climax was a speech by Speaker Bankhead, who left the chair to deliver his remarks. Bankhead expressed violent opposition to the discharge resolution and read a letter from President Roosevelt attacking the referendum proposal. Ludlow's motion was defeated 188 to 209, although all isolationists except

[40]Detzer to Bankhead, dtd May 7, 1937, House Records (Committee on Foreign Affairs), File 75A–H 12.4; JR 62,A (Legislature of Wisconsin), dtd May 25, 1937, House Records (Committee on the Judiciary), File 75A–H 8.7; National Committee on the War Referendum Papers, *passim;* National Council for the Prevention of War Papers, Drawer 82.

[41]Ludlow to all Congressmen, dtd April 6, 1937, House Records (Committee on the Judiciary), File 75A–D 20; Ludlow's progress in procuring signatures is shown in the records of the National Committee on the War Referendum.

Maverick, Tinkham, and Mrs. Rogers supported it. The closeness of the vote was regarded as a challenge to the Administration and as a sign that the Ludlow Amendment had widespread support. The issue before the House, however, was simply whether the referendum should be considered and discussed. Had House Resolution 199 actually been brought to the floor, it is likely that the distrust of the President and of Congress implicit in the resolution would have led to its defeat by a more substantial margin.[42]

A major drive for a war referendum was now begun in the Senate. La Follette, Clark, and Capper sponsored separate referendum resolutions there, without achieving any immediate results. In the next session, a new measure was introduced by Senator La Follette for himself and Senators Bone, Capper, Clark, Nye, Wheeler, Frazier, Vic Donahey of Ohio, Herbert E. Hitchcock of South Dakota, Ernest Lundeen and Henrik Shipstead of Minnesota, and James E. Murray of Montana. Congress adjourned before any action could be taken.[43]

[42]*Congressional Record*, 75th Cong., 3rd sess., 276–283 (January 10, 1938). Most accounts of the episode leave the erroneous impression the narrow Administration victory came on the issue of the adoption of the amendment; Langer and Gleason state "the much-debated Ludlow Amendment...was defeated in the House by a narrow margin of twenty-one votes, despite all efforts of the Administration to mobilize opposition against it" (*op. cit.*, 14). Hull's *Memoirs*, I, 364 [sic] are given as the source. Hull described the event correctly (*Memoirs*, I, 563–564), though the last part of his description is open to misinterpretation. Dexter Perkins, also apparently using Hull as a source, attaches much significance to the outcome of the vote and implies it was the amendment that was so narrowly defeated (*The New Age of Franklin Roosevelt, Chicago History of American Civilization*, Daniel J. Boorstin, ed. (Chicago, 1957), 101–102). Bailey speaks more correctly of the amendment's being "shelved " (*Diplomatic History*, 746n). Actually, it merely remained shelved.

[43]The other proposals were Senate Joint Resolution 218 (La Follette), Senate Joint Resolution 221 (Clark), and Senate Joint Resolution 223 (Capper).

Early in 1939, Clark and Ludlow again offered war referendum amendments. So did Senator Alexander Wiley of Wisconsin. The resolution sponsored by the twelve Senators in the previous Congress was reintroduced, this time with the added endorsement of Senator D. Worth Clark of Idaho.[44] A subcommittee of the Senate Committee on the Judiciary again held public hearings on the matter, and ultimately reported out both the La Follette and Wiley Resolutions without recommendation. Neither measure was taken up on the floor and both died quietly on the Senate calendar.[45] Still, the belief in the desirability of such legislation persisted in isolationist circles.

The only justification for a constitutional amendment requiring a national referendum on the issue of war or peace was the belief that Congress and the President could be forced by well-organized pressure groups into declaring war even when such a step was contrary to the interests and wishes of a majority of the American people. Moreover, supporters of such an amendment were certain a declaration of war would never be approved by the voters. Ludlow appealed for support of his proposal on this basis from the outset, and Representative Dunn estimated in 1935 that any popular vote would run 9 to 1 against war. In 1937, Ludlow described his amendment in these terms:

It changes the Constitution so that the trigger that starts the war machinery will be pulled, not by a little group subject to being cajoled and bullied by selfish special interests, but by all the people....I sincerely believe that it would keep America

[44]These were Senate Joint Resolution 4 (Clark), House Joint Resolution 89 (Ludlow), Senate Joint Resolution 140 (Wiley), and Senate Joint Resolution 84 (La Follette *et. al.*).

[45]*Senate Reports,* Nos. 749 and 750 (Committee on the Judiciary), 76th Cong., 1st sess. (1939).

out of all foreign wars, and indeed, out of all wars, unless the occasion should arise for a righteous war of defense.

Senator Capper expressed the identical opinion.[46]

"My war-referendum peace resolution...," the indefatigable Ludlow declared shortly thereafter, "is intended to prevent our precious boys—the flower of American manhood—from being drawn into another world war which appears at this moment to be looming over the world horizon." He struck the same note again and again in his book *Hell or Heaven,* published in 1937, which also contained a lengthy indictment of the munitions makers. Hamilton Fish, writing in 1938 to Alida K. L. Milliken, chairman of the Public Action Committee, Inc., of New York, expressed his intention to "do everything in my power to isolate the American people and the United States from participating in unnecessary foreign wars. The best and surest way is to give the people the final vote to determine the issue themselves." Even Senator Borah gave serious consideration to the war referendum. Expressing the opinion that twenty-five men had brought on the First World War, he favored giving a greater voice to the people in such matters, perhaps through the implementation of Ludlow's scheme.[47]

Witnesses appearing before a subcommittee of the Senate Judiciary Committee in 1939 supported the Ludlow Amendment for the same reasons. Major-General William C. Rivers

[46]Ludlow to all congressmen, dtd April 6, 1937, House Records (Committee on the Judiciary), File 75A–D 20; House, *To Amend the Constitution; Hearings,* (1935), 44; *Congressional Record,* 75th Cong., 1st sess., App. 1028 (April 29, 1937); Capper to Frank E. Gannett, dtd July 3, 1937, National Council for the Prevention of War Papers, Drawer 82.

[47]*Congressional Record,* 75th Cong., 1st sess., 7710 (July 27, 1937); *ibid.,* 75th Cong., 3rd sess., App. 10 (January 4, 1938); Louis Ludlow, *Hell or Heaven* (Boston, 1937), *passim;* Borah to G. Krause, dtd February 28, 1938, Borah Papers, Box 417.

regarded adoption of the proposal as virtually synonymous with the prevention of war. Representative Caroline O'Day of New York supported the war referendum with the rhetorical question: "Why should our men be sent overseas to fight for countries not their own and for causes that have their roots in ancient quarrels in which the United States were [sic] not involved?" Representative James F. O'Connor of Montana thought the Ludlow Amendment would "allay the activities of the powerful lobbyists on behalf of the munitions makers." Stuart Chase was sure it would "prevent us from being rushed into war by a belligerent, frightened or acquisitive minority." Senator Capper believed its adoption "would be a long step toward preventing the first steps that lead to foreign entanglements that lead to participation in foreign wars." Gerald Monsman of the Keep America Out of War Congress, Dorothy Detzer of the Women's International League for Peace and Freedom, and Mrs. Florence Brewer Boeckel of the National Council for the Prevention of War also appeared before the subcommittee in order to argue for the Ludlow Amendment.[48]

The support given it by the pacifists characterizes the war referendum as a device intended to make American participation in war less likely. Yet, the only specific purpose the Ludlow Amendment could have served would have been that of reducing the effectiveness of small groups seeking to involve this country in wars against the interests and wishes of most Americans. Isolationists fought for the referendum proposal because they saw in this measure another means for exorcising the devils who, they were certain, had dragged the United States into disaster in 1917.

The devil theory of war was a basic part of isolationism

[48]Senate Judiciary Committee, Subcommittee, *War Referendum; Hearings*, 76th Cong., 1st sess. (1939), 34, 36, 47, 57, 125, 143, 156, 158.

during the Roosevelt Era. It explained why America entered the First World War despite the absence, in the eyes of most isolationists, of valid national interests that required military intervention. Moreover, it showed what steps had to be taken to prevent a similar tragedy in the future. Attempts to curb the activities of international bankers and munitions makers, to take the profits out of war, and to deprive the President and Congress of the power to declare war without specific authorization by a majority of the people were made on the assumption America could be kept out of war in this way. Yet such measures could be effective only if wars were the work of small, malevolent minorities. The vigor with which most isolationists supported these measures belies any disclaimers some of them may have made of the devil theory itself.[49]

The legislation that isolationists generally supported on the eve of the Second World War placed restrictions on the activities of munitions makers, bankers, and businessmen. None of the isolationist measures that failed of adoption would have done more. Such legislation could neither engender a genuine spirit of neutrality in the American people nor prevent the United States from becoming a factor in any major foreign conflict. The isolationists failed to appreciate that enforced nonaction by American bankers and businessmen, or by the American government, might tacitly align this country with the policy of imposing economic sanctions, and thus, for all practical purposes, with the League of Na-

[49]All isolationists favored the placing of some restrictions on the activities of munitions makers and bankers. That some of them did not favor the specific measures proposed for taking the profits out of war has been noted earlier. The only significant isolationist opposition to the Ludlow Amendment came from the American Legion and other veterans organizations (see House Records [Committee on the Judiciary], File H 76A-13.19).

tions. They failed to see that the policy they supported might give aid and comfort to foreign nations fighting for causes that were unpopular in America. In short, they did not see clearly enough that United States involvement in world affairs in the twentieth century was not due primarily to ill-conceived policies or inadequate precautions, but rather to the objective facts of the economic and potential military power of this country, to advances in technology, and to the shift of the balance of power in Europe and Asia.

By insisting that internal devils, rather than the realities of the international situation, were propelling the United States toward war and by adhering to the principle that only unilateral actions could serve American interests, the isolationists created serious dilemmas for themselves whenever they sought to apply their policies to specific situations. But they could not abandon these propositions without abandoning isolationism itself.

VI

THE ISOLATIONIST DILEMMA

▶▶▶▶▶▶▶▶▶▶▶▶▶▶▶▶▶▶◀◀◀◀◀◀◀◀◀◀◀◀◀◀◀◀◀◀

THE isolationists of the Roosevelt Era were firmly committed to unilateralism and to the avoidance of war. They were committed to unilateralism because they respected the advice of Washington and Jefferson and distrusted the motives and actions of foreign nations. They yearned for the conditions that prevailed in the nineteenth century, when American unilateralism kept European rivalries and power politics from interfering with the territorial and economic expansion of the United States. Isolationists were committed to the avoidance of war because they regarded the First World War as an object lesson, teaching that modern war disrupts the economies of participating countries and threatens political liberty, that America could not solve the problems of Europe, and that military intervention was a one-way street leading to further undesirable entanglements.

The combination of unilateralism with pragmatic pacifism made isolationism attractive to most Americans prior to 1935. But the application of this combination of principles to the international crises of the thirties involved isolationists in dilemmas they were never able to resolve fully. Their failure to do so ultimately cost them majority support. The

Prof. is not realistic —

dilemmas developed, on the one hand, because isolationist theories did not fit the realities of the world situation and, on the other hand, because unilateralism and *ad hoc* pacifism frequently proved incompatible with each other in practice.

The isolationists tried hard to demonstrate that no conceivable war involved specific American territorial or economic interests, that virtue was not the monopoly of Great Britain and France nor vice that of the Axis Powers, and that the Western Hemisphere was well-nigh impregnable, regardless of the outcome of foreign wars. These assertions could not be definitely proven false and seemed plausible to most Americans for a time. They did not, however, constitute an adequate response to all the international problems of the United States.

America was not propelled toward war in the thirties merely by the necessity of defending specific rights, the desire to uphold good against evil, or fear for its own safety in case of an Axis victory. Two other factors, greatly underestimated by the isolationists, played a prominent role. One was the sympathy most Americans, isolationists no less than others, had for one of the contending parties in Europe or Asia, a sympathy not wholly explainable in moralistic terms. The other was the economic and potential military strength that made the United States a factor in world affairs and affected, through American acts of omission as well as of commission, the outcome of every full-scale war.

2 reasons for war: Sympathy + US strength

American sympathies raised the temptation to intervene whenever the favored side seemed to be losing. Confirmed isolationists fought this temptation by reminding themselves and others of the horrors of war. But this did little to overcome the unneutral attitude of the American people, an attitude likely to have dangerous consequences. The noticeable, if unintended, effect of American policies on the course of foreign wars offered the additional temptation to tailor

Emotional Conflict

these policies so as to help the seemingly more deserving belligerent. Interventionists openly favored such a course and sought to distinguish between aggressors and their victims. Isolationists attacked this as leading to war, but were caught in a dilemma whenever the policies they favored inadvertently aided the side whose aims they opposed. The dilemma was compounded when policies unintentionally helpful to one side in a conflict brought retaliatory action from the other side and thus exposed the United States even more directly to the danger of war.

Another dilemma was created by the isolationists' insistence that war be avoided through unilateral action. Restrictions on American trade, which formed the core of neutrality legislation intended to implement the isolationist position, either undermined the economic sanctions the League of Nations was attempting to impose or else bore, in their application, a striking resemblance to such sanctions. In the first case, it was conceivable that neutrality legislation increased the possibility of American involvement in war by frustrating the attempts of other nations to prevent wars altogether. In the second case, it could be argued that if American policy paralleled that of the League in any event, the wisest course would be one of cooperation to make this common policy more effective.

Confirmed isolationists refused to be swayed by such arguments but were never able to counter them convincingly. Their inability to do so eventually lost them the support both of those unilateralists who realized that true independence in foreign affairs required the strength and willingness to risk war in defense of rights and principles, and of those pacifists who saw that America could avoid war only by cooperating with other nations to prevent wars from breaking out. Increasingly, it also lost them the support of the politically disinterested, who had accepted isolationism as a safe and easy course but now discovered that it was both difficult and dangerous.

America's neutrality legislation encountered its first test almost at once. The Act of 1935 was signed by the President on August 31. On October 3, Mussolini launched his long-expected attack on Ethiopia. Two days later Roosevelt issued the obligatory American declaration of neutrality. The Italo-Ethiopian War, coming at a time when discussion of new antiwar legislation was already under way in America, afforded a good test of the validity of the isolationist position. The initial results of this test were not promising. In the first place, the war in Africa was not likely to involve the United States unless, through the action of the League of Nations, it turned into a general conflict. That was improbable from the outset and became ever less likely as the discussions in Geneva progressed. The Neutrality Act therefore had little relevance to the issue of war or peace for America in this situation. Second, it was immediately apparent that the Act did not affect both belligerents in the same manner. American neutrality policy thus became a factor in the conflict and tended to entangle, rather than to disassociate, the United States.

Neither Italy nor Ethiopia normally acquired arms or ammunition in this country and neither was, therefore, directly affected by the arms embargo Hull issued on Roosevelt's orders on October 5. Italy, however, produced munitions in sufficient quantities to prosecute the war in which it was engaged, while Ethiopia did not and was legally barred from making up this deficiency through purchases in the United States. Though Ethiopia lacked the financial means to buy substantial quantities of arms, and transportation problems made sizable shipments from America impossible, the arms embargo still posed more of a problem to the African empire than it did to the Fascist dictatorship. Moreover, Italy's military effectiveness depended to a considerable extent on imports of American raw materials such as oil, cotton, and iron ore. By prohibiting the sale of guns to Ethiopia while supplying Italy with increasing quantities of strategic supplies, the United States was, in a sense, supporting the aggressive tactics of Mussolini.

Roosevelt and Hull, however, thought that American policy was detrimental to Italy, and hence might help to delay an Italian victory and make an equitable settlement of the conflict possible. Their hopes in this regard were based on the largely unwarranted assumption that all trade with Italy would suffer as a result of the arms embargo. The initial declaration of neutrality was accompanied by a warning against all commercial relations with belligerents. On October 10, Hull made this warning more explicit. On November 15, the Secretary of State admitted that trade in strategic materials had increased and proceeded to enumerate the items which should not be exported to belligerents. He implied that failure to heed this moral embargo would bring positive steps by the Administration to cut down on undesirable trade. Hull's threat of such actions drew an immediate charge of unneutrality from the Italian ambassador, who claimed "it is well-known that their practical result would be actually to impair the freedom of trade only with Italy." No such protest had greeted the imposition of the arms embargo.[1] The steps actually taken by the Administration, though intended to express disapproval of Italian aggression and to resemble possible economic sanctions by the League, did no appreciable harm to Italy. But they were further proof that

---

[1]Cordell Hull, *Memoirs*, I, 410, 414–415, 429–431; Elliott Roosevelt, ed. (with Joseph P. Lash), *F.D.R., His Personal Letters* (2 vols., New York, 1950), 446, 505; U.S. Department of State, *Peace and War: United States Foreign Policy 1931–1941* (Washington, 1943), 283, 292–294; Robert A. Divine, *The Illusion of Neutrality* (Chicago, 1962), 122–127.

neutrality legislation, as designed by the isolationists, did little to insulate America against the danger of war.

In some respects, the Italo-Ethiopian War fitted neatly into the isolationists' concept of foreign wars and their relation to the United States. The United States had no territorial and only slight economic interests in Africa. Though Mussolini's action was clearly aggressive and unprovoked, it seemed little different from what Great Britain and France had been doing in Africa for nearly a century. The fact that Ethiopia, unlike Algeria or Rhodesia, was a Christian country and a member of the League of Nations was largely ignored by the isolationists, who had scant respect for the League and regarded the African nation simply as an uncivilized country inhabited by dark-skinned natives. Italy's attempt to gain a colony there appeared to be an effort to redress legitimate grievances stemming from the First World War and a necessary step toward relieving dangerous internal population pressures. Moreover, Italy had shown no animosity toward the United States and, though Mussolini was unquestionably a dictator, Emperor Haile Selassie could hardly qualify as a champion of democracy or his spear-carrying tribesmen be considered defenders of American values and principles.

The isolationists were certain, therefore, that the United States had no reason to become involved in the conflict, either for practical or for moral reasons. They were not prepared to admit that the Neutrality Act was unnecessary to insure American noninvolvement in this instance, and showed great concern about the unequal effects of the law on the two belligerents. As a consequence, they intensified their search for means to improve existing legislation in order to produce genuine American neutrality in future conflicts. The most logical step in this direction was a mandatory embargo on strategic materials other than arms ammunition,

Strong step for neutrality

to take effect immediately upon the outbreak of war anywhere in the world.

A wide split developed in isolationist ranks over this issue.
Borah and other belligerent isolationists categorically opposed all embargoes, and had accepted the ban on the sale of
arms in 1935 only because they regarded trade in implements
of war as inherently undesirable. They were unalterably
opposed to the further surrender of neutral rights. Some
timid isolationists, who basically favored additional trade
restrictions, had compunctions about changing American
neutrality rules while a war was in progress. Moreover, most
isolationists were uncomfortably aware of the fact that imposing an embargo on raw materials at this time resembled
the League's proposal for economic sanctions on Italy. While
they did not object to parallel actions on principle, if no
specific American commitment was involved, they nevertheless regarded even such actions with suspicion. Yet, they also
saw a danger in the growing trade in oil and other strategic
materials. Not only might this give the United States an
economic stake in the war, it would also put this country in
the anomalous position of becoming Italy's chief source of
supply if the League of Nations were to impose sanctions
while America adhered to its existing policy. The isolationists
reached no agreement on the relative importance of these
contradictory factors.

The Neutrality Act was to expire on February 29, 1936,
and Congress spent much of January and February in a
debate on what measure was to replace it. The State Department, seeking a compromise between President Roosevelt's
desire for neutrality legislation that could be used as a
foreign policy tool and Congressional insistence on a bill that
would keep America uninvolved in foreign conflicts, proposed extension of the arms embargo, a ban on long-term
credits to belligerents, and a quota system limiting the export

volume of specified war materials to pre-war levels. The quota system was to apply to all warring nations, but the materials to be included under the system were to be enumerated by the President at his discretion.[2]

Nye, Maverick, and Clark introduced resolutions paralleling the Administration measure, but making the quota system mandatory for all essential war materials. Their proposal *Cash+carry* also included a cash-and-carry provision requiring all trade with belligerents to be carried in foreign ships, and only after title to the goods had been transferred to the purchaser or shipper. Ludlow introduced a bill to place an absolute embargo on trade with warring nations.[3]

As finally reported out of the Committee on Foreign Relations, the proposed Neutrality Act of 1936 contained the Administration-sponsored section prohibiting the sale of any articles other than food, clothing, or medical supplies to belligerents

President's power to embargo whenever during any war in which the United States is neutral, the President shall find that the placing of restrictions on the shipment from the United States to belligerent countries of certain articles or materials used in the manufacture of arms, ammunition, or implements of war, or in the conduct of war, will serve to promote the security and preserve the neutrality of the United States, or to protect the lives and commerce of nationals of the United States, or that to refrain from placing such restrictions would contribute to a prolongation or expansion of war.[4]

Rejected This section of the Pittman Bill and its substantial counterpart in the McReynolds Bill introduced in the House were unacceptable to almost all isolationists. Even those who

[2]House, *American Neutrality Policy; Hearings* (1936), 1–6.
[3]*Congressional Record,* 74th Cong., 2nd sess., 87–89 (January 6, 1936), 163–164 (January 8, 1936).
[4]This was the controversial Section 4a of the Pittman Bill; See Senate, *Neutrality; Hearings* (1936), 2.

favored further embargoes objected to the wide discretionary powers granted the President and to the implication that one of the purposes of neutrality legislation was to influence the outcome, or at least the extent, of a foreign conflict.

Even before the Pittman Bill became an issue, Professor Borchard made his position clear in an article praising the nineteenth-century conception of international law. "Men of that age had long ago abandoned the delusion, once rather common in theological circles," he wrote in *Today*, "that assistance to the righteous belligerent was privileged, that there was a right and wrong side in every war, or that collective sanctions against the 'aggressor' constituted a practical procedure, or that taking sides in foreign wars could shorten them or produce pacification either of the sword or of the spirit." Discretionary embargoes, he argued, give the President the opportunity to provoke war and thus cause him to assume a function properly left to Congress. Two months later, he told the Foreign Relations Committee embargoes were generally undesirable.[5]

Much of the same attitude was expressed by John Bassett Moore, who objected to the Pittman Bill on the grounds it put this country in line with the League of Nations. Moreover, Moore thought, the measure gave unlimited power to the President to put the United States into war through an unneutral selection of commodities to be embargoed. At the same time, Frank H. Simonds declared flexible neutrality was playing Britain's game and urged retention of the Neutrality Act of 1935 without major changes. "If the law stands," he assured *Saturday Evening Post* readers, "the danger which

[5]Edwin M. Borchard, "We Can Remain Neutral," *Today*, IV (October 5, 1935), 6, 23; House, *American Neutrality Policy; Hearings* (1936), 51–53.

has overhung the country since the World War will have been exorcised."[6]

The attack on discretionary embargoes was supported by Congressional isolationists. The traditional friendship between the United States and Italy partly accounted for this response, since Italy was certain to be the first victim of presidential discretion. More generally, however, isolationists objected to the basic unneutrality of a flexible policy and to the added powers that the Pittman Bill gave the President. "Now, I do not care anything about Mussolini," Representative Tinkham told his colleagues on the Foreign Affairs Committee, "I do not like his form of government....But the American people and the Italian people are friendly. We should remain friendly until the Italian people show hostility to us. This provision is a declaration of an unneutral policy. It denotes an intention to take one side or the other whenever trouble may arise in the world....That is not neutrality." On the floor of the House he claimed the proposed bill "makes the United States a puppet state of Great Britain and a subsidiary of the League of Nations."[7]

Similar sentiments were expressed by Representative Arthur D. Healy of Massachusetts in a speech urging retention of the existing law. "Surely the American people recognize too great a debt of gratitude to Italy for its contribution to the Nation in the development of our common country and our civilization...," he insisted, "to pass legislation which, by all accepted principles of international law, would amount to an unfriendly and hostile act toward a traditionally friendly nation." Hamilton Fish, claiming to speak for the

[6]Senate, *Neutrality; Hearings* (1936), 174–182; Frank H. Simonds, "John Bull's Holy War," *Saturday Evening Post,* CCVIII (December 21, 1935), 60.

[7]House, *American Neutrality Policy; Hearings* (1936), 17; *Congressional Record,* 74th Cong., 2nd sess., 1403 (February 3, 1936).

The Isolationist Dilemma 179

Republican party, added the final dimension to the isolationist argument against the Pittman Bill when he declared:
"We do not propose to give any additional power whatever
to the President of the United States, discretionary or otherwise, to involve us in foreign entanglements. The policy of
the Republican Party is that we will spend millions for
defense but not one dollar to send American troops to
foreign lands to fight other people's battles; and that is
what is involved if we give the President this discretionary
power." The old law was fine, Fish argued, and additional
embargo provisions were not required.[8]

Many other isolationists were convinced, however, that
the Italo-Ethiopian War demonstrated the need for more
embargoes, though not for discretionary ones. Dorothy Detzer, while expressing confidence in President Roosevelt,
opposed discretionary embargoes because they might give
Vice-President Garner or some future Republican president
the power to involve the United States in war. She clearly
favored further restrictions on trade with belligerents, however. "The test of the legislation, it seems to me," she told
readers of the *Nation,* "would be to make it so tight and
rigid that America could not be drawn into this present
war through the gate of economic sanctions." A mandatory
embargo on strategic materials would meet this test.[9]

"There is only one way to be neutral," Representative Ludlow told a nationwide radio audience in February, 1936, "and
that is to be neutral. We cannot be both neutral and accessory
to war at the same time. The only way to protect America's
neutral position in the world is to cut off all trade and all
financial transactions with warring nations." Like Miss Det-

[8]*Congressional Record,* 74th Cong., 2nd sess., 2246 (February 17,
1936), 1613 (February 6, 1936).
[9]Dorothy Detzer, "What Neutrality Means," *Nation,* CXLI (December, 1935), 642 and *passim.*

zer, Ludlow trusted Roosevelt but feared what another President might do. He showed utter contempt for the discretionary embargo provisions of the Pittman and Mc-Reynolds bills:

I make the assertion that in the manner of its operation it is pro-British. I make the assertion that when we pass it we will be playing Great Britain's international game to the *n*th degree. The title of this resolution should be changed. It should be entitled 'A joint resolution to make the United States of America an ally of Great Britain in any war in which Great Britain may be engaged.'[10]

The combined opposition of those who objected to all embargoes, those who feared presidential discretion, and non-isolationists who were generally skeptical of the value of neutrality legislation prevented acceptance of the Pittman Bill. Eventually, the Neutrality Act of 1935 was simply extended for fourteen months and a provision added banning loans to belligerents. Three other suggestions offered by isolationists were rejected.

Extension of 1935 bill not Pittman

The first was keeping American ships and goods owned by Americans out of the war zones by placing all trade with belligerents on a cash-and-carry basis. This idea had appeared in rudimentary form in a bill introduced by Ludlow early in 1935, and had been developed and popularized by Bernard Baruch, who believed the United States might "mumble, jumble, fumble, or tumble into war" unless such a policy was adopted. The cash-and-carry principle was strongly supported by Representative Kloeb and was incorporated into resolutions sponsored by Senators Nye and Clark, and Congressman Maverick.[11] Its ramifications were not seriously

3 choices rejected

---

[10]*Congressional Record,* 74th Cong., 2nd sess., 216 (January 9, 1936), 2243 (February 17, 1936).

[11]Bernard M. Baruch, "Cash and Carry," *Today,* V (November 2, 1935), 6; House, *American Neutrality Policy; Hearings* (1936), 32, 50,

considered until the following year, however, and no measure embodying the cash-and-carry idea came to a vote in 1936.

A second and somewhat simpler alternative to an embargo on strategic materials was offered as an amendment to the Neutrality Act of 1935 by Senator Bone. Bone's amendment provided for a mandatory declaration that all goods shipped from this country to belligerents go at the risk of the trader and do not enjoy the actual or implied protection of the American government. Only eighteen Senators, among them Bone, Nye, Frazier, Clark, Donahey, La Follette, and Rush D. Holt of West Virginia, voted for this proposal.[12] Belligerent isolationists were strongly opposed to it. Borah, for example, had attacked an earlier trade-at-your-own-risk proposal before the Foreign Relations Committee by stating: "I do not consider that neutrality is synonymous with cowardice." Hiram Johnson had threatened a filibuster against the Pittman Bill on the grounds that it surrendered American rights. Neither man could condone Bone's amendment, which would have yielded one of the most elementary of rights and advertised to the world that, in the words of Senator Tom Connally of Texas, "we are a bunch of white-livered people who will not protect our own citizens."[13]

The last effort to obtain more comprehensive neutrality legislation in the Seventy-Fourth Congress was made by Senator Clark, who proposed to extend the existing law only to June 1, 1936. He hoped to marshal the supporters of mandatory embargoes during the three-month grace period thus provided and to secure the enactment of a stronger measure than that now proposed. Nye and Wheeler had so little faith

84; *Congressional Record,* 74th Cong., 2nd scss., 87–89 and 124–125 (January 6, 1936). Ludlow's 1935 bill was HR 7572.

[12]*Congressional Record,* 74th Cong., 2nd sess., 2293 and 2306 (February 18, 1936).

[13]Senate, *Neutrality; Hearings* (1936), 81, 144; New York *Times,* January 14, 1936 and January 30, 1936.

in this amendment's chances of passage that they were absent
when it was voted on. Among the sixteen Senators who supported the three-month extension were Capper, Frazier, Vandenberg, Bone, Clark, Donahey, Holt, and La Follette. After
the defeat of the Clark amendment, the Neutrality Act of
1936 passed the Senate without a roll-call vote. It had been
approved by the House a day earlier by a margin of 353 to 27.
Most of the Representatives opposing it were isolationists who
objected to the absence of further mandatory embargo provisions. Seven Wisconsin Progressives, as well as Ludlow,
Lemke, Dirksen, and Maverick were among those voting
nay.[14]

The split among isolationists over the embargo question
was a purely tactical one implying no disagreement on long-
term objectives. It did, however, reveal a basic weakness in
the isolationist position. The Italo-Ethiopian War clearly
indicated that the United States would be a factor in any war
involving a major power, regardless of the means adopted
by Congress to prevent American involvement. In the neutrality debate of 1936, belligerent isolationists, who relied on
international law, appeared willing to accept this as inevitable and insisted only on the impartial application of any
policy the United States might adopt. More timid isolationists still believed they could lessen America's weight in the
international power balance by removing defects in existing
legislation. All admitted by implication, however, to the
existence of a flaw in the oversimplified picture of America's
world role they generally drew in their arguments. If, as
isolationists now recognized, restrictions on trade affected the
belligerents unequally, the United States could not be insured against involvement in war by the simple expedient
of curbing the activities of munitions makers and bankers.

[14]*Congressional Record,* 74th Cong., 2nd sess., 2287 and 2292 (February 18, 1936), 2253 (February 17, 1936).

The neutrality debate of 1936 gives some support to Lubell's contention that anti-British and pro-Axis sentiments were basic ingredients of isolationism during the thirties.[15] Some of the statements previously quoted were clearly hostile to Great Britain and friendly to Italy, and many similar expressions of sentiment can be found. The refusal of belligerent isolationists to support measures that would have restricted the sale of strategic materials to Italy can be regarded in the same light. However, a substantial group of isolationists strongly urged adoption of mandatory embargoes which were as anti-Italian as the economic sanctions voted by the League of Nations on October 11, 1935. The actual harm done Mussolini's forces by an American embargo on strategic materials would have been slight. The Italo-American trade agreement required twelve months' notice of an intention to abrogate it, and any embargo act would presumably have contained a clause maintaining the sanctity of existing treaties.[16] Nevertheless, the isolationists' support of an embargo on war material in 1936 demonstrates that admiration or distrust for any given nation was at best a secondary factor in isolationist thinking.

The defeat of the discretionary embargo and the unsuccessful effort to secure a mandatory one were, as far as the isolationists were concerned, simply attempts to avoid war through unilateral action. Granting the President discretion in the selection of nonexportable goods gave him the right to impose what amounted to economic sanctions. Considering Roosevelt's attitude, this meant conscious cooperation with the League and the likelihood of American involvement if

[15]See Samuel Lubell, *The Future of American Politics* (2nd rev. ed., Garden City, 1956), 141.

[16]Such a clause was contained in Section 16 of the McReynolds Bill. Its probable effects were pointed out by Kloeb. See *Congressional Record,* 74th Cong., 2nd sess., 1485 (February 5, 1936).

war came. Belligerent isolationists, who were certain that international cooperation could not prevent war, sought to avoid both cooperation and war by opposing all embargoes and relying on international law to keep American commerce within the accepted standards of neutral behavior. Timid isolationists favored a mandatory embargo on strategic materials. Such an embargo might help one of the belligerents and might parallel League of Nations' efforts, but it was also an independent policy requiring no direct contacts with European powers. It had the further virtue of reducing contact with all belligerents and thus served to avoid dangerous incidents that might lead to war for the United States.

The key to isolationist thinking was not liking or dislike for particular foreign powers, but studied indifference to all of them. The isolationists attacked the League powers and defended Italy during the Ethiopian crisis because they feared America could be involved in a war of Great Britain and France against the Fascist state and wanted to demonstrate that no logical reason for such a step existed. Had their stand resulted primarily from sympathy for Italy or hatred of England, the isolationists would automatically have opposed British policy and championed Axis aims in every subsequent crisis. They did not do so.

Their response to the civil war that broke out in Spain in July, 1936, makes this very plain. The Italo-Ethiopian War was an international conflict of limited scope. The rebellion led by General Francisco Franco, though an internal conflict, seemed likely to develop into a general war. Portugal, Germany, Italy, and the Soviet Union were active in Spain from the outset, and it was possible that the involvement of these powers would produce a world-wide struggle. The authors of America's neutrality legislation had not prescribed an embargo on arms, ammunition, or credit to factions engaged in civil strife. Yet the dangers isolationists feared so greatly in international wars were clearly present in the Spanish situation.

The first clear statement of the isolationists' reaction to the Spanish Civil War was contained in a telegram sent by ten members of Congress to President Roosevelt on August 14. It read:

In view of our neutrality legislation, the clear interest of Congress and the expressed will of the people of this country we wish to go on record urging every possible effort on the part of the government to prevent shipment of war supplies to Spain. We urge that you make a statement to this effect in your Chautauqua address.

Senator Nye and Representatives Ludlow, Koppleman, Sisson, Hildebrandt, and Byron N. Scott of California were among the signers. Another telegram to the same effect was sent on August 25.[17] These communications were sent at the same time that Britain and France proposed an embargo on arms shipments to Spain, a proposal that led to the meeting of the twenty-seven-nation Non-Intervention Committee in September, 1936. The isolationists' concurrence with the chief League powers was, of course, wholly unintended.

The Spanish situation presented the most serious difficulties to liberals and radicals among the isolationists. Despite their avowed indifference to foreign quarrels, they could not fail to see a moral issue in a conflict so clearly pitting Fascists against Socialists. Moreover, in the existing situation, an embargo on arms to Spain would aid Franco's forces. Under international law, as previously applied by the United States to various political upheavals in Latin America, it was entirely proper to continue normal commercial relations with the duly elected government of Spain, while barring trade with those groups seeking its overthrow. To stop trade altogether would mean placing both sides in the same legal position and would implicitly grant the Insurgents a degree

[17]Copies of both telegrams are in FDRL OF 1561.

of recognition. Furthermore, the Insurgents were adequately supplied by Germany and Italy and had little reason to seek war materiel from the United States. The Spanish government, on the other hand, was short on strategic supplies. It would lose the right to buy arms with which to defend itself if the Neutrality Act were applied. America's "neutrality" would thus become a factor in a foreign conflict for the second time.

The liberals had been willing to accept this fact in the Ethiopian crisis. But they had not then identified themselves either with the government of Mussolini or with that of Haile Selassie. The Spanish situation presented itself to them as an attack by forces of which they disapproved on a government controlled by men whose political views they shared. The liberals and radicals among the isolationists were torn, therefore, between their desire to keep America unentangled and their fervent hope that nothing would be done by the United States that would be disadvantageous to the Loyalists.

This dilemma was clearly revealed on August 31, in a long telegram from Norman Thomas to President Roosevelt. The leader of the Socialist party, normally an ardent champion of mandatory neutrality legislation, did not plead for a ban on the shipment of strategic materials to Spain. Instead, he urged the American government to take the partisan, though legal, step of forbidding ships sailing under its flag to enter rebel-held ports. In a letter of December 29, Thomas went even further. He now strongly opposed the imposition of an arms embargo on Spain. "It is true," he wrote to Roosevelt, "that the sale of implements of war to the Spanish government at this juncture means that some Americans are making profits out of another nation's civil war, but nevertheless in vital respects the situation that now confronts the United States is very different from that created by a war between nations."

Despite valiant efforts, he could not explain these "vital respects" convincingly in isolationist terms. He could merely point out that this was not "a simple world wherein a principle useful to keep the United States out of international war must be automatically and inexorably applied in civil insurrections," and conclude:

In the long run it is not peace for the world, even for America, which will be served by applying to the Spanish rebellion a general principle which should be asserted more rigorously than is yet the case in Congressional legislation concerning neutrality in international law.

The basic contradiction in this reasoning revealed the weakness of the radical isolationists' position.[18]

Roosevelt would have rejected Thomas' argument even if it had not contained a logical flaw. The President believed an embargo on arms shipments to Spain to be a painless and, for once, popular method of cooperating with Great Britain and France. Moreover, he thought an American embargo would be advantageous to the Loyalists. In 1941, Roosevelt admitted his Spanish policy had been wrong. But he still insisted at that time that "the Rebels in Spain had control over more shipping than did the Loyalists. As a result, if American war materials had been allowed to be sold to the participants in the Spanish conflict, the overwhelming probability was that the Rebel forces would have received greater assistance through American implements of war than would have the Loyalists of Spain." This opinion was probably shared by Hull in 1936, but not by other members of the Cabinet. It was not shared by the liberal, pro-Loyalist American Ambassador to Spain, Claude G. Bowers, or by the majority of Americans favoring the legitimate government of

[18]The telegram and the letter are in FDRL OF 422-C.

Spain.[19] It was certainly not shared by the liberals and radicals among the isolationists.

When the Foreign Affairs Committee held public hearings on neutrality legislation in 1937, Norman Thomas sent a long letter to Chairman McReynolds. Once again the Socialist party leader supported mandatory legislation that would make any attempt to select "guilty" nations impossible. But he opposed the application of such laws to the Spanish Civil War.

There is little or no danger [wrote Thomas] that the United States will be involved in war by permitting democratically elected governments to buy supplies (if desirable on the cash-and-carry plan) to use in the struggle against armed Fascist insurrection. Congress should judge problems arising from civil wars as they arise. We respectfully but urgently submit that your judgment in denying to the Spanish government rights freely granted Japan, Italy, Germany, and the Chinese dictator Chiang, is not an example of non-intervention, but intervention. . . . The inconsiderable danger to peace of permitting to Spain the usual rights of governments dealing with armed rebellion is blotted out by the enormous danger of this encouragement of Fascism.

The Socialist party's Executive Secretary, Roy E. Burt, supported this position in testimony before the Committee. Burt thought the Spanish Embargo was contrary to the interests of "the workers" and admitted he would favor helping rebels who attacked a "capitalist" government.[20] Since Burt could

[19]See Note to "Proclamation Forbidding Export of Arms to Spain, May 1, 1937," *The Public Papers and Addresses of Franklin D. Roosevelt* (Samuel I. Rosenman, comp.), 1937 vol. (New York, 1941), 192–193; Hull, *Memoirs*, I, 476–485; Harold Ickes, *The Inside Struggle, 1936–1939, The Secret Diary of Harold Ickes*, II (New York, 1954), 380, 569–570; Thomas H. Greer, *What Roosevelt Thought* (East Lansing, Michigan, 1958), 176; Divine, *op. cit.*, 168–170; Cole, *Nye*, 113.

[20]House, *American Neutrality Policy; Hearings* (1937), 131–132; Thomas to McReynolds, dtd March 5, 1937, House Records (Committee on Foreign Affairs), File 75A–D 13.

explain no better than Thomas why large-scale civil wars were different from international conflicts, his arguments weakened the isolationists' contention that the United States had no essential interest in the outcome of foreign wars. They thus weakened isolationism itself.

The Socialists' views on the Spanish embargo reveal a distinct anti-German and anti-Italian bias. Since Great Britain favored an arms embargo an anti-British bias was not necessarily absent, but it is certain that a desire to see the Axis Powers triumph played no part in determining the position of liberal and radical isolationists. The response of other isolationists to the Spanish embargo indicates they were also not motivated by such a desire.

When Congress reconvened in January, 1937, it considered the Administration's proposal for such an embargo. The Senate passed the measure 81 to 0 after a brief discussion. Many isolationists voiced misgivings, however. Senators Clark of Missouri and Vandenberg of Michigan expressed preference for a law covering all civil wars on the grounds that singling out Spain constituted an unneutral act. Nye objected because the resolution lined the United States up with Great Britain and France. He was not worried about this per se, but foresaw entangling difficulties in the event these nations decided to change their policies. Moreover, Nye pointed out that the United States had refused to change its neutrality laws to the detriment of Italy the previous year but was now prepared to change them in a manner that would aid General Franco. This, he emphasized, made this country appear pro-Fascist. The North Dakota Senator's charge was taken seriously and drew a specific denial from Senator Pittman, whose remarks mirrored the views of the Administration.[21]

In the House, Maverick pointed out that the United States had always supported the legitimate government of a nation

[21]*Congressional Record,* 75th Cong., 1st sess., 74–80 (January 6, 1937).

in previous civil wars and called the embargo resolution unfair to the elected leaders of Spain. He was supported in this
assertion by Hamilton Fish and by Gerald J. Boileau and
Thomas O'Malley of Wisconsin. Representative Thomas R.
Amlie of Wisconsin went even further. The militant Progressive charged that the supporters of the Spanish embargo
were "not interested in maintaining the neutrality of the
United States. These people are pro-Fascist, and they would
like to have the United States take a stand that would help
the Rebel-Fascist forces of Spain." Despite these misgivings,
Amlie voted for the resolution, which was adopted 411 to 1.
The lone dissenter was Minnesota's John T. Bernard, a
Corsica-born labor organizer and militant anti-Fascist.[22]

The isolationists' doubts about the wisdom of the Spanish
embargo were not stilled by passage of the measure. In January, 1937, Borchard informed Villard that "the Spanish Arms
Embargo, just enacted, is an intervention statute and not a
neutrality statute." "It means," he added, "that we shall treat
the lawful government of Spain and the insurgents whose
belligerency we do not recognize, as having precisely the same
status." In February, Representative Voorhis presented a
statement, signed by thirty-one members of the House, favoring strict neutrality legislation but pointing out "if an
embargo is enforced against the Spanish Government, but
not against other nations shipping to the Spanish rebels, the
United States is placed in the position of actively or con-
structively acting as cobelligerent with the forces attempting
to overthrow the Spanish Government." Among the signers,
in addition to Voorhis, were Burdick, Hildebrandt, Withrow,
Maverick, Amlie, Ludlow, Koppleman, Sauthoff, and Mrs.
O'Day.[23]

[22]*Ibid.*, 86–99 (January 6, 1937).
[23]Borchard to Villard, dtd January 12, 1937, Villard Papers, File 305;
Congressional Record, 75th Cong., 1st sess., App. 130 (February 2, 1937).

In March, Borchard again condemned the embargo as a violation of international law, this time in a letter to Borah. Nye now introduced Senate Resolution 100, asking the Secretary of State whether the Neutrality Act could be used to proclaim embargoes against nations engaging in the civil wars of others. Two weeks later, he explained the meaning of this question on the floor of the Senate. Italy, he declared, was at war in Spain and the President should stop arms shipments to Italy at once. In support of his assertion, he quoted a Washington *Post* editorial which charged existing American policy was "not neutrality at all but merely disguised assistance to a Fascist rebellion."[24]

At the end of April, Nye raised objections to a provision in the proposed Neutrality Act of 1937 that would have made the export of medical supplies subject to Presidential approval. To underscore his position, he cited telegrams from such pro-Loyalist organizations as the League for Industrial Democracy, the Medical Bureau to Aid Spanish Democracy, the United Youth Committee to Aid Spanish Democracy, the American League Against War and Fascism, the Kansas City Committee to Aid Spanish Democracy, the New England Society for Technical Aid to Spanish Democracy, and the American Friends to Spanish Democracy. Nye's stand also won the endorsement of the Massachusetts Branch of the Women's International League for Peace and Freedom. Soon afterward, Borah explained his position in great detail to Clyde Miller, a professor at Teachers College, Columbia University. It was unneutral, Borah concluded, to refuse to sell arms and ammunition to those within Spain while continuing to supply weapons to Germany and Italy.[25]

[24]Borchard to Borah, dtd March 1, 1937, Borah Papers, Box 405; *Congressional Record*, 75th Cong., 1st sess., 3315–3317 (April 9, 1937).
[25]*Congressional Record*, 75th Cong., 1st sess., 3958–3959 (April 29, 1937); Borah to Miller, dtd June 2, 1937, Borah Papers, Box 405.

The Joint Resolution of January 8, 1937, found a state of
civil strife to exist in Spain and placed an embargo on the
shipment of arms and ammunition to Spanish ports. It gave
the President authority to rescind the embargo only if the
war should end. The Neutrality Act of 1937, on the other
hand, left it to the President to decide when a civil war
became dangerous enough to warrant an embargo. Roosevelt unhesitatingly proclaimed the embargo on May 1, 1937,
the very day on which the new law took effect. He still did not
share the fears of isolationists and others that such a step
would undeservedly handicap the Loyalists. On August 26,
the indefatigable Norman Thomas once more wrote to the
President. This time, he urged invoking the Neutrality Act
against Portugal and Germany, and especially against Italy,
which was openly boastful "over the triumph of Italian arms
in Santander."[26]

[handwritten: Discretionary Powers to stop embargo] The Neutrality Act of 1937 also authorized the President
to rescind the arms embargo whenever, in his judgment, a
state of civil strife no longer existed or no longer endangered
the peace of the United States. A number of prominent isolationists urged Roosevelt to take this step with respect to
the conflict in Spain. It was once again Senator Nye who
acted most decisively. On May 2, 1938, he introduced Senate
Joint Resolution 288 for the purpose of repealing the Joint
Resolution of January 8, 1937, and "conditionally raising the
[handwritten: Repeal of Span-embargo] embargo against the Government of Spain." He attached
the condition that any goods sent to Spain must pass out of
American possession before leaving this country and could
not be transported on vessels sailing under the American
flag.[27]

[26]Thomas to Roosevelt, dtd August 26, 1937, FDRL OF 422-C.
[27]*Congressional Record,* 75th Cong., 3rd sess., 6017 and 6060 (May 2,
1938).

Nye thus favored retention of the cash-and-carry principle favorable to Great Britain while proposing to lift the embargo in order to help the anti-Fascist government of Spain. In answer to an inquiry from Pittman, Hull made it clear the Administration favored retention of the embargo. He thus *Embargo* took a stand much less clearly anti-Italian than that of the *not* Senator from North Dakota. Not until November 28, 1938, *lifted* did Roosevelt even consider permitting arms to be sent to Spain; and did not actually allow them to go until after Franco had won.[28]

The isolationists' stand on the Spanish embargo indicates they were not motivated by high regard for the Axis Powers. In many ways, their statements and actions were more clearly anti-Italian and anti-Fascist than those of Administration spokesmen who introduced and supported the embargo. The *US to* isolationists were motivated, instead, by their desire to adopt *stay clear* a course independent of, though not necessarily opposed to, *of League* that proposed by the League of Nations, a course that would, *actions* above all, keep this country out of war. Both the aims of the isolationists and the dilemma they faced found eloquent expression in a letter sent by Borah to Professor Ignatius W. Cox of Fordham University. Wrote Borah:

It is earnestly contended by one side that to lift the embargo is to favor communism and tacitly approve the mass murders and persecutions of religionists in Spain. On the other hand, it is contended that if we do not lift the embargo, we are favoring Franco, who is supported by the fascists.

I want nothing to do with either outfit and I do not want, if

[28]Hull to Pittman, dtd May 12, 1938, U.S. State Dept., *Peace and War*, 419–420; Memorandum from Roosevelt to Attorney General Homer S. Cummings, Elliot Roosevelt, ed., *op. cit.*, 832–833. By contrast, Stephen Raushenbush was a member of the Washington Committee to Lift the Embargo against Republican Spain by early 1939. See letter to Senator Norris, dtd March 7, 1939, Norris Papers, Tray 31, Box 6.

it is possible, to favor either of these forces. The fascists and communists are all the same when I come to consider the interests of my own country. . . .

At this writing, I do not know what my course will be.[29]

The minds of some isolationists were made up by their desire to maintain a traditional American policy: the extension of aid and recognition to a duly elected, democratic government. The liberals and radicals also acted out of sympathy for the Loyalists. To the extent that they permitted this sympathy to affect their judgment on neutrality policy, they were yielding to forces whose importance they always denied. These same forces played a major role in undermining the isolationist position and in ultimately involving America in the Second World War.

Though isolationists were suspicious of the Spanish embargo in part because it represented a policy paralleling that of Great Britain, anti-British bias had little to do with determining their actions. Britain applied an embargo on arms shipments to Spain but directed its principal effort toward persuading those nations actually supplying the opposing factions in the civil war to stop doing so. Many isolationists favored embargoes against Italy and Germany that had the same aim. Thus, they were themselves advocating a policy paralleling that of Great Britain. Moreover, the British policy was intended to aid the Loyalists, and many American advocates of strict neutrality had similar intentions.

Anti-British bias cannot be ruled out as a basic factor in isolationism as clearly as pro-Axis sympathies. The state of the world during the thirties makes this impossible. Since the United States was threatened with war only as an ally of Great Britain and France, isolationists had to oppose consistently all American moves that explicitly supported the

[29]Borah to Cox, dtd January 13, 1939, Borah Papers, Box 427.

European democracies in their struggle with the dictatorships, and therefore threatened further entanglement. But
the reaction to the Spanish embargo indicates that genuine
anti-British sentiments were at most only secondary factors in
the formation of isolationist attitudes.

The debate on the cash-and-carry policy points even more
strongly to the same conclusion. The proposal to prohibit the
carrying of strategic materials to belligerents in American
ships and to insist that title must pass to the shipper or purchaser before export, clearly favored the leading maritime
powers, Great Britain, France, and Japan. It had to be un-
equivocally opposed by any group acting largely from anti-
British motives. Yet it was willingly accepted by most isolationists and vigorously supported by some. Representative
Kloeb defended cash-and-carry on the grounds that it "does
not differ from the situation if we have complete freedom
of the seas, because a nation that controls the seas is the one
that makes a blockade." The policy also won the approval of
Representative Voorhis and of Mrs. Florence Brewer Boeckel,
speaking for the National Council for the Prevention of
War.[30]

In 1937, the neutrality bills proposed in both the House
and Senate, House Joint Resolution 242 and Senate Joint
Resolution 51, contained discretionary cash-and-carry provisions. Senate isolationists made an effort to eliminate this discretionary feature. When they failed, they rallied to the
support of the entire resolution. The only attack on the cash-
and-carry principle as such came from Senators Borah and
Johnson. While these two belligerent isolationists sought to
win support by calling the proposal a "British measure," their
real objection stemmed from the fact that they regarded cash-

---

[30]House, *American Neutrality Policy; Hearings* (1936), 50; House,
American Neutrality Policy; Hearings (1937), 59, 91.

Johnson
Borah

and-carry as a cowardly and unpatriotic surrender of freedom of the seas] "What sort of government is this and what sort of men are we," asked Johnson, "to accept a formula which will enable us to sell goods and then hide?" Borah and Johnson made no converts and the neutrality bill passed the Senate 63 to 6. Not a single isolationist joined the two belligerent stalwarts in opposing cash-and-carry.[31]

The debate in the House was somewhat more stormy. A minority report submitted by the Foreign Affairs Committee and signed by Fish, Martin, and Mrs. Rogers, among others, attacked discretionary cash-and-carry as "weak, timorous, and un-American." On the floor, many Congressmen expressed their belief that the proposed policy was an insufficient restriction on wartime trade and thus would not prevent American involvement through the gate of economic interest. But the only modification made did not affect the principle involved. The cash-and-carry provision was limited to two years, and the resolution was then passed 376 to 13. Burdick, Dirksen, Ludlow, Robsion, and Tinkham, among the isolationists, opposed it, but many others voted yea.[32] The Senate-House conference committee accepted the cash-and-carry provision despite the presence on the committee of Borah and Fish. The House immediately accepted the conference report. In the Senate, the Nye group now protested the greater discretion given the President by the compromise measure. Nevertheless, the Neutrality Act of 1937 passed 41 to 15. Bone, Bridges, Capper, Clark, Frazier, Holt, and Nye were

[31]*Senate Reports,* No. 118 (Foreign Relations Committee), 75th Cong., 1st sess. (1937), *passim; Congressional Record,* 75th Cong., 1st sess., 1677–1683 (March 1, 1937), 1778–1779, 1798–1801 and 1806–1807 (March 3, 1937); See also, Borah to Archibald MacLeish, dtd March 15, 1937, Borah Papers, Box 405.

[32]*House Reports,* Nos. 320 and 363 (Foreign Affairs Committee), 75th Cong., 1st sess. (1937), *passim; Congressional Record,* 75th Cong., 1st sess., 2377–2406 (March 18, 1937).

among those opposing it. Of these men, only Bridges objected to the cash-and-carry idea as such.[33]

Most isolationists thus willingly accepted a principle favorable to Great Britain in the interest of maintaining American neutrality. Although Borah called it "sordid" and "cowardly" and Borchard complained that "we have now apparently become a colony again, without even the advantages of a self-governing dominion," their position was strongly supported only by largely nonisolationist East and West Coast shipping interests and by the opponents of all neutrality legislation. To those isolationists who favored mandatory embargoes on all shipments to belligerents in the interests of American peace, the cash-and-carry provision appeared to be the best compromise they could obtain while working for more satisfactory arrangements at a future date. To those who favored economic disentanglement but feared the adverse effects of embargoes on the domestic economy, the compromise seemed to offer a workable, if not entirely satisfactory, escape from their quandary. Bernard Baruch, for example, who deemed it desirable "to keep out of war at almost any cost—except invasion," but whose ties to the business community made him reluctant to strike a body blow to American trade, advanced the cash-and-carry idea as the best available.[34] Many conservatives supported him in the hope of forestalling even more drastic commercial restrictions.

The unfortunate fact that the proposal clearly favored

---

[33]*Senate Reports,* No. 723 (House-Senate Conference Committee), 75th Cong., 1st sess. (1937); *Congressional Record,* 75th Cong., 1st sess., 3937–3962 (April 20, 1937).

[34]Borah to Archibald MacLeish, dtd March 15, 1937, and Borchard to Borah, dtd March 1, 1937, Borah Papers, Box 405; Bernard M. Baruch, "Neutrality and Common Sense," *Atlantic Monthly,* CLIX (March, 1937), 371.

the great maritime powers produced some uneasiness in isolationist ranks. Much of this was overcome, however, by the
placing of a two-year limit on the cash-and-carry provision
and by the realization that those nations having the largest
merchant fleets would, in any case, carry on the greatest trade
with the United States. "It has been said," declared Representative Earl C. Michener of Michigan, "that the passage
of this legislation will make the United States an ally of Great
Britain in the Atlantic and of Japan in the Pacific. . . . This is
one of the phases of the proposal that I do not like. However,
no law is perfect in every particular, and this is but a 2-year
experiment." George Cless, a strong advocate of cash-and-
carry neutrality, expressed the feelings of many isolationists
when he wrote in 1938:

I dislike to be inconsistent and I dislike exceedingly the thought
of being allied automatically with England or Japan, but, in my
opinion, this inconsistency in the principle of neutrality advocated is justified by the fact that it is merged into a vastly larger
principle.

The larger principle was that of keeping America out of
war. If the cash-and-carry provision would reduce contacts
with belligerents and, through the requirement for immediate payment, limit trade in strategic materials, it might prevent the United States from being drawn into a foreign
conflict. If it did that, it was desirable legislation even if it
hurt American business somewhat and basically favored the
cause of Great Britain.[35]

The Neutrality Act of 1937 was not a measure designed to
aid Germany and Italy. Neither the cash-and-carry provision
nor the discretionary powers granted a President who strongly

[35]*Congressional Record*, 75th Cong., 1st sess., 2404 (March 18, 1937);
George H. Cless, Jr., *The Eleventh Commandment* (New York, 1938),
303.

favored the cause of the democracies permit the contrary conclusion. But the act, like all the neutrality legislation, gave
indirect encouragement to the Axis Powers. It declared
American unwillingness to intervene actively in defense
of world order, and it told Britain and France they could
expect no direct American help if they took a firm stand
against the dictators. That this was another incidental result
of such legislation and not its basic aim, was clear to a man
who had every reason to hope otherwise. "From the German
standpoint," Hitler's ambassador in Washington, Dr. Hans
Heinrich Dieckhoff, reported to Berlin in December, 1937,
"the position taken and the stir created by supporters of the
isolationists are to be welcomed since, in view of the present
temper of the United States, we can under no circumstances
expect America to intervene on our side in case a world
conflict breaks out. . . . But," he added emphatically, "we
must clearly understand one thing: the pacifists—aside from
some few groups, especially of German-Americans—have
their attitude in no way determined by friendship or sympathy for Germany."[36]

In 1939, the issues in regard to neutrality legislation were
somewhat more complicated. War was imminent. The cash-
and-carry provision had expired. The Administration now
offered a new cash-and-carry proposal that would have
covered arms and ammunition. The purpose of this move
was to secure repeal of the absolute embargo on such commodities that had been in effect since 1935. Nearly all isolationists correctly regarded this as an attempt to weaken the
system of neutrality legislation and opposed the Administration measure vigorously. The Senate Foreign Relations
Committee defeated the bill with the help of Vandenberg,

[36]Dieckhoff to Foreign Office, dtd December 7, 1937, *Akten,* D, I, 534
(translation mine).

La Follette, Johnson, Borah, Capper, and Clark of Missouri. Fish, however, voted for the proposal in the House without giving any explanation for his action and Taft wrote to F. J. Libby: "I do believe that it is consistent with neutrality, and I do feel strongly against Mr. Hitler."[37]

The minority report of the Foreign Affairs Committee clearly shows that the isolationists attacked repeal of the arms embargo and not the cash-and-carry principle. Nye, Bone, and Clark, in fact, proposed Senate Joint Resolution 106 as an alternative to the Administration's plan. SJR 106 called for retention of the existing neutrality law and re-enactment of the old cash-and-carry clause, which contained no reference to arms or ammunition. General Hugh S. Johnson spoke for most isolationists when he told the Foreign Relations Committee again that the fact that cash-and-carry favored England and Japan was not important in itself. "It is certainly not our business," he explained, "to try to rectify and equalize the economic relations of nations either in peace or war."[38]

Willingness to accept the cash-and-carry principle was not induced by admiration for Japan. Most isolationists were highly critical of Japanese aggression in China, though they differed on the Far Eastern policy the United States should adopt. The President had not declared a state of war to exist between China and Japan and the Neutrality Act of 1937

[37]*Congressional Record,* 76th Cong., 1st sess., 8512–8514 (June 30, 1939); a letter from Presidential Secretary Stephen Early to Myron C. Taylor, dtd September 6, 1939, containing the results of the vote by the Foreign Relations Committee is in FDRL OF 1561; Taft to Libby, dtd May 1, 1939, Pinchot Papers, Box 64.

[38]*House Reports,* No. 856 (Foreign Affairs Committee), 76th Cong., 1st sess. (1939). *passim;* Senate, *Neutrality, Peace Legislation, etc.; Hearings,* 283. See also, Baruch to Pittman dtd April 22, 1939, Senate Records (Committee on Foreign Relations), File 75A–F 9-1.

was, therefore, not applied to that conflict. Roosevelt believed that applying the arms embargo would primarily hurt China, which would be cut off from desperately needed American supplies by such a step. A minority of isolationists, including Representatives Thomas O'Malley and Bernard J. Gehrman of Wisconsin, shared the President's view. Senator Borah, who expressed his basic sympathy for China on frequent occasions but opposed any action which, by cutting off trade with Japan, would parallel the steps being considered by the League of Nations, was certain that the United States could protect its interests in the Orient "by following a policy of our own" and agreed that the President's course, in this instance, was the correct one.[39]

The majority of isolationists disagreed with this assessment of the situation, but not with the sympathy for China it reflected. Soon after the commencement of large-scale hostilities in 1937, a group of Congressmen that included Koppleman, Voorhis, Sauthoff, Amlie, Ludlow, Fish, and Knutson urged the President to declare China and Japan to be at war. "Invocation of the Neutrality Act," the lawmakers insisted, "so far as the nations involved in the conflict are concerned, will make their situation more equal. Japan can at any time blockade China and prevent it from obtaining munitions in this country." Nye, Bone, and Clark took substantially the same position. They insisted that Roosevelt's course did not harm Japan in any way and professed to see a danger that continued shipments of war material to the Pacific might involve the United States in war. In 1938, Sauthoff introduced House Resolution 351, requesting the President to

[39]*Congressional Record,* 75th Cong., 1st sess., 8057–8058 (August 2, 1937); *ibid.,* 76th Cong., 1st sess., App. 3195 (July 12, 1939); Borah to Philadelphia *Inquirer,* dtd October 7, 1937, and to International News Service, dtd October 9, 1937, Borah to Mrs. T. E. Kinney, dtd November 18, 1937, and various other communications in Borah Papers, Box 405.

declare that a state of war existed between China and Japan.[40]

Jeanette Rankin, representing the National Council for the Prevention of War, took a position that was even more definite and more partisan. "Until the neutrality law is applied," she asserted in a handbill circulated among members of Congress, "we are definitely helping Japan."[41] The Women's International League for Peace and Freedom called on the President to invoke the Neutrality Act in the Far Eastern crisis and demanded additional embargoes on oil, scrap iron, and other war materials which Japan was importing in large quantities. Senator Norris felt so strongly about the Far Eastern situation that he ignored the advice of Borchard and others and came out strongly in favor of a boycott of Japanese goods to "supplement application of the neutrality act."[42]

Since most isolationists willingly accepted the cash-and-carry principle for commodities other than arms and ammunition, despite their realization that such a course favored Great Britain, France, and Japan, their stand indicates adherence to principles more fundamental to isolationism than antipathy to any nation or group of nations. Anti-British feeling cannot be ruled out as a contributing factor in the development of the isolationist position on the basis of such evidence. But it was clearly a factor of secondary importance.

The isolationists' response to the crises in Ethiopia, Spain, and China, and their acceptance of the cash-and-carry princi-

[40]*Congressional Record,* 75th Cong., 1st sess., App. 2196–2197 and 2187 (August 19, 1937); A copy of Sauthoff's bill is in the National Committee on the War Referendum papers.

[41]A copy sent to Representative Virginia E. Jenckes of Indiana is in FDRL OF 1561.

[42]Senate, *Neutrality, Peace Legislation, etc.; Hearings,* 528; Borchard to Norris, dtd January 3, and January 7, 1938, Norris to Borchard, dtd January 4, 1938, and to Freda Kirchwey, dtd March 19, 1938, Norris Papers, Tray 104, Box 4.

ple not only demonstrate the existence of isolationist beliefs
that were unrelated to admiration or hatred for a given
country; they also throw considerable light on a basic isolationist dilemma: [measures designed to disentangle the United
States from world affairs brought results running counter to
that aim whenever they were applied to a specific situation.]
In every existing conflict, and in all those that could be fore-
seen, American neutrality legislation had the effect of aiding
one side or the other. [Since isolationists had tried to eliminate
this dangerous contingency through Congressional action,
their efforts to promote true neutrality through legislation
must be considered a failure.]

No other result could reasonably have been expected.
Under international law, neutrality is simply the condition of
a state or government which refrains from taking part, directly or indirectly, in a war between other powers, and which
is recognized as immune from invasion or use by belligerents.
Such a condition cannot be produced by domestic legislation.
It is, in any case, unattainable for a great power in the
modern world. What was called neutrality legislation in the
thirties had little to do with genuine neutrality. It was
merely a device for curbing the activities of American bankers
and businessmen, for reducing America's direct economic
stake in future wars, and for decreasing the chance that isolated, dangerous incidents would involve the United States
in war.

The isolationists' efforts to tinker with neutrality legislation reveal their awareness of its inadequacy. But this inadequacy was due less to the absence of specific provisions
than to a flaw in the theory on which it was based. The
United States could change its role in world affairs by nonaction, but it could not eliminate that role. And as long as
this country played any important role, it could not insulate
itself against war. The isolationists realized to their sorrow

that the Neutrality acts did not significantly decrease America's importance as a factor in foreign conflicts, but they failed to draw the logical inference from this fact.

As crisis followed crisis during the thirties, the isolationists discovered it to be impossible to find a policy that would have absolutely no effect on the course of a foreign war. They discovered too, that they were no more indifferent than other Americans to the side that was to be aided by the "neutrality" of the United States. Senator Nye opposed the Spanish embargo on the grounds that it helped the Fascist powers. Miss Rankin wanted the Neutrality acts applied to the Sino-Japanese War in order to help China. Both of them, along with many other isolationists who used similar arguments, implicitly recognized the existence of American interests, unrelated to the desires of bankers and businessmen, in the outcome of these struggles. They were not prepared to admit, however, that the existence of such interests undermined the devil theory of war, and with it much of the isolationist position.

If the United States had genuine interests beyond its own borders and was inevitably a factor in foreign wars, only two courses of action could possibly assure American safety. Either this country could pursue its interests with vigor and seek safety in strength, or it could make its position secure by taking all possible steps to prevent war from breaking out anywhere. The isolationists were unprepared to fully accept either alternative. The root of their difficulty was the combination of unilateralism with *ad hoc* pacifism that initially had made the isolationist position such an attractive one. The isolationists, even those of the Borah-Fish-Johnson variety, could not entirely espouse a unilateralism relying on strength because they were too fearful of the effects of military involvement on the United States, and for that reason, when all was said and done, too strongly committed to the avoidance of war.[43] Yet, they could not condone cooperation with other nations to prevent war because of their commitment to unilateralism itself. They were, therefore, compelled to attempt the impossible: to insulate a great power against events outside its borders. *Insulation*

They succeeded only in creating a situation in which the question of peace or war in the world was left to the decision of the other powers, and the question of American intervention to the fortunes of war. Each of the international crises that preceded the Second World War showed this to be a policy of drift, not of independence. Each crisis indicated, moreover, that it was not a policy likely to keep America out of war. The course of world events was steadily undermining the isolationist position. *events get closer to home*

[43]See below, Chapter VII.

VII

CHALLENGE AND RESPONSE

➤➤➤➤➤➤➤➤➤➤➤➤➤➤➤➤➤➤➤◀◀◀◀◀◀◀◀◀◀◀◀◀◀◀◀◀◀◀

THE twenty-seven months between the German invasion of
Poland and Japan's attack on the naval base at Pearl Harbor
have been characterized as the period of the "Great Debate."
They have been described as a time during which a President,
convinced of the need for American aid to the democracies,
waged a battle against powerful isolationist sentiment, with
the future of the United States, perhaps even of the civilized
world, hanging on the outcome. Yet, however difficult the
struggle may have seemed, there was, in fact, a continuous
and relatively rapid retreat from isolationism after the start
Rapid move of the Second World War. The arms embargo was repealed
toward war in November, 1939. The first peacetime selective service act
in American history was passed in September, 1940. The
Lend-Lease Bill was approved in March, 1941.

Within eighteen months of the outbreak of war in Europe,
Congress thus largely dismantled the structure of neutrality
legislation which embodied the effort of the isolationists to
avoid war through unilateral action. It legalized the sale of
implements of war to belligerents, recruited an army far
larger than could conceivably be required to ward off invasion, and rendered the ban on loans to belligerents ineffective

by making seven billion dollars' worth of American goods available to Great Britain and her allies as a virtual gift.

For years isolationists had argued successfully that if America became an important supplier of belligerents, it could avoid neither war nor its accompanying entanglements. Yet, within a short time after Hitler's armies had begun to turn all of Europe into a Greater Germany, the United States became, in President Roosevelt's felicitous phrase, "the great arsenal of democracy." This rapid transformation was partly due to the President's qualities of leadership. But it owed more to the fact that the isolationism which seemed so flourishing early in 1939, was even then little more than an imposing façade. The events in Ethiopia, Spain, and China had revealed a basic flaw in the isolationist concept. German activities, beginning in 1938, destroyed the validity of the entire concept for most Americans.

The coherence of the isolationist position depended on belief in the absence of clearly defined moral issues in any approaching conflict, and confidence in the impregnability of the Western Hemisphere. Buttressing these assumptions was the reassuring faith that Great Britain and France could defeat Germany and Italy without the help of the United States, a faith still maintained by 86 per cent of all Americans in September, 1938.[1] No one saw more clearly that this position had been undermined by world events and would be unlikely to withstand further shocks than the German Ambassador to the United States.

As early as October 9, 1937, the perspicacious Dieckhoff cabled Berlin that, though the Quarantine Speech was not likely to lead to immediate activation of American foreign policy, "the weight of the United States of America would

[1] "American Institute of Public Opinion—Surveys 1938–1939," *Public Opinion Quarterly*, II (October, 1939), 599.

be thrown on the English side of the scale" soon after the outbreak of any world conflict involving Great Britain. He used virtually the same words again the following week in a lengthy report on Roosevelt's remarks.[2]

On December 7—four years to the day before the United States actually became involved in war—Dieckhoff surveyed the state of American isolationism for the benefit of his Foreign Office. The Ambassador admitted that "at least up to now" the greater part of the American people were against every entanglement and agreed that the activities of the isolationists should be welcomed by the Reich government. But he went on to explain that, except for isolated cases, the "pacifists" were not motivated by friendship or sympathy for Germany. "Their supporters," he pointed out, "are to be found, in the first place, among large elements of the population, especially in the Midwest, who are indifferent to foreign policy and whose only wish is to be left in peace and, in the second place, in all the peace organizations, particularly those drawing support from liberal and labor circles." He added these prophetic words:

> If they should ever be roused out of their lethargy or arrive at the realization that their doctrinaire concept is either unworkable or will help the opponents of liberalism and democracy, the jump from a policy of isolation to one of intervention will not be very great. . . . In a conflict in which the existence of Great Britain is at stake, they will throw their weight on the English side of the scale.[3]

Dieckhoff realized that Hitler's activities were likely to produce such a result. On December 20, 1937, he set forth his views in a detailed letter to his friend Ernst, Freiherr von

[2]Dieckhoff to Foreign Office, dtd October 9, and October 15, 1937, in *Akten*, D, I, 518–519, 522–524 (translation mine).

[3]Dieckhoff to Foreign Office, dtd December 7, 1937, *ibid.*, 533–535 (translation mine).

Weizsäcker, then head of the Political Section of the German
Foreign Office. "The United States position in regard to
foreign affairs," he wrote, "is determined by American public
opinion, on which both the President and Congress are
dependent." He listed three basic reasons why public opinion
had turned strongly against Germany—and therefore away
from isolationism—in recent months.

|Germany's closer association with Italy and Japan and its
intervention in the Spanish Civil War, Dieckhoff pointed out,
had raised American fears that the "aggressor nations" would
permanently threaten the peace of the world. The activities
of the German-American Bund and the evidence of Nazi subversion in Brazil and other Latin-American countries had
made all German activities suspect, and had led Americans to
fear the possible "export" of fascism and national socialism
from Europe. And, finally, the basic differences between
German and American principles were more clearly recognized. There was an increasing tendency, the Ambassador
explained, to see the coming struggle in Europe as one
between democracy and dictatorship, between freedom and
despotism, and even between Christianity and neopaganism.

"One could say, perhaps, that it should make no difference
to us what the American public thinks about Germany. But
I believe we should remember that the development of public
opinion in America against us was once before disastrous in
its consequences—and that only 20 years ago. . . . I do everything," Dieckhoff added resignedly, ". . . to enlighten [Ameri-
ca] in regard to German policy. But the three factors I have
mentioned form a wall against which I cannot do very much
from here."[4]

The already weakened isolationist position was further

[4]Dieckhoff to Weizsäcker, dtd December 20, 1937, *ibid.*, 537–539
(translation mine).

undermined by Hitler's annexation of Austria in March,
1938. The destruction of an independent nation in the heart
of Europe by an act of unprovoked aggression could not be
convincingly excused as the act of a "have-not" power attempting to ease internal population pressures. Nor could
most people consider it in the same light as British activities
in Afghanistan or India. "I do not know," Dieckhoff wrote
to Weizsäcker, "whether in other parts of the world the reuni-
fication with Austria has produced such a fantastic hate
campaign by the press as the one which has made itself felt
here for the last eight days. . . . Dorothy Thompson has really
had an attack of hysterics and screams herself hoarse in
articles published throughout the country." To the Foreign
Office he reported a week later: "Even though the [Neu-
trality] Act continues in force, it is impossible to speak of a
true neutrality on the part of the United States."[5]

When Germany brought the world to the verge of war by
its demand for the Sudeten district of Czechoslovakia in
September, 1938, few Americans had doubts as to who was
the guilty party. The injustices of the Treaty of Versailles
were inadequate to justify such an act. The abject surrender
of Great Britain and France at the conference table in
Munich could not easily be used to support the assertion that
the dismemberment of a peaceful, democratic country was
simply another chapter in the age-old struggle over the
boundary lines of Europe, which was of no concern to the
United States. When Hitler violated his solemn pledge and
absorbed the remainder of Czechoslovakia in March, 1939,
very few Americans regarded this deed as morally no more
objectionable than the failure of the Allies to pay the debts
stemming from the First World War.

If additional evidence was needed to demonstrate the exist-

[5]Dieckhoff to Weizsäcker, dtd March 22, 1938, and Dieckhoff to
Foreign Office, dtd March 30, 1938, *ibid.*, 566, 570 (translation mine).

ence of at least some moral difference between the democracies and the dictatorships, it was supplied by the renewed outbreak of religious and racial persecution in Germany late in 1938. The increasing harassment of the Catholic Church and other religious bodies, and, more importantly, the senseless and savage persecution of the Jews, which was marked not only by the withdrawal of civil and religious liberty, but also by the wanton destruction and willful confiscation of property and the imprisonment of thousands of persons in so-called concentration camps, were in direct violation of cherished American principles. Beside such activities, French denial of voting rights to the Moslems of Morocco paled into insignificance and lost much of its force as an argument designed to show that all European nations disregarded American ideals.

After the "Crystal Night" of November 9, 1938, when synagogues were put to the torch throughout Germany, the American Ambassador in Berlin, Hugh Wilson, was recalled. He never returned to his post. A poll conducted in December found 94 per cent of all Americans opposed to Hitler's treatment of the Jews and 97 per cent to his anti-Catholic measures. At the same time, Senator Pittman, whose views on foreign policy had heretofore differed little from those of the isolationists, issued an extraordinary public statement in which he declared: "The people of the United States do not like the Government of Germany."[6]

In the face of such events, one of the basic premises of the isolationist faith became logically untenable for most Americans. No country dedicated to principles of domestic justice and international peace was likely to pretend any longer that the Axis Powers and the democracies showed substantially equal disregard for such ideals. Nor could any amount of

[6]"American Institute of Public Opinion—Surveys 1938–1939," 598; New York *Times*, December 23, 1938.

argument dissuade the majority of the American people from the conclusion that this country had a clear moral interest in frustrating Hitler's further designs. A survey conducted by *Fortune* in October, 1937, found 62 per cent of Americans neutral in their attitude toward Germany. Immediately after the Munich Conference, 56 per cent favored a boycott of German goods. This figure rose to 61 per cent after the anti-Jewish violence of November 10, 1938, and to 65 per cent after the German annexation of Czechoslovakia four months later.[7]

In February, 1939, 69 per cent of Americans polled favored all aid to England short of war. By April, 66 per cent were prepared to supply Great Britain with arms and ammunition in case of war, despite the existence of neutrality legislation forbidding such action. When war broke out in Europe seven months later, 82 per cent of those questioned by the American Institute of Public Opinion blamed Germany for what had happened. Only 3 per cent pointed to the guilt of England and France, and only a like proportion saw the new conflict as an inevitable result of the injustices contained in the Treaty of Versailles. *Fortune* found in October that 83.1 per cent wanted England and France to win the war, 1 per cent favored Germany, and only 5 per cent expressed indifference to the outcome. In December, the same magazine discovered that only 10.5 per cent of those polled regarded the war as merely another manifestation of Europe's ceaseless quarrels.[8] However imprecise these early public opinion polls

[7]These statistics were reproduced in Philip E. Jacob, "Influences of World Events on U.S. 'Neutrality' Opinion," *Public Affairs Quarterly*, IV (January, 1940), 51–52. Jacob's conclusions substantiate the interpretation given here.

[8]"American Institute of Public Opinion—Surveys 1938–1939," 600; "Public Opinion Surveys," *Public Opinion Quarterly* IV (January, 1940), 99. A report on the *Fortune* poll of October 20, 1939 is in House Records (Committee on Foreign Affairs), File 76A–F 17.3.

may have been, the cumulative picture they convey is sufficiently clear and consistent to warrant the assumption that the general conclusion to which they point is largely correct.

World events had thus convinced most Americans by the end of 1939 of the existence of moral issues which made the cause of the European democracies that of the United States. Yet, it was still possible to maintain that American aid to Great Britain and France should not be carried to the point of actual military intervention. Though an Axis victory was now clearly considered to be undesirable, United States involvement in war might be worse. As long as a large proportion of Americans regarded the Western Hemisphere as impregnable, the isolationist position, in somewhat modified form, could continue to command considerable support.

The success of German blitzkrieg tactics soon undermined America's faith in its safety from attack. The fall of Poland in only twenty-seven days gave rise to the first doubts. These misgivings were somewhat allayed by the subsequent lull in the fighting, which lasted until April 9, 1940. But the rapid conquest of Denmark, Norway, Holland, Belgium, and Luxembourg which followed again raised American fears that the nation's vaunted impregnability was largely mythical. The surrender of France within six weeks of its invasion confirmed these fears. By June, 1940, Germany and Italy controlled virtually the entire European coast, Great Britain seemed on the verge of invasion and defeat, Dakar and other potential stepping stones to the New World were nearly defenseless, and the United States was becoming increasingly aware of espionage and subversion within its own borders. Under such circumstances, the isolationists' insistence on the safety of this nation, regardless of events in Europe, became less and less persuasive.

On September 28, 1939, the day after the surrender of Warsaw, a poll conducted by the American Institute of Public

Opinion found 63 per cent of Americans convinced that Germany would eventually attack the United States if it was victorious in Europe. By June 2, 1940, fifteen days before the fall of France, the figure stood at 65 per cent. A month later, *Fortune* discovered that 63.1 per cent of those questioned expected an immediate attempt to seize territory in the Western Hemisphere to be the consequence of an Axis triumph. And 42.5 per cent expected an immediate attack on the United States.[9]

Another basic tenet of isolationism had thus been severely challenged and rejected by a majority of Americans long before the United States actually entered the war. The proposition that this country had no direct stake in the outcome of the conflict could be defended only with great difficulty after the fall of France. Significantly, the most influential anti-isolationist organization established in the United States called itself the Committee to Defend America by Aiding the Allies. It was organized in May, 1940.

As world events sharpened the moral issues in the European conflict and challenged the concept of American impregnability, popular faith in isolationism declined rapidly. The Princeton Public Opinion Research Project, headed by Hadley Cantril, found that by May, 1940, fully 33 per cent of those polled wanted the United States to underwrite a British victory even at the risk of war. Thirty-eight per cent were anxious to refrain from military intervention, but believed more American aid should be given the democracies. Only 23 per cent displayed true isolationist sentiment. They opposed both direct involvement in the conflict and indirect involvement through the extension of aid to one of the contending parties. By September, the isolationist group was

[9]"Public Opinion Surveys," *Public Opinion Quarterly,* IV (January, 1940) 102; *ibid.* (July, 1940), 550; *ibid.* (October, 1940), 712.

reduced to 12 per cent of the total, and 53 per cent now believed the defeat of Hitler to be more important than staying out of war. The findings of the American Institute of Public Opinion confirmed this shift. Dr. Gallup's organization conducted a continuing survey of opinion on the relative importance of helping England and avoiding military involvement up to the time of the Pearl Harbor attack. By January 2, 1941, it found 68 per cent of all Americans favoring all-out aid even at the risk of war. The figure remained nearly constant for the remainder of the year.[10]

The declining faith in isolationism is reflected in Congressional attitudes toward an arms embargo. Early in 1939, the Administration attempted to obtain new neutrality legislation that would, among other things, have repealed the embargo provisions of the Act of 1937. However, the House of Representatives adopted an amendment offered by Republican Representative John M. Vorys of Ohio, which restored the embargo on arms and ammunition. The Vorys amendment was approved by a vote of 214 to 173 on June 30. Although this result clearly indicates the continuing strength of isolationist sentiment, it is of greater significance that 123 Congressmen who had supported an arms embargo two years earlier now voted against it. Seven of these Representatives had even favored a resolution to prohibit the peacetime export of arms and ammunition, which Hamilton Fish had introduced in 1937.[11]

The Administration proposal was subsequently shelved by the Senate Foreign Relations Committee. The majority of the

[10]Hadley Cantril, "America Faces the War: A Study in Public Opinion," *Public Opinion Quarterly*, IV (July, 1940), 395, 401; Hadley Cantril, Donald Rugg, and Frederick Williams, "America Faces the War: Shifts in Opinion," *ibid.* (October 1940), 652.

[11]*Congressional Record*, 76th Cong., 1st sess., 8511–8512 (June 30, 1939); *ibid.*, 75th Cong., 1st sess., 2409 and 2410 (March 18, 1937).

members of that committee favored repeal of the arms embargo, however. The 12 to 11 vote for postponing consideration of neutrality legislation revision resulted from the action
of Democratic Senators Guy M. Gillette of Iowa and Walter
F. George of Georgia. Both men favored repeal of all
neutrality legislation, but both were bitter political foes of
President Roosevelt, who had attempted to purge them in
the primary elections of 1938. When Senator Clark offered
them the chance to vote against Roosevelt without voting
directly against repeal of the arms embargo, they eagerly
accepted it.[12]

After war had broken out in Europe, sentiment in favor
of repeal of the arms embargo became even stronger. A
Gallup poll taken in mid-September showed 57 per cent of
those questioned approving such a step. After Roosevelt had
delivered an address to Congress on the issue on September
21, this percentage rose to 62. On September 28, the Senate
Foreign Relations Committee, responding to pressure by the
Administration and by public opinion, approved, by a vote
of 16 to 7, a bill incorporating repeal of the arms embargo.
Despite strenuous efforts by Senators Borah, Vandenberg,
Lodge, and Holt, the Senate approved this bill by the substantial margin of 63 to 30. It had earlier voted down a new
embargo provision offered by Senator Clark, 60 to 33. When
the Vorys amendment was once again offered in the House a
week later, it was rejected by 179 to 245. Forty-five Congressmen who had supported the amendment in June voted
against it only four months later.[13] Strong pressure exerted by

Vorys defeat [margin annotation]

[12]T.R.B., "Politics at the Water's Edge," *New Republic*, XCIX
(August 2, 1939), 360; New York *Times*, July 9, and July 12, 1939;
Robert A. Divine, *The Illusion of Neutrality* (Chicago, 1962), 277–278.
    [13]"Public Opinion Surveys," *Public Opinion Quarterly*, IV (March,
1940), 105–108; New York *Times*, September 29, 1939; *Congressional
Record*, 76th Cong., 2nd sess., 1022–1024 (October 27, 1939), 1343
(November 2, 1939).

the Administration undoubtedly affected the outcome of these votes. But the world events that changed public opinion were also not without influence on the members of Congress.

The progressive thinning of isolationist ranks soon became apparent outside of Congress. Although its publisher, Senator Robert M. La Follette, Jr., remained a staunch isolationist, *The Progressive* of Madison, Wisconsin, carried an editorial on October 28, 1939, in which editor William T. Evjue expressed strong doubts about the wisdom of the policies which the weekly had long supported.

Doesn't it seem silly and unwise [he asked rhetorically] for the United States to deny munitions to the nations that are fighting Hitler and his totalitarian concept of government and then to spend billions of dollars for the fight on Hitler after he has destroyed the British Empire and is stronger than ever? If Hitler defeats England and the British fleet is destroyed, what becomes of our splendid isolation, with Hitler on the Atlantic side and Japan and Russia on the Pacific side?[14]

In July, 1940, *Common Sense* noted editorially that Western civilization was tied to Great Britain and France through the provisions of Magna Charta and the ideals of *Liberté, Egalité,* and *Fraternité.* Its editor now believed the achievement of the socialist democracy he had always advocated to depend on the defeat of Hitler. At the same time, the *New Republic* dropped its most fervently isolationist columnist, John T. Flynn. By October, this formerly pacifist journal was advocating an all-out effort to support the cause of the democracies.[15]

Oswald Garrison Villard, who had already lamented "the

[14]Copy in House Records (Committee on Foreign Affairs), File 76A–F 17.3.

[15]"A Foreign Policy for American Democracy," *Common Sense,* IX (July, 1940), 3–6; "The Threat from the Axis," *New Republic,* CIII (October, 1940), 466–467.

apostasy of the *Nation* and the temporary insanity of [its editor] Freda Kirchwey," now despairingly informed Harry Elmer Barnes that "Bliven has lost his bearings precisely like Freda Kirchwey. They have all gone mad."[16] In January, 1941, the editors of *Common Sense* celebrated their conversion to active internationalism by giving an elaborate dinner honoring Mrs. Franklin D. Roosevelt.[17]

Defections from isolationist ranks were not limited to the liberal and radical press. The American Legion had reiterated its traditional opposition to any steps that might conceivably lead to war at its Chicago convention in October, 1939. It reversed its position during 1940. By July, the South Carolina Department of the Legion was urging Congress to aid Britain in the battle against the aggressors on the grounds that the protection of American rights and of the dignity of man was more important than keeping out of war. At their Boston meeting in September, 1940, the Legionnaires spoke nostalgically of "our former gallant comrades in arms," and adopted a foreign policy resolution which read in part:

We urge that the Government of the United States exercise all lawful means to prevent the shipment of war materials to the aggressor nations and that it continue to extend to all peoples who are resisting aggression the fullest cooperation consistent with our obligations, our security, our liberty and our peace.[18]

The American Legion still opposed going to war. But by recognizing the existence of aggressors and victims in the European struggle and urging the United States to aid the

[16]Villard to Alfred M. Bingham, dtd August 8, 1940, Villard Papers, File 670; Villard to Barnes, dtd August 19, 1940, Villard Papers, File 137.
[17]The seating plan and other material relating to this event are in the *Common Sense* Papers, Yale University Library.
[18]Resolution of American Legion, Department of South Carolina, dtd July 23, 1940, House Records (Committee on Military Affairs), File 76A–16.1; O. K. Armstrong, "The American Legion and Involvement," *Scribner's Commentator*, IX (November 1940), 31–32.

righteous cause, it broke sharply with its isolationist past. By this time too, the Veterans of Foreign Wars had reached the conclusion that "England—single handed and alone—is carrying the torch for Liberty, Civilization, and Christianity against these forces of evil," and advocated the sending of destroyers and the cancellation of the British debt to the United States.[19]

On February 2, 1940, Senator Vandenberg began his slow conversion to the internationalist persuasion. On that date, he noted in his diary that "probably the best we can hope for from now on is 'insulation' rather than isolation. I should say that an 'insulationist' is one who wants to preserve all of the isolation which modern circumstances will permit." Early the following year, Alfred M. Bingham voiced his desire for a British victory. The consequences to America of a war to assure this victory, he told Stuart Chase, might not be so terrible after all. A month later, Bingham indignantly informed Professor Wilson L. Godshall of Lehigh University, who had asked him to present the isolationist view in a panel discussion, that he now believed the outcome of the war to be of decided concern to the United States. A German victory, Bingham asserted, would imperil democracy everywhere.[20]

Senator George W. Norris of Nebraska had voted against American entry into the First World War and had frequently pointed to the bitter lessons this country had learned after 1917. He had favored the cutting of American trade in order to avoid entanglements and had consistently opposed mem-

[19]Resolution of Robert O. Purdy, Jr., Post #3034, Veterans of Foreign Wars, dtd August 12, 1940, House Records (Committee on Military Affairs), File 76A–H 16.1.

[20]Arthur H. Vandenberg, Jr. (with Joe Alex Morris), ed., *The Private Papers of Senator Vandenberg* (Boston, 1952), 4; Bingham to Chase, dtd January 6, 1941, and Bingham to Godshall, dtd February 6, 1941, *Common Sense* Papers.

bership in the World Court. Though he had begun to worry about the threat posed to the United States by Japanese expansion as early as 1938 and expressed concern over a possible combination of Stalin, Hitler, Mussolini, and Japan soon thereafter, he still opposed the Selective Service Act of 1940 because he feared the militarization of the United States and was certain that mobilization meant war. Yet, by early 1941, Norris had come to admit that things were not the same as they had been twenty-four years earlier. He consequently came out in favor of the Lend-Lease Bill and moved to a position scarcely distinguishable from that of the interventionists.[21]

By February, 1941, Representative Herman P. Koppleman of Connecticut, one of the earliest and most outspoken of the isolationists, had reached the conclusion that "if we don't become an arsenal for democracy and send sufficient help in sufficient time, it may be the last mistake free America will ever make." At the same time, Representative Voorhis told his colleagues he had "an interest in the way of life wherein free men can freely struggle to better their conditions, freely worship and believe according to their own consciences.... I know," he continued, "that this is not possible in a Nazi- or Communist-dominated nation. So it seems to me that the importance of aid to Great Britain, of aid to other nations attempting to resist the totalitarians, has become part of American policy." In accordance with their changed views,

[21]Norris to R. Mauthey, dtd October 14, 1935, and J. G. Randall to Norris, dtd February 7, 1935, Norris Papers, Tray 31, Box 1; Norris to W. K. Klopp, dtd March 14, 1936, to John T. Flynn, dtd January 4, 1938, to Freda Kirchwey, dtd March 19, 1938, to A. W. Peterson, dtd February 3, 1938, to G. Shellenberger, dtd June 26, 1940, to W. A. Jones, dtd July 19, 1940, to G. A. Moon, dtd July 23, 1940, to J. P. Goehring, dtd March 13, 1941, to A. Cortney, dtd March 15, 1941, and to H. Chresman, dtd May 23, 1941, Norris Papers, Tray 104, Boxes 1 and 4.

both Koppleman and Voorhis subsequently supported the Lend-Lease Bill.[22]

Within a relatively short time after the outbreak of war in Europe, and many months before the United States entered the struggle, the isolationists were reduced to minority status. Yet, isolationism remained a strong and significant factor in shaping American policy. The remaining isolationists pressed their case vigorously in Congress and elsewhere. Isolationist organizations flourished and received substantial financial support. The most ambitious of all anti-interventionist groups, the America First Committee, was formed in September, 1940.

This paradoxical situation arose because the world events which challenged basic isolationist assumptions did not absolutely disprove them. Hitler's increasingly reprehensible conduct did not make the cause of Great Britain and France seem righteous to everyone. Nor could the military threat an Axis victory would pose to the United States be accurately assessed while the war was still in progress. The possible economic threat of such a victory was even less clearly definable, since it could be argued that a war-ravaged world would have to rely on American resources, regardless of who exercised political control. Moreover, the same world events which undermined isolationist assumptions also increased the possibility of American involvement in war. They thus lent greater urgency to the arguments of those who still believed the United States could be insulated against foreign dangers. Though many Americans now abandoned isolationism as impractical and unsafe, others found this shift in opinion totally incomprehensible. Villard thought the editors of the *Nation* and the *New Republic* had simply lost their senses.

[22]*Congressional Record,* 77th Cong., 1st sess., 532 and 559 (February 4, 1941), 815 (February 8, 1941).

Senator Nye went so far as to question his own powers of reasoning. "Sometimes as I watch and listen to others, intelligent, conscientious, and forceful, as they work themselves into fevers over what they allege to be the grave emergency confronting this country of ours," he told his colleagues on August 23, 1940, "I come up wondering if I am 'all there,' if I have lost my reason, if I ever had the power of reasoning well. I will swear to real concern when I find myself failing to respond, and feeling the fears which others do feel and show."[23]

The arguments employed by the remaining isolationists during the "Great Debate" did not, therefore, reflect the course of world events, but were strikingly similar to those used in the prewar period. Behind them still lay the questions asked by generations of American statesmen, and the implicit answers that were part of the American tradition, accepted as articles of faith since the early days of the Republic. "Why...," Alexander Hamilton had asked in 1795, "should we by a close political connection with any power of Europe, expose our peace and interest, as a matter of course, to all the shocks with which their mad rivalship and wicked ambition so frequently convulse the earth? 'T were insanity to embrace such a system." "Are we, sir," John Randolph of Roanoke had wanted to know thirty years later,

to go on a crusade in another hemisphere, for the propagation of two objects as dear and delightful to my heart as to that of any gentleman in this or any other assembly—Liberty and Religion— and in the name of those holy words—by this powerful spell, is this nation to be conjured and beguiled out of the high way of heaven—out of its present comparatively happy state, into all the

[23]Villard to Harry Elmer Barnes, dtd August 19, 1940, Villard Papers, File 137; *Congressional Record,* 76th Cong., 3rd sess., 10804–10820 (August 23, 1940); Cole, *Nye,* 170.

disastrous conflicts arising from the policy of the European powers, with all the consequences which flow from them?[24]

Even after the surrender of France in June, 1940, isolationist arguments differed little from those found in Secretary of State William H. Seward's declaration of 1863. Seward had explained America's refusal to aid the Poles in their struggle for independence in these terms:

In view of the location of this Republic, the character, habits, and sentiments of its constituent parts, and especially its complex yet unique and very popular Constitution, the American people must be content to recommend the cause of human progress by the wisdom with which they should exercise the powers of self-government, forbearing at all times, and in every way, from foreign alliances, intervention, and interference.[25]

Isolationists still agreed with Carl Schurz that "this Republic, on its Continental fastness, is impregnable, if not substantially unassailable" and that "no old-world power will think of going to war with us, unless kicked into it by some absolutely unendurable provocation on our part." Some of them still subscribed to the view advanced by Henry Clay in support of his American System: "If we had no intercourse with foreign states, if we adopted the policy of China, we should have no external wars."[26] The men who held fast to isolationism after 1939 simply failed to see that world events during the 1930's cast serious doubts on the assumptions underlying such statements. As a result they continued to

[24]Henry Cabot Lodge, ed., *The Works of Alexander Hamilton* (12 vols., New York and London, n.d.), V, 184–185; *Annals of Congress*, 18th Cong., 1st sess., 1182 (January 24, 1824).

[25]Quoted in D. A. Graber, *Crisis Diplomacy* (Washington, 1959), 123.

[26]Frederick Bancroft, ed., *Speeches, Correspondence and Political Papers of Carl Schurz* (New York and London, 1913), VI, 371–372; Daniel Mallory, ed., *The Life and Speeches of the Hon. Henry Clay* (2 vols., Hartford, 1853), I, 471.

oppose, with arguments earlier found serviceable, involvement in what they still regarded as other nations' quarrels.

After the annexation of Czechoslovakia, it was difficult to
accept German activities as the justifiable, or at least understandable, actions of a "have-not" nation. Yet Borchard still
assured Borah that "Hitler or Germany has a case in destroying the Treaty of Versailles, and its unwise political division
of territory," and won the Senator's approval to the proposition that it would be futile and foolish to go to war to prevent
that "reconstruction." Former Congressmen Fred J. Sisson
of New York and Henry C. Luckey of Nebraska made the
same point in testimony before the Foreign Affairs Committee. William R. Castle, who had served in the State Department from 1919 to 1933 and had once occupied the post
of Assistant Secretary, told the Committee that "when, and
if, war comes to Europe, it will not be, as repeatedly asserted,
a war of the dictatorships against the democracies. It will
rather be an attack by the have-not nations on the nations
which have something the others want."[27]

Three weeks later, Dorothy Detzer appeared as representative of the Women's International League for Peace and
Freedom, World Peaceways, and the Keep America Out of
War Congress before the Foreign Relations Committee. "The
Germans were starved into signing the Versailles Treaty,"
she told the Senators, "and I think...that that policy was
the chief thing that finally created Hitler." The controversy
between the democracies and the dictatorships, she insisted,
was nothing more than a part of "the age-old struggle to
control Europe, the Mediterranean and the Near East." It
had to be understood in these terms.[28]

[27]Borchard to Borah, dtd April 18, 1939, and Borah to E. W.
Murphy, n.d., in Borah Papers, Box 426; House, *American Neutrality
Policy; Hearings* (1939), 293, 304, 110.
   [28]Senate, *Neutrality, Peace Legislation, etc.; Hearings,* 531, 535.

Shortly before the outbreak of the war he regarded as possible though not probable, Boake Carter argued that the European crisis "is the same old struggle for advantage between the 'haves' and the 'have-nots.' It is the same old struggle for advantage at the expense of some other nation. It is a struggle in which democracies and dictators, aggressors and potential victims, treaty upholders and treaty violators, are so inextricably mixed up that it would overtax the powers of a Solomon to discover where right and justice lie." "Austria," he maintained, "never should have been made a completely independent state." It had voluntarily sought economic union with Germany long before the advent of Hitler, a point readily conceded by Senator Borah, and its "government was not a democracy but a form of dictatorship under Italian influence." President Wilson and British Prime Minister David Lloyd George, Carter pointed out, had opposed giving the Sudetenland to Czechoslovakia in 1919, and "long before the Munich crisis of September 1938 responsible British (and even French) statesmen were apparently agreed that the incorporation of the Sudetenland into Germany was fair and desirable." He regarded Hitler's violation of the Munich agreement as a regrettable mistake, but supported German claims to Memel and Danzig.[29]

John Foster Dulles' *War, Peace and Change* made the same argument in a more sophisticated and pretentious manner. Dulles was not a confirmed isolationist. But he proceeded on the assumption that the *status quo* was unjust and that the "exponents of force are the inevitable product of a society within which change can occur only through force." His blueprint for the avoidance of war pictured the activities of the

[29]Boake Carter, *Why Meddle in Europe?* (New York, 1939), 78–84; Borah to D. F. Bacon, dtd March 21, 1938, Borah Papers, Box 417.

"have-not" nations as understandable and, to some extent, justifiable.[30]

Such sentiments found support in Congress. "Are we to take sides over Danzig," Hamilton Fish asked indignantly, "95 per cent German, and stolen from Germany by the Versailles Treaty?" Together with many of his isolationist colleagues, Fish regarded repeal of the arms embargo as a prelude to American participation in a war of the "haves" against the "have-nots." It would be far better for the United States and for the world, these men were certain, to determine the objectives of Germany, Italy, Japan, and other so-called war-desiring nations, to assess the reasonableness of these objectives, and to explore the prospects of amicable settlement.[31] Nothing that had happened, at the Munich Conference and afterwards, had shaken their belief that the totalitarian states had legitimate grievances and could be persuaded to accept an equitable settlement.

The outbreak of hostilities in Europe made the "have-not" argument less serviceable. Isolationists, who dreaded war and its consequences everywhere, could not entirely excuse Hitler's recourse to violence. Although in January, 1941, President William C. Dennis of Earlham College still described the German attack on Poland as an attempt to settle a "legitimate grievance,"[32] isolationists after September, 1939, generally confined their efforts to demonstrate the absence of moral issues in the European war to denigrating the cause of Great Britain and its allies, and to characterizing the conflict as a traditional Old World power struggle. ("Sir," John

[30] John Foster Dulles, *War, Peace and Change* (New York and London, 1939), ix–x and *passim.*, esp. 143–151.

[31] *Congressional Record*, 76th Cong., 1st sess., 7984 (June 27, 1939). See also the remarks of Representatives Harold Knutson of Minnesota and Andrew C. Schiffler of West Virginia in *ibid.*, 8153 (June 28, 1939) and 8236 (June 29, 1939).

[32] House, *Lend-Lease Bill; Hearings*, 575–577.

Randolph had exclaimed in 1824, "England has been for centuries the game cock of Europe. It is impossible to specify the wars in which she has been engaged for contrary purposes; and she will, with great pleasure, see us take off her shoulders the labor of preserving the balance of power."[33])

The isolationists never ceased belittling the virtues of Great Britain and magnifying her vices. In a nationwide radio address in April, 1939, and in a Senate speech delivered four months later, Senator Borah blamed the British, at least in part, for Hitler's annexation of Czechoslovakia.[34] At the same time, Benjamin C. Marsh, executive secretary of The People's Lobby, professed to see a glaring inconsistency in United States efforts to frustrate modern aggressors by defending the fruits of past illegitimate conquests. He referred to Great Britain as "the mother of aggression," and called those Americans "damned fools" who sought to safeguard, with American money, what he regarded as British interests.[35] L. D. Stillwell of Dartmouth College told the Foreign Relations Committee that the coming war would be fought to maintain dictatorships in Poland, Greece, Rumania, Turkey, Portugal, and Russia, and expressed the opinion that "when all the petty tyrannies of Europe start lining up with Britain and all the free democracies of Europe...avoid British 'protection' as if it were the plague, we Americans better all move to Missouri and stay there." General Hugh S. Johnson urged substantially the same view on the assembled Senators.[36]

In Congress and elsewhere the charge that England and France had themselves been guilty of repeated aggression was

[33]*Annals of Congress,* 18th Cong., 1st sess., 1187 (January 24, 1824).
[34]William E. Borah, "What Our Position Should Be," *Vital Speeches of the Day,* V (April, 1939), 398–399; *Congressional Record,* 76th Cong., 1st sess., 8674–8675 (July 6, 1939).
[35]House, *American Neutrality; Hearings* (1939), 295.
[36]Senate, *Neutrality, Peace Legislation, etc.; Hearings,* 563, 282.

ceaselessly repeated. Isolationists again and again compared
the annexations of Ethiopia by Italy and of Czechoslovakia by
Germany to the British conquest of the Boer Republic, and
pointed to the absence of significant moral distinctions among
these actions. They even challenged the fact that Britain and
France shared a common system of government with the
United States and were deserving of American support on
that basis. "Would it not help in your next speech," Oswald
Garrison Villard asked Senator Wheeler, "to point out that
France is no longer a democracy and may never again be
one?"[37]

In October, 1939, Poland had already been conquered. But
isolationists continued to stress the selfishness and amorality
of the European democracies. The English were in the war to
prevent the rise of a powerful rival in Europe, H. L. Mencken
wrote in a Baltimore *Sun* editorial. "It is a rational reason,
but it is as devoid of moral content as a theorem in algebra or
a college yell."[38] In the Senate debate on repeal of the arms
embargo, Robert M. La Follette, Jr., pointed out that the
British and French governments had failed to support the
cause of democracy in Manchuria, Ethiopia, Spain, and postwar Europe in general. Moreover, he insisted, the very
countries whom the United States was now being asked to
support had betrayed democratic Czechoslovakia into Hitler's
clutches at Munich. D. Worth Clark of Idaho went even
further. "Paint me a picture of the six years of persecution of
the Jews, the Catholics, and the Protestants in Germany," he
challenged the interventionists, "paint it as gory and bloody

[37]See, for example, the remarks of Representatives Paul W. Shafer
of Michigan and William Lemke of North Dakota in *Congressional
Record,* 76th Cong., 1st sess., 8240 and 8244 (June 29, 1939); Villard
to Wheeler, dtd March 23, 1939, Villard Papers, File 4151.
[38]H. L. Mencken, "Notes on a Moral War," reprinted in Porter
Sargent, *Keeping US Out of War* (Boston, 1941), 137.

as you please, and I will paint you one ten times as brutal, ten times as savage, ten times as bloody in the 500 years of British destruction, pillage, rape, and bloodshed in Ireland." Clark's charges that the British Empire provided the outstanding example of aggression in the history of the world were seconded by Senator Rush Holt of West Virginia, who also added the French bombing of Damascus in 1925 to the list of crimes perpetrated by the democracies.[39]

The events of 1940 did nothing to alter the views of confirmed isolationists of both the right and the left. The Socialist party's national convention, held in New York in April, adopted a foreign policy resolution which was introduced into the *Congressional Record* by Hamilton Fish. It read in part:

The cause for which Hitler has thrown the German masses into war is damnably unholy. But the war of Chamberlain and Reynaud is not thereby rendered holy. The fact that Hitler is the opponent does not make the Allied war a fight for democracy....
The Allied Governments have no idealism in the conflict, no war aims worthy of the sacrifice of the democracy and life of their peoples, no purpose of overthrowing fascism except to replace it by a more desperate and brutal government, if need be, that would crush the economic demands of the German workers, and leave England and France free to pursue their star of profit. The American people have no stake in such a victory.[40]

Norman Thomas expressed his regrets over the conquest of the Scandinavian countries and France, but continued to deny that "the march of history can be pictured in terms of war between light and darkness," and that "the tragic fate of this hour comes altogether upon innocent people." Senator Lundeen voiced similar thoughts on the American Forum

[39]*Congressional Record*, 76th Cong., 2nd sess., 332 (October 12, 1939), 446 and 447 (October 16, 1939), 549–550 (October 18, 1939).
[40]*Ibid.*, 76th Cong., 3rd sess., App. 2293 (April 11, 1939).

of the Air,[41] and Colonel Lindbergh informed the Foreign Affairs Committee that he believed "the fault of the war is about evenly divided in Europe, and the causes of it." Senator Capper again told readers of *Scribner's Commentator*, at this time the organ of extreme and largely right-wing isolationism, that the United States had nothing in common with the European democracies.[42]

Isolationists continued to insist, as they had done before the outbreak of war, that the democracies had forfeited the good will and assistance of the United States by their failure to meet the financial obligations stemming from the First World War. They still condemned the *status quo* as unjust and professed to see little or no difference between Axis fascism, Russian communism, and British imperialism. Senator Nye, for example, thought the United States was in the process of allying itself with "the most aggressive aggressor the world has ever known." He paid tribute to England as the "mother of parliaments" and the "capital in Europe of democracy." But he urgently warned against the "other Britain," which represented "the very acme of reaction, imperialism and exploitation." His catalogue of Britain's sins filled ten pages of the *Congressional Record*.[43]

The expression of such views was by no means confined to the floor of Congress. Writing in *Uncensored*, a magazine

[41]Norman Thomas, "America's Contribution to an Enduring Peace," *The Annals of the American Academy of Political and Social Science,* CCX (July, 1940), 44; *Congressional Record*, 76th Cong., 3rd sess., App. 3754 (June 11, 1940).

[42]House, *Lend-Lease Bill; Hearings*, 378; Arthur Capper, "Time to Think American," *Scribner's Commentator*, IX (February, 1941), 72.

[43]*Congressional Record,* 77th Cong., 1st sess., 543 (February 5, 1941), 598 and 620 (February 5, 1941), 1412 (February 20, 1941), 1295 and 1296 (February 24, 1941), 1414 and 1432 (February 26, 1941), 1724–1733 (March 4, 1941).

in newsletter form which had been founded by isolationist "refugees" from the *New Republic,* Harry Elmer Barnes called the European war "fundamentally a clash between totalitarian aggression and democratic dry-rot," with neither side worthy of American assistance. In July, 1941, Robert M. Hutchins still felt it necessary to remind his readers of the "victims of aggression before 1939," including Indo-China, Africa, the Malay States, and, above all, India. At the same time, General Johnson denounced "American neck-stickers-out on our Eastern seaboard" and once again raised the issue of British ingratitude for America's help in the First World War, as demonstrated by the failure to make war debt payments. Great Britain's sole aim in the war, he insisted, "is to maintain her dominant Empire position with her own kinsmen and also over black, brown and yellow conquered and subject peoples in three continents."[44]

Similar ideas were offered in three books published in 1941, by authors who had little in common except their isolationism. Theodore Dreiser's *America Is Worth Saving* was largely devoted to bitter denunciations of England, based on the assumption the "the British Empire is not a democracy and never has been." Great Britain, Dreiser argued, "now holds 500,000,000 of its world-scattered colonials as well as 29,000,000 of its natives in educationless, moneyless, and privilegeless bondage." America could put its own house in order only by avoiding alliance with such a country and by remaining out of "a European war that has at this writing no more to do with the problem of democracy or civilization

[44] Harry Elmer Barnes, "Where Are We Headed?" *Uncensored,* Supplement to No. 73 (February 21, 1941), 1; Robert M. Hutchins, "The Proposition is Peace," *Scribner's Commentator,* X (July, 1941), 95; Hugh S. Johnson, "Is Britain Fighting Our War?" in Nancy Schoonmaker and Doris F. Reid, eds., *We Testify* (New York, 1941), 94, 99–100.

in Europe or the world than it has to do with the state of the inhabitants of Mars, if any."[45]

In *We Have a Future,* Norman Thomas also argued that the United States could save itself only if it avoided alliance with Great Britain. Though Thomas realized that "a partial democracy and the whole liberal culture" would be affected by the outcome of the war in Europe, he did not believe the conflict was a struggle over American principles. American intervention would not rescue Britain, but might easily result in the loss of liberty and democracy in the United States. In a similar vein, the indefatigable General Johnson pointed out in *Hell-Bent for War* that Great Britain was fighting her own war, "in part for continued imperial domination over weaker and exploited, subdued and subject peoples." If America became involved militarily, he concluded, it might "possibly wreck what we now laughingly call 'Western Civilization'—no matter who wins."[46]

Isolationists thus continued to characterize the war as a struggle to preserve the British Empire long after the fall of France. The alternative contention, that it might be a battle between communism and fascism, was made temporarily unserviceable by the Hitler-Stalin Pact of August, 1939. Nevertheless, some disappointed liberal isolationists thought in January, 1940, "the war may yet become an alliance of Britain and France with Hitler's Germany and Mussolini's Italy against the Soviet Union, let democracy fall where it may." They argued against American intervention on that basis.[47]

When Germany resumed its drive toward the East in June,

[45]Theodore Dreiser, *America Is Worth Saving* (New York, 1941), 41–43 and *passim.*

[46]Norman Thomas, *We Have a Future* (Princeton, 1941), 32–33; Hugh S. Johnson, *Hell-Bent for War* (Indianapolis and New York, 1941), 49.

[47]*Uncensored,* No. 15 (January 13, 1940), 3.

1941, the America First Committee was quick to revive the Communist-versus-Fascist argument. Its Bulletin #350 read in part:

The entry of Communist Russia into the war should settle once and for all the intervention issue here at home. The war party can hardly ask the people of America to take up arms behind the red flag of Stalin. With the ruthless force of dictatorship and aggression now clearly aligned on both sides the proper course for the United States becomes even clearer. We must continue to build our own defenses and take no part in this incongruous European conflict.[48]

At the same time, aircraft manufacturer Igor Sikorski warned that giving aid to "godless Communist murderers" would be "a betrayal of the very foundation of Christian idealism." John T. Flynn's pamphlet *Should America Fight to Make Europe Safe for Communism* contained the negative replies of Herbert Hoover, Milo J. Warner of the American Legion, Norman Thomas, and Senators Clark, Wheeler, La Follette, and Taft. "Apparently," Taft wrote with wry humor, "we are to follow Bundles for Britain with Packages for Petrograd."[49]

Just as they had done during the years from 1935 to 1938, isolationists still concluded that events in other parts of the world were simply manifestations of endemic rivalries. The United States, they continued to argue, could not solve the world's problems and had no real interest in making the attempt. Dean Helen Taft Manning of Bryn Mawr College informed the Foreign Relations Committee that the existing alignment of the powers of Europe differed "in no respect"

---

[48] Quoted in Wayne S. Cole, *America First* (Madison, 1953), 85.

[49] Igor Sikorski, "The Nature and Objectives of the Communist Government," in Schoonmaker and Reid, eds., *op. cit.*, 169, 183; John T. Flynn, *Should America Fight to Make Europe Safe for Communism*, copy in America First File, Swarthmore College Peace Collection.

from that which had existed since the fifteenth century, and other witnesses supported her testimony.[50] Throughout 1939, both in the regular session of Congress and during the special session called after the outbreak of war in Europe, isolationist Senators and Representatives of both major parties reminded their colleagues continually that the states of the Old World had been at war for over 2,000 years over questions of trade and boundary lines, and insisted that nothing else was involved in the existing conflict. To Senator Borah, for example, the attempt to frustrate Hitler's aggressive designs still appeared as "nothing more than another chapter in the bloody volume of European power politics, the balance of which, John Bright, the great commoner of England [sic], once declared was the curse of any possible European peace." "If we admit at all that we should take an active interest," Senator Taft added prophetically, "we will be involved in perpetual war."[51]

In desperately seeking to establish that international relations had not changed significantly and that the United States should therefore adhere to its traditional, nineteenth-century attitudes in dealing with foreign powers, the isolationists were moving further and further away from reality. To most Americans, and indeed, to many former isolationists,

[50]Senate, *Neutrality, Peace Legislation, etc.; Hearings,* 260. See also the testimony of Philip Marshall Brown of the American Peace Society and of Bainbridge Colby in *ibid.,* 380 and 512, and the testimony of William R. Castle in House, *American Neutrality Policy; Hearings* (1939), 110.

[51]*Congressional Record,* 76th Cong., 1st sess., 8243, 8259, and 8261 (June 29, 1939), 8486 (June 30, 1939), 8276 (June 29, 1939); 76th Cong., 2nd sess., 45 and 73 (October 2, 1939), 268 (October 11, 1939), 313 (October 12, 1939), 1179 (November 1, 1939), 1100 (October 31, 1939), 1295 and 1316 (November 2, 1939); Kendall Hoyt, ed., *A Republican Program: Speeches and Broadcasts by Robert A. Taft* (Cleveland, 1939), 4.

it was clear by this time that the war that had broken out in Europe was of far more direct concern to this country than any previous war had been. [They recognized what the remaining isolationists continued to deny: that the interests of the United States had expanded and that, at the same time, the ability of foreign nations to interfere with these interests had dramatically increased. As a result, this isolationist argument, which had been so effective in earlier years, now lost much of its force, and far from making converts, continued to alienate its erstwhile supporters. More promising was the argument that, even if American interests were involved, the United States was powerless to protect these interests by intervention.]

Immediately after the invasion of Poland, Oswald Garrison Villard informed the readers of the *Nation:* "Let no one think for a single moment that the prospect of a Europe dominated by Hitler, with his brutal, aggressive doctrines, leaves me any peace of mind. But the United States cannot settle the future of Europe; only Europe itself can do that." In *A Foreign Policy for America,* Charles A. Beard argued once more for a continentalism which he defined as "a concentration of interest on the continental domain and on building here a civilization in many ways peculiar to American life and the potentials of the American heritage." Such a policy, he believed, was finding increased support because of a more general "recognition of the hard fact that the United States, either alone or in coalition, did not possess the power to force peace on Europe and Asia, to assure the establishment of democratic and pacific governments there, or to provide the social and economic underwriting necessary to the perdurance of such governments."[52]

[52]Oswald Garrison Villard, "Issues and Men," *Nation,* CIL (September, 1939), 247; Charles A. Beard, *A Foreign Policy for America,* (New York, 1940), 12, 152.

In a letter to Alfred M. Bingham, Villard observed that
the assumption that "if we get into the war we will win it is
on a par with the absurd over-confidence of the British
Government last Fall." "And I'll bet you a nice, large, red
apple," be added, "we won't help preserve any precious
values if we get in." In December, 1940, William Henry
Chamberlin warned readers of the *American Mercury* that
"the greatest and most irretrievable error into which American liberalism could fall today would be to be lured into
supporting another crusade, another aggressive war in
Europe, or Asia, or both, prompted by a general dislike of
the totalitarian idea and by the pathetic illusion that all
the broken pieces of Europe, Asia and Africa could be neatly
put back in place by such a war."[53]

Both liberal and conservative isolationists continued to
argue in this vein down to the day of the Pearl Harbor attack.
Senator Vandenberg found Europe's power politics "devious
with deep intrigue" and "beyond our ken." Taft told the
National Republican Club of New York City that the United
States could not hope to find a permanent solution to
Europe's problems. Senator David I. Walsh of Massachusetts
was certain that American principles of justice would not be
understood or respected in Europe. Colonel Lindbergh, just
emerging from a period of personal isolation to become the
favorite spokesman for anti-interventionist groups, informed
a Keep-America-Out-of-War rally in Chicago in August, 1940,
that the problems of Europe cannot be solved by the interference of America. Amos Pinchot told Rabbi Stephen S.
Wise flatly: "Going into the war won't help the Allies."[54]

[53]Villard to Bingham, dtd September 27, 1940, Villard Papers, File
679; William Henry Chamberlin, "War—Shortcut to Fascism," *American Mercury*, LI (December 1940), 400.

[54]Robert A. Taft, "Our Foreign Policy," *Vital Speeches of the Day*,
VI (March, 1940), 347; *Congressional Record*, 76th Cong., 2nd sess., 97

By the end of the same year, the America First Committee was distributing copies of a lengthy poem by Oliver Allstrom, entitled "The War—'Over there' 1917–1940." The literary value of this opus was slight, but its basic message was clear enough. It read in part:

'Over there,' there's mud, and shedding of blood,
   And tongues confusing and strange,
So why lend a hand to an alien band
   Whose dreams we can never change?

· · · · ·

No, no comes the cry from the U.S. sky,
   We'll never be allied tools
Nor again parade in a foreign brigade,
   Like saps in a squad of fools!

· · · · ·

And Europe may strut through its bloody rut,
   And scheme with her Babel-snares,
But we'll stay at home, this side of the foam
   And mind our own affairs![55]

Norman Thomas opposed the Lend-Lease Bill in January, 1941, as well as other measures designed to help Great Britain, because he felt that proponents of such a course were "entirely too optimistic about our wisdom and our power to set the whole world right by this method. We shall make a worse job of it than in the first World War." His statement was enthusiastically applauded by Representative Fish and was seconded by Colonel Hanford MacNider, a former Assistant Secretary of War and Minister to Canada, who was a member of the board of the America First Committee.[56] In

---

(October 4, 1939); 76th Cong., 3rd sess., App. 449 (February 1, 1940); Charles A. Lindbergh, "An Appeal for Peace," *Vital Speeches of the Day*, VI (August, 1940), 644; Pinchot to Wise, dtd June 14, 1940, Pinchot Papers, Box 67.
   [55]Pamphlet in FDRL OF 4330.
   [56]House, *Lend-Lease Bill; Hearings*, 320, 321–322, 350.

the Congressional debate over the Lend-Lease Bill the same argument was made again and again. Europe's wars would continue, no matter what the United States did, "until the angel Gabriel places one foot on the land and one foot on the sea and proclaims to the world 'Time is no more.' "[57]

By the middle of 1941, some isolationists were not only convinced that the basic problems of Europe were insoluble through outside intervention, they also thought the United States too weak and unprepared to affect the outcome of the war. "The fact is," wrote Lindbergh, "that America is not in a position to wage a successful war in Europe under present conditions....I believe that for us to enter the conflict in Europe at this time would result in defeat and humiliation." Herbert Hoover agreed on the grounds that "America is as yet unprepared even for adequate defense; that our people are not united." John T. Flynn found "something almost grotesque in our quixotic proposals to carry democracy to all corners of the world, with the planes we have not got and the tanks we have not yet produced."[58]

In line with their views on the futility of American intervention, some isolationists also began to speak more frequently and more hopefully about the possibility of a negotiated peace. Even before the war in Europe had broken out,

[57]The words are those of Representative Robsion of Kentucky *(Congressional Record,* 77th Cong., 1st sess., 642 [February 5, 1941]). See also the remarks of Representative Tinkham of Massachusetts and Senator Bulow of South Dakota in *ibid.,* 626 (February 5, 1941) and 1254 (February 21, 1941).

[58]Lindbergh, "Letter to Americans," in Schoonmaker and Reid, eds., *op. cit.,* 74–75; Hoover, "The Immediate Relation," in *ibid.,* 4; John T. Flynn, "The Great Retreat," in *ibid.,* 159–160. For even earlier expressions of similar sentiments see Pinchot to Tinkham, dtd May 3, 1940, to Arthur Krock, dtd May 17, 1940, and to Roy Howard, dtd July 2, 1940, Pinchot Papers, Box 68, and speech by Henry Cabot Lodge, Jr., delivered in October, 1940, America First File, Swarthmore College Peace Collection.

the Women's International League for Peace and Freedom, as well as other similar groups, had supported mandatory embargoes as a device for forcing the democracies and the dictatorships to compromise their differences. In October, 1939, Borah expressed the hope that American nonintervention might help the "anti-Hitler group" in Germany and the pacifists in England to gain control and to end the war. By December, 1940, Amos Pinchot was arguing confidently that there would be a negotiated peace if the United States stayed out of the war, and that Hitler would grant Great Britain generous terms with regard to the Empire, the Mediterranean, France, and Scandinavia.[59]

By this time, very few Americans wished to see Germany win the war. Those who did were understandably in the isolationist camp, but they did not constitute a majority even there. The admirers of Hitler generally gathered in Nazi-financed organizations which shared German racial and religious theories and were clearly outside the main stream of isolationism. Anglophobes congregated in considerable numbers around the America First Committee. It was, however, the consistent policy of that organization to discourage the expression of anti-British sentiments as such.[60]

Despite their continued attacks on the European democracies, most isolationists greatly preferred to see Great Britain and France defeat the Axis Powers. They were merely unwilling to do much to bring about this denouement. William C. Dennis made this clear in testimony before the Foreign Relations Committee in January, 1941. "I would like to see Great Britain win," he told the Senators, "although I think

[59]Mrs. M. M. Willey to Senator Shipstead, dtd June 24, 1939 Senate Records (Committee on Foreign Relations), File 75A–F 9; Borah to Nye, dtd October 24, 1939, Borah Papers, Box 426; Pinchot to Frank Gannett, dtd December 13, 1940, Pinchot Papers, Box 67.

[60]Cole, *America First*, 35–36.

a negotiated peace would be best for the world. But I would not like to see her win at the expense of our diverting ourselves from our plain duty as I see it to be—neutral." Among the many isolationists who expressed their preference for a British triumph at this time were Amos Pinchot, Senators Taft, Wheeler, and Charles L. McNary of Oregon, as well as Representatives Fish and James F. O'Connor of Montana. O'Connor estimated that 98 per cent of his colleagues shared that preference.[61]

General Wood stated the official position of the America First Committee and the unofficial position of most isolationists in a speech to the Advertising Men's Post No. 38 of the American Legion. "We sympathize with Britain," he declared, "we hope she will not be defeated, we favor sending her aid. But we do not favor this aid going to the point of stripping ourselves of our own defenses, of putting the entire economic resources of the United States at the disposal of Britain for an indeterminate period, to be paid for by our people, and, above all, of sending our manpower to her aid."[62] These statements, and the entire isolationist position during the "Great Debate," do not reflect a basic feeling of attachment for one power or overriding hatred for another. As in the years before 1939, isolationists simply resented world events that seemed to tie American fortunes to those of other countries and, as a result, lashed out at those nations with whom involvement was imminent. "I come before you tonight," Lindbergh told a Mutual Broadcasting System

[61]House, *Lend-Lease Bill; Hearings,* 576–577; *Congressional Record,* 77th Cong., 1st sess., 547 (February 4, 1941); Pinchot to F. D. Roosevelt, dtd February 9, 1941, Pinchot Papers, Box 69; speech of Senator Taft before New York State Bar Association, January 25, 1941, and McNary to M. M. Sharp, dtd January 24, 1941, McNary Papers, Box 14; Wheeler to "Dear Friends," January or February 1941, and radio speech by Hamilton Fish, dtd January 21, 1941, Pinchot Papers, Box 69.

[62]Copy in FDRL PPF 1365.

audience in October, 1940, "to enter a plea for American independence. . . . Why. . . ," he asked, "with one hundred and thirty million people, are we being told that we must give up our independent position, that our frontiers lie in Europe, and that our destinies will be decided by armies fighting on European soil?"[63] (John Adams claimed to have told the Continental Congress in 1775 that "our real if not our nominal Independence would consist in our Neutrality," that otherwise "we should be little better than Puppetts danced on the wires of the Cabinetts of Europe" and "the Sport of European Intrigues and Politicks."[64])

The basic unilateralism of the isolationist position was never more clearly expressed than by Lindbergh. But a belief in unilateralism was implicit in most anti-interventionist statements made during the two years preceding Pearl Harbor. The isolationists had no desire to prevent a British victory. They simply refused to "subordinate" American interests to those of Great Britain by committing America's resources to a struggle that had begun without America's consent and was being waged far from American shores. They were willing to give some aid to England, provided the United States did not have to weaken its own defenses in order to supply it. But they were unalterably opposed to broad, general commitments that would keep this country in virtual alliance with Hitler's enemies for an indefinite period.

When the Administration introduced House Resolution 1776, the Lend-Lease Bill, in January, 1941, isolationists offered a counterproposal. Representative Mundt suggested extending a credit of two billion dollars to Great Britain for

[63]Charles A. Lindbergh, "A Plea for American Independence," *Scribner's Commentator*, IX (December, 1940), 69–70.

[64]"The Autobiography of John Adams," The Adams Papers (on microfilm in three parts, Boston, 1954–1956), Pt. III, No. 180.

the purchase of war materiel in the United States. Hamilton
Fish then proposed recommitting H.R. 1776, with instruc-
tions to the Foreign Affairs Committee to prepare a new bill
calling only for a loan. Fish's motion to this effect had the
support of all isolationists. It was defeated 160 to 263. In
the Senate, Taft proposed the loan measure as a substitute
in the form of an amendment to the Lend-Lease Bill. His
motion was voted down 29 to 62. Bulow, Capper, Clark of
Missouri, Johnson of California, La Follette, Reynolds, Shipstead, Taft, Vandenberg, Wheeler, and C. Wayland Brooks
of Illinois were among the overwhelming majority of isolationists who favored the substitute.[65]

The difference between the Administration proposal and
the isolationist-supported counterproposal was not that one
favored Great Britain, the other the Axis Powers. It was
simply that the proposed credit did not represent a commitment of indefinite scope. It did not give the President the
power, as the Lend-Lease Bill did, to integrate the American
economy with the British war effort. Nor would it tempt the
chief executive to insure the safe delivery of goods to be lent
or leased, a move that might well lead to military involvement.

The proposal to extend credit to Great Britain represented
a shift in the position previously taken by the isolationists.
It violated the principles of the Johnson Act of 1934 and of
the Neutrality Acts of 1936 and 1937. It meant setting out on
a road which, according to the Nye Committee, had led to
war in 1917. The political realism of most Congressional isolationists was a major factor in producing this apparent
change of heart. The majority of Americans sympathized with
the hard-pressed British in 1941, and absolute refusal to aid

[65]*Congressional Record,* 77th Cong., 1st sess., 711 (February 6, 1941),
814–815 (February 8, 1941), 2079–2082 (March 8, 1941).

Great Britain was not likely to be rewarded at the polls. Moreover, given the sentiments of the majority of Congressmen, the Lend-Lease Bill could be defeated, if at all, only by offering a counterproposal that promised to accomplish the same things without involving the same risks. Faced with these realities, the isolationists abandoned their earlier stand and proposed extension of the credit as the lesser of two evils.

This move was not wholly incompatible with the overall position of the isolationists. Isolationists never admitted that the welfare of the United States depended on the defeat of the Axis Powers. But they generally recognized that a world dominated by Hitler would not be as safe and comfortable for this country as one controlled by the democracies. The direct and unilateral interest of the United States might, therefore, be served by rendering aid to Great Britain, and isolationists were willing to give such assistance. Aid had to be limited, however, to funds and supplies that could be readily spared. And all aid had to be given in the manner least likely to involve America in war.

Isolationists continued to insist, up to the day of the Pearl Harbor attack, that defeat of the Axis Powers, while desirable, was not essential to the future well-being of the United States. Their justification for this assertion was still, as it had been throughout the thirties, the alleged absence of compelling moral issues in the conflict, and the enduring belief that no conceivable military developments in Europe or Asia could threaten the impregnability of the Western Hemisphere. The persistence of the latter concept, despite Axis successes in Europe and the Japanese advance in China, remains to be demonstrated.

VIII

THE PERSISTENCE OF
ISOLATIONISM

>>>>>>>>>>>>>>>>>>><<<<<<<<<<<<<<<<<<<

WORLD events between 1939 and 1941 persuaded most Americans that the conflict in Europe revolved about significant moral issues and that the United States had an interest in its outcome. They consequently came to favor increased aid to Great Britain, even at the risk of war. At the same time, the minority who remained true to isolationism continued to insist that neither side was fighting for principles so vital to America as to require the assumption of greater risks. Axis military successes raised the possibility that Great Britain would be defeated and the United States thus left to face an ambitious and apparently invincible conqueror alone. Most Americans, therefore, became convinced that the course proposed by the isolationists was not only cowardly but also foolhardy, since it gave Hitler the opportunity to defeat the democracies one by one without having to overcome the united strength of all. Yet a vocal minority continued to maintain that, regardless of what happened elsewhere, the United States could not be invaded or defeated. Belief in the impregnability of the Western Hemisphere and doubts about the intention of any European ruler to test this impregnability were basic to isolationism throughout the thirties. The outbreak of war in Europe and the rapid defeat of Poland did not destroy this belief entirely. In October, 1939, Senator Henry Cabot Lodge, Jr., of Massachusetts attacked the Administration's attempt to repeal the arms embargo by pointing out that "even if Germany were victorious and desired to conquer the United States, she could never do so. No European power can occupy or vanquish the United States, and it is fanciful to suggest that it could." Senator Clark of Missouri was certain that we did not need the British Navy or the French Army to defend the Western Hemisphere. Hiram Johnson reassured his colleagues by asserting that Hitler could never successfully attack this country because he would leave revolt behind him everywhere. "Let us not get jittery and alarmed," added William J. Bulow of South Dakota, "for fear that Hitler is coming over here and haul down the Stars and Stripes, the emblem of a free people, and raise in its stead the Swastika flag. That time will never come."[1]

At the same time, *Uncensored* added a special supplement entitled "American Impregnability," which offered the conclusion that "the invasion of the United States by a European or Asiatic power is a practical impossibility."[2] In June, 1940, when Germany controlled virtually all of Europe, the same publication observed editorially that the possibility of a Nazi invasion was "fantastic" in the face of what it considered to be "the realities of Hitler's position in Europe and the fundamental strategic factors that make up America's impregnability." Two months later, Senator Burton K. Wheeler still

[1]*Congressional Record,* 76th Cong., 2nd sess., 250 (October 10, 1939), 268 (October 11, 1939), 631 (October 20, 1939), 315 (October 12, 1939). See also Kendall A. Hoyt, ed., *A Republican Program: Speeches and Broadcasts by Robert A. Taft* (Cleveland, 1939), 7.

[2]"American Impregnability," *Uncensored,* Supplement to No. 5 (November 4, 1939), 1 and *passim.*

thought that an armed invasion of the United States in the foreseeable future was a "slim possibility indeed," even assuming the defeat of Great Britain. Senator Taft suggested that the existing alliance between Germany, Italy, and Japan might be temporary and expressed doubt that any of these nations would attack the United States. Even were they to do so, he was certain, the armed forces of the United States were capable of warding off the danger.[3]

Writing in the *Virginia Quarterly Review*, Harry Elmer Barnes characterized the idea that "we are certain to be invaded and overrun by a victorious coalition of Nazis, Fascists, etc.," as one of the current "myths." "Save for the vaporings of disgruntled renegades and sensational journalists," he concluded, "there is no evidence that the totalitarians even remotely contemplate any onslaught against us." If we maintain an adequate defense, Amos Pinchot told Hiram Johnson, "America can become as secure as though Germany were located on the moon." In December, General Wood expressed similar views in the pages of *Scribner's Commentator*.[4]

Early the following year, *Uncensored* observed that the Lend-Lease Bill reflected Administration fears that the Germans would invade the United States if the British Navy were defeated. "The possibility that Hitler can ever acquire the bases in this Hemisphere which he must have for a successful attack against the Americas," the magazine countered, "is

[3]*Ibid.*, No. 35 (June 1, 1940), 1–2; *Congressional Record*, 76th Cong., 3rd sess., 10222 (August 13, 1940), 10307–10308 (August 14, 1940); see also Norris to L. Henricksen, dtd December 17, 1940, Norris Papers, Tray 104, Box 1.

[4]Harry Elmer Barnes, "Europe's War and America's Democracy," *Virginia Quarterly Review*, XVI (Autumn, 1940), 552, 554; Pinchot to Johnson, dtd August 31, 1940, Pinchot Papers, Box 67; Robert E. Wood, "War or Peace—America's Decision," *Scribner's Commentator*, IX (December, 1940), 78.

extremely slight." Lindbergh gave the same assurance to the Foreign Affairs Committee and Senator Capper to the readers of *Scribner's Commentator*. Addressing an American Legion Post in Chicago, General Wood still insisted that "it does not make sense that Germany, at the end of a long exhausting war, will, even if victorious, undertake the perilous and costly adventure of attacking a nation of 130,000,000 people across 3,000 miles of ocean." At the same time, Villard urged Senator Wheeler to continue "pounding on the line that the United States *can* be defended easily and is not in danger."[5]

Such sentiments were expressed in Congress with increasing frequency. The opponents of the Lend-Lease Bill based much of their argument on the supposed safety of the United States and the consequent superfluity of the proposed legislation. Both Hamilton Fish and Representative Bartel J. Jonkman of Michigan developed this theme at length in February, 1941. "Mr. Chairman," declared Harold Knutson, "in my consideration of H.R. 1776 I have been entirely free from any fear that it is within the range of possibility that the United States of America can be invaded by any single nation or combination of nations in Europe, or Asia, or both." "Hitler, with all his power," observed Representative Knute Hill of Washington, "cannot cross 20 miles of English Channel and penetrate England. How can he possibly cross the Atlantic and land troops in the Western Hemisphere?"[6]

Isolationist Senators offered their answers to this question. Asserted Bennett C. Clark:

[5]*Uncensored,* No. 68 (January 18, 1941), 3–4; House, *Lend-Lease Bill; Hearings,* 381; Arthur Capper, "Time to Think American," *Scribner's Commentator,* IX (February, 1941), 73–74; Robert E. Wood, "What Now America?" in FDRL PPF 1365; Villard to Wheeler, dtd January 24, 1941, Villard Papers, File 4151 (italics in original).

[6]*Congressional Record,* 77th Cong., 1st sess., 487 (February 3, 1941), 528–529 (February 4, 1941), 590 and 620 (February 5, 1941).

The failure of the Germans during a period now of nearly a year with complete superiority in the air and a state of high preparation, to be able to cross 20 miles of the English Channel and land as much as one man on the British Isles, to my mind makes it preposterous that the Germans at any time within the reasonable future could cross 3,000 miles of sea from Europe to the United States, or, by a roundabout course coming through Africa and South America, cross some nine or ten thousand miles of sea and jungle to attack the United States, provided we attend to our own business and preserve the means for defense which we now have and which are in the course of preparation.[7]

independent mood

"I do not believe," added Robert La Follette, "and I reject the assertion, that the fate of 130,000,000 Americans will either now or in the future be dependent upon or be determined by the outcome of war in Europe, Asia, or Africa." "I know that there are those who insist that Hitler, in addition to all his other qualities, is some sort of magician," declared Senator Nye, "and that he would find some miraculous way of overthrowing all military and naval obstacles if he should win this war, and would then attack this country. Well, Mr. President, we have seen no evidence so far that Hitler is a military magician." It was Senator Bulow, however, who added the final note of assurance, when he exclaimed: "If I were as certain of a place in Heaven as I am that Herr Hitler will never invade, or attempt to invade the United States, I would feel very safe; I would feel just as if I were already in God's pocket."[8]

In May, 1941, Senator Wheeler told an America First Rally in New York's Madison Square Garden that unless Hitler could invade the Western Hemisphere within the next few months he could never do it even though he captured

[7] *Ibid.*, 1108 (February 18, 1941).
[8] *Ibid.*, 1300 (February 24, 1941), 1435 (February 26, 1941), 8256 (February 21, 1941).

the entire British fleet and the remainder of the French and Italian fleets. "We are safe now," he declared, "—and for years to come." Robert Maynard Hutchins was still certain that Germany would not attack a prepared America, and that the United States could survive—though not comfortably—in a totalitarian world. Herbert Hoover insisted that "America cannot be defeated," and General Wood asserted: "I can find in 'Mein Kampf' a program for German expansion in Europe but not one for conquering the world or the Western Hemisphere."[9]

Less than two months before Pearl Harbor, former Senator David A. Reed of Pennsylvania informed the Foreign Relations Committee that the United States and its possessions were safe "from any conceivable attack that Hitler might make in the reasonably near future." At the same time, the isolationist belief in American impregnability received impressive support in the pages of *Army Ordnance*. Writing in September, 1941, Lieutenant-Colonel T. R. Phillips declared flatly: "Land-based airpower has made the United States impregnable to seaborne invasion." Lindbergh carried this message to 35,000 persons assembled in the Hollywood Bowl, and various isolationist organizations gave much publicity to the Phillips article. The America First Committee also circulated copies of a pamphlet compiled by John T. Flynn. Its title raised the question "Can Hitler Invade America?" The answer it offered was an emphatic no.[10]

⁹Burton K. Wheeler, "The American People Want No War," *Vital Speeches of the Day*, VII (June, 1941), 490; Wheeler, "What If Germany Seizes," Hutchins, "War and Four Freedoms," Hoover, "Immediate Relation," and Robert E. Wood, "America's Foreign Policy Today," in Nancy Schoonmaker and Doris F. Reid, eds., *We Testify* (New York, 1941), 193, 39, 12, 111.

¹⁰Senate Foreign Relations Committee, *Modification of the Neutrality Acts of 1939*; Hearings, 77th Cong., 1st sess. (1941), 77; reprint of Phillips' article and John T. Flynn, *Can Hitler Invade America?* in

The events of 1939–1940 thus did not destroy the theory of American impregnability. Indeed, it remained a basic element of isolationist belief. But it was no longer accepted by the majority of Americans who now regarded Hitler as a malevolent being and feared for the safety of their country. Moreover, more and more Americans were awakening to the danger that the economic encirclement of the United States by hostile powers posed for the internal development of the country. Even without military attack or invasion, it was now argued, Hitler and Japan might bring the United States to its knees through the world-wide application of something like Napoleon's "Continental System." This realization turned many more Americans away from isolationism, but it was by no means convincing to all of them.

Isolationists who were not themselves shaken in their beliefs were prone to blame the defections from their ranks, not on the weaknesss of their own position, but on insidious propaganda unleashed by the traditionally suspect pressure groups. As a result, the devil theory of war gained new prominence. "Already," Representative James C. Oliver of Maine warned his colleagues in June, 1939, "the propagandists of the international bankers and of others seeking profit bring forth their song of Circe in eagerness to befuddle and beguile the minds of the American people, to soften them for the killing." At the same time, Harold Knutson saw "the same group of international bankers ply their disloyal and nefarious practices," and William Lemke noted that "the munitions manufacturers and the war lords are again in the saddle."[11]

Pinchot Papers, Box 68; Charles A. Lindbergh, "Time Lies With Us," *Scribner's Commentator,* XI (November, 1941), 89. See also America First File, Swarthmore College Peace Collection.

[11]*Congressional Record,* 76th Cong., 1st sess., 8169 (June 28, 1939), 8236 and 8244 (June 29, 1939).

The Socialist party reaffirmed its support for the Ludlow Amendment, providing for a national referendum to precede an American declaration of war, in April, 1940. Representative Karl Mundt found that "the chant of the international meddlers and profit seekers is beginning again with its insidious and deadly monotony." In December, Henry Ford recalled he had learned from his Peace Ship expedition of 1915 "that a very small group of individuals was promoting the World War for selfish purposes." He suggested the same thing was happening again. *Uncensored,* meanwhile, found something sinister in the fact that William Allen White's Committee to Defend America by Aiding the Allies had the support of Thomas W. Lamont and of J. P. Morgan and Company.[12]

In 1941, isolationists renewed their drive for some kind *war* of war referendum. They also attempted to establish through *referendum* privately conducted polls that America's visible movement toward war was caused by the activities of well-organized groups representing only a minority of the people. Ludlow and Capper introduced resolutions calling for a war referendum amendment to the Constitution as soon as the Seventy-seventh Congress convened. Ludlow supported his proposal with a speech displaying the same vigor—and the same sentiments—as all of the others he had made in this cause since 1935.[13]

When the proposals for a constitutional amendment were buried in committee, a group of isolationist Senators offered a simpler alternative. Senate Concurrent Resolution 7, intro-

[12]*Ibid.,* 76th Cong., 3rd sess., App. 2294 (April 11, 1940), App. 2897 (May 13, 1940); Henry Ford, "An American Foreign Policy," *Scribner's Commentator,* IX (December, 1940), 5; *Uncensored,* No. 60 (November 23, 1940), 1.

[13]*Congressional Record,* 77th Cong., 1st sess., A 1971–1972 (April 25, 1941). The bills were Senate Joint Resolution 47 (Capper) and House Joint Resolution 1 (Ludlow).

duced jointly by Nye, Wheeler, Clark of Idaho, La Follette, and Shipstead on March 27, called for an advisory referendum to be taken in the event Congress was asked to declare war. Although no further action was taken on this proposal, the America First Committee officially endorsed it on June 23. At the same time, the Committee proceeded to conduct a public opinion poll on the issue of war in selected Congressional districts.[14]

Questionnaires sent out under the franks of Fish, Hill, Sauthoff, and Shafer showed 80 per cent of those responding to be opposed to war. Despite the fact that only 15,000 of the 96,000 registered voters in Hill's district responded, and that the poll planned for North Carolina, using the frank of Senator Reynolds, was canceled out of fear of an adverse result, the isolationists cited these polls in support of their assertion that the United States was being dragged into war by a greedy, selfish minority. The devils were at work again. Late in 1941, Theodore Dreiser devoted two entire chapters of a book to the proposition that American financiers had aided Hitler's rise to power and now favored military action to solve the international problems they had helped create.[15]

A new candidate for the devil's role was put forward as American involvement in war became more imminent. From the very beginning, Nazi propagandists had blamed the Roosevelt Administration's increasing attachment to the cause of Great Britain and France on the Jews, who were alleged to be exerting a disproportionate influence on American policy. Father Coughlin and other anti-Semites had frequently repeated this charge. By 1941, it had also gained credence in more respectable quarters.

[14]*Ibid.,* 2610 (March 27, 1941), 4640 (June 2, 1941), A 3612 (July 29, 1941).

[15]Wayne S. Cole, *America First* (Madison, 1953), 57–60; Theodore Dreiser, *America Is Worth Saving* (New York, 1941), Chapters 14 and 15.

In the early thirties, there had been numerous Jews in the isolationist camp. Some of them, notably Lessing J. Rosenwald, subsequently a leading member of the American Council on Judaism, remained there to the end, but many others experienced a change of heart when confronted by the fate of their European coreligionists. Hitler's racial policies understandably made most American Jews bitterly anti-German *~~U.S.~~ Jewish* and led them to support policies designed to bring about the victory of Great Britain and France. This was particularly true of those who regarded themselves as liberals or radicals. Borah had, as early as 1939, told Rabbi Morris M. Rose of Brooklyn that "your people" wanted to line the United States up with Great Britain, and had expressed his surprise at this, in view of British "perfidy" in Palestine. In February, 1941, Villard communicated his hopes of reviving "the old *Nation*" to Mauritz Hallgren. But he expressed doubts about his ability to raise the necessary funds because "many of the liberals and Jews who supported the *Nation* are now for war, particularly the Jews."[16]

The America First Committee attracted anti-Semites in considerable numbers. The leadership was worried by this development and took some effective countermeasures. It refused contributions from notorious anti-Semites, placed a Jew on the national committee, and made efforts to weed out known Coughlinites and such other undesirables as former Representative Jacob Thorkelson.[17] Despite such a policy, numerous persons with anti-Semitic leanings continued to be prominent in the Committee's affairs. "The Jews and the organizations such as B'nai B'rith," wrote the leader of the

[16]Borah to Rose, dtd March 8, 1939, Borah Papers, Box 426; Benjamin Akzin [editor of *American Jewish Chronicle*] to Borah, dtd November 1, 1939, Borah Papers, Box 425; Villard to Hallgren, dtd February 12, 1941, Villard Papers, File 1493.

[17]Cole, *America First*, 8, 10, 105, 117, 132–135.

Florida chapter to national headquarters, "are primarily responsible for our being so far along the path to war.... Under Mr. Roosevelt's administration...the nine million Jews [sic] are directing the affairs of the entire one hundred and thirty million."[18]

The isolationists' reputation on this score suffered further when a subcommittee of the Senate Interstate Commerce Committee, headed by Burton K. Wheeler and ostensibly investigating "interventionist" tendencies in the motion picture industry, spent most of August, 1941, pointing out that persons of the Jewish faith controlled many of the largest film companies. It reached its nadir after the speech Colonel Lindbergh delivered in Des Moines, Iowa, on September 11, 1941. Lindbergh found it impossible to condone Hitler's racial policies, and his remarks were not wholly unfavorable to the Jews. But, in attempting to identify the elements "responsible for changing our national policy from one of neutrality and independence to one of entanglement in European affairs," he asserted that the "three most important groups who have been pressing this country toward war are the British, the Jewish and the Roosevelt administration." He called interventionist Jews shortsighted and declared that they constituted "a danger to this country" because of "their large ownership and influence in our motion pictures, our press, our radio, and our government."

Lindbergh's most reprehensible and most frequently criticized remarks were those warning the Jews of the risk they ran by urging the United States to enter the war. "Instead of agitating for war," he declared, "the Jewish groups in this country should be opposing it in every possible way, for they will be among the first to feel its consequences. Tolerance is a virtue that depends upon peace and strength. History shows

[18]Quoted in *ibid.*, 139.

that it cannot survive war and devastation."[19] These remarks could be interpreted as threatening reprisals against America's Jewish population, and the choice of words clearly displays Lindbergh's political naïveté. Yet, in essence, they simply illustrate a general isolationist view with a specific example. Isolationists of all kinds, including some Jews, repeatedly warned of the loss of civil liberties in wartime. Logically, minority groups would be the first to feel the effects of such a loss, and should, therefore, show the greatest reluctance about going to war. What Lindbergh foolishly said aloud was thus clearly implied by the statements of others, many of whom could not conceivably have been anti-Semites.

Although its existence offers further proof of the persuasiveness of the devil theory of war, anti-Semitism was only a minor, if particularly unfortunate, ingredient of the isolationist position. It became an ingredient of some importance when world events pushed most Jews into the interventionist camp. But it must be considered in the same light as the apparent Anglophobia of those who were not necessarily prejudiced against England, but who saw in the denigration of the British Empire the only hope of avoiding entanglement for America.

Anti-semite
isolationism

Most responsible isolationist leaders rejected anti-Semitism even on this basis. Lindbergh himself was shocked by the furor his remarks caused and, hastily scribbling the draft of a telegram to Wood on the back of a New York restaurant menu, explained that he "did not attack England or the Jews, British or otherwise, on the basis of race and religion." Pinchot, who thought Lindbergh's speech "helpful" and defended the Colonel in a widely distributed letter to S. Stanwood Menken, assured his correspondents that "we are certainly none of us anti-Semitic." The America First Com-

[19]New York *Times*, September 12, 1941.

mittee refused to reprimand Lindbergh and instead deplored what it called "racist smears" directed against him, but the Des Moines speech was vigorously attacked by the director and the governing committee of the Keep America Out of War Congress and by Norman Thomas and the Socialist party. It was strongly criticized by the Hearst newspapers and repudiated by the Chicago *Tribune,* usually the most pro-Lindbergh publication in the United States. Expressions of disapproval also came from many America First leaders, including Herbert K. Hyde, Irving S. Cobb, John T. Flynn, and General Hugh S. Johnson. John Haynes Holmes expressed shock at what he considered to be a gratuitous attack on an already much maligned and much oppressed people.[20]

Nye defended Lindbergh's speech, but insisted that there "was not a shred of anti-Semitism in a single fibre of the being of this courageous American." The North Dakota Senator had earlier defended himself against charges that he was an anti-Semite in an impassioned letter to William Stern, a Jewish banker of Fargo, North Dakota, who had been best man at Nye's wedding in 1940. He had promised to battle against racial prejudice and anti-Semitism if Jews were ever to be persecuted in America, and was subsequently to refuse Gerald L. K. Smith's invitation to embark on a lucrative speaking tour by declaring that he could not in good conscience take a hand in stirring up class strife "against the Jewish race [sic] or any other race of people."[21]

[20]Cole, *America First,* 147–149; Lindbergh's draft of telegram to Wood, dtd September 16, 1941, Pinchot Papers, Box 87; Pinchot to Wood, dtd September 15, 1941, to Menken, dtd October 4, 1941, and to Holmes, dtd October 29, 1941, Pinchot Papers, Box 69; Press Release from National Committee, America First, dtd September 24, 1941, America First File, Swarthmore College Peace Collection; Holmes to Pinchot, dtd November 10, 1941, Pinchot Papers, Box 69.

[21]Wayne S. Cole, *Senator Nye and American Foreign Relations* (Minneapolis, 1962), 189–190, 218–219.

The theory that the devil was represented not by bankers, munitions makers, or Jews, but by President Roosevelt himself was popularized in the postwar period by Charles A. Beard, Harry Elmer Barnes, and others. It was less widely propagated before Pearl Harbor. Isolationists did attack Roosevelt's foreign policy vigorously and never tired of pointing out that this policy was at variance with the plans the President had expounded prior to 1938 and was likely to lead the United States into war. Increasingly, they also began to question Roosevelt's motives, imputing to him the desire to make himself a dictator through the emergency situation produced by war. "The President, I regret to say," Hiram Johnson had stated privately as early as May, 1939, "has been most anxious to take us into war." Within a year, Pinchot was making this charge publicly in a letter to the President himself, and Representative Tinkham introduced the letter into the *Congressional Record* under the provocative title "President Roosevelt Desires War and Dictatorship for the United States."[22]

Attacks on the President were particularly bitter during this campaign year of 1940. In a violently partisan speech delivered in May, Representative George H. Bender of Ohio accused Roosevelt of "old-fashioned chauvinism" in leading the nation down the path to war. He charged that "a Democratic President in 1914, already predisposed to regard one side of a European war as holy and the other as tainted, finds his counterpart in a Democratic President in 1940 equally determined to champion one side as against its enemies." At the same time, George N. Peek, the former head of the Agricultural Adjustment Administration and long-time president of the Moline Plow Company, launched a vigorous at-

[22]Johnson to Pinchot, dtd May 7, 1939, Pinchot Papers, Box 66; *Congressional Record*, 76th Cong., 3rd sess., 10875 (May 29, 1940).

tack on American foreign policy. Peek was basically at odds
with the Administration over the New Deal farm program,
but he believed that the charge of "socialism," which Hoover
and others had made in 1936, was ineffective and that the only
hope of upsetting the New Deal now lay in exploiting the
"warmongering" issue. Peek subsequently joined the America First Committee, was elected to the national committee of
that organization, and became honorary chairman of the
Moline, Illinois, chapter.[23]

Villard told Porter Sargent in July, 1940, that the responsi-
bility for America's entanglement was "80 per cent Franklin
Roosevelt's and frankly I think he will put us into the war
before election day if he thinks that Willkie is leading him."
Mary W. Hillyer, executive director of the Keep America
Out of War Congress, warned the members of the Foreign
Affairs Committee the following year that the United States
would be brought into the conflict "not by the people but by
Mr. Roosevelt and the people whom he has gathered about
him."[24]

Such expressions of sentiment were relatively rare, however. At least in their official and semiofficial pronouncements, few isolationists charged the President with
deliberately leading the nation to war to further his own
ambitions, even when they were convinced the Roosevelt
policies would bring about that result. In July, 1941, Peek
himself laid the real blame on "those who profit most from
international trade—the international bankers, ocean transportation companies, marine insurance companies, exporters
and importers, and so forth." He regarded Roosevelt, Hull,

[23]*Ibid.*, 2896 (May 13, 1940); Gilbert C. Fite, *George N. Peek and the
Fight for Farm Parity* (Norman, Oklahoma, 1954), 294–297.
[24]Villard to Sargent, dtd July 30, 1940, Villard Papers, File 3395;
House Foreign Affairs Committee, *Arming American Merchant Vessels; Hearings,* 77th Cong., 1st sess. (1941), 65.

and Willkie merely as spokesmen for these interests.[25] The attacks on the President were thus simply a variant of the devil theory and indicate the persistence of that theory in isolationist thought.

The demonstrated consistency of the basic isolationist argument throughout the years from 1935 to 1941, despite world events that challenged its validity and decreased its effectiveness, raises a fundamental question. If most Americans surrendered their belief in the amorality of international relations and the impregnability of the Western Hemisphere, why did not all do so? How could a sizable and by no means unintelligent minority continue to adhere to the virtually unchanged tenets of isolationism? Isolationists insisted that their fellow-countrymen had been seduced by the traditional devils or misled by the devious tactics and clever manipulations of President Roosevelt, but these explanations are clearly inadequate and an alternative answer must be sought.

It is very likely that a majority of Americans had never been isolationist because of a reasoned adherence to the principles underlying isolationist thought. The majority had merely given tacit approval to such principles as long as domestic problems were pressing and it seemed easier to put off serious consideration of foreign affairs. When the internal economic situation of the United States improved and, at the same time, conditions in Europe reached the critical stage, this approval was simply withheld. The minority who genuinely believed in isolationist principles, however, continued to do so. The basic tenets of isolationism had never had more than questionable validity in the twentieth century. Those who regarded them as valid upon mature reflection must, therefore, have been largely immune to world events.

[handwritten margin notes: Public opinion / Domestic crisis 1st 1930's]

[25]*Congressional Record,* 77th Cong., 1st sess., 3527–3528 (July 21, 1941). But see also draft of American First article, dtd September 26, 1941, Pinchot Papers, Box 87.

This immunity persisted despite the violence of the contagion that swept the world in the thirties. It can be fully explained only in terms of the attitudes and experiences of individual isolationists, by evaluating factors which, though not in themselves of primary importance, have cumulative effects when present in proper combination. Such an explanation lies in the realms of sociology and psychology as much as in that of history. There can be little doubt, however, that a major cause of the immunity of all confirmed isolationists to world events was the inordinate fear of war which had led them to make the avoidance of armed conflict the primary aim of their political activity.

Isolationists had always expressed their profound dread of a large-scale war and of the effects of such a war on the future development of the United States. They continued to do so with ever increasing vigor until the day of the Pearl Harbor attack. Other Americans also wished to avoid war and regarded its imminence with considerable apprehension. But they feared it less and had more confidence that democratic institutions would survive it. This does not mean that isolationism can be equated with pacifism. There were many pacifist isolationists, but there were others, such as Senator Borah, who were theoretically willing to defend American interests by force. [All isolationists, however, believed that involvement in war was the greatest conceivable disaster, far greater and more damaging to America than that of a world dominated by Hitler.] It was the strength of this belief that ultimately set isolationists apart from other Americans.

Basic ✱
isolationist
belief ✱

Fear of war's consequences had not been widespread in the early days of the Republic. Americans who had challenged the might of Great Britain in 1776 were prepared to go to war with either Britain or France for forty years thereafter. John Adams' stratagems for remaining at peace with France, though salutary, were never popular, nor were the embargo and nonintercourse policies by which Jefferson and Madison sought to avoid war. Most Americans were eager for conflict in 1812, when they believed the assurance of freedom of the seas and the conquest of Canada to lie within their power. Jackson's victory at New Orleans compensated for the general dampening effect of the War of 1812, and Americans rushed into the Mexican War in 1846, prepared to challenge France over Maximilian's Mexican Empire in 1866, and marched into battle over Cuba thirty-two years later without seriously considering the consequences of possible defeat or the repercussions of war itself on the domestic scene.

Yet there had always been warning voices. Alexander Smyth of Virginia, for example, opposed American involvement in the Greek War for Independence in 1824 by pointing out such a step would jeopardize the basic mission of the United States. "The cause of freedom, the hope of mankind," he told his fellow Congressmen,

depends on the ultimate success of the hitherto successful experiment in the science of government, now making in the United States. When we consider the importance of the interests confided to us, it must appear unpardonable wantonly to hazard the success of that experiment. If there be a mode of destroying civil liberty, it is by leading this Government into unnecessary wars.[26]

Sixty-five years later, Carl Schurz offered the same warning to the readers of *Century Magazine*. "To be just to their highest responsibility and duty," he wrote, "the American people should...avoid as much as possible everything, however flattering it may be to their ambition, that may be apt to make their democratic government at home less honest, less just, less beneficent and thereby less respectable and less attractive in the eyes of the world. One of the most prolific

[26] *Annals of Congress*, 18th Cong., 1st sess., 1211 (January 24, 1824).

agencies of evil in this respect is war, for whatever purpose it may be undertaken."[27]

The remarks reportedly made by President Wilson just before he asked for the declaration of war against Germany were even more foreboding. Wilson had reached his decision to call Congress into special session to hear the war message only after much genuine soul searching. The strain of the attempt to reconcile ideals that seemed to call for contradictory courses of action was evident in the President's behavior during these critical days. On April 1, 1917, he sent for Frank Cobb, editor of the New York *World*. After explaining that he saw no alternative to military intervention, Cobb later recalled, Wilson "began to talk about the consequences to the United States. He had no illusions about the fashion in which we were likely to fight the war...."

"Once lead this people into war," he said, "and they'll forget there ever was such a thing as tolerance. To fight you must be brutal and ruthless, and the spirit of ruthless brutality will enter into the very fibre of our national life, infecting Congress, the courts, the policeman on the beat, the man in the street,"...

He thought the Constitution would not survive it; that free speech and the right of assembly would go. He said a nation couldn't put its strength into a war and keep its head level; it had never been done.

["If there is any alternative, for God's sake, let's take it,"] he exclaimed.[28]

The isolationists of the thirties subscribed wholeheartedly to such views. Moreover, war had become so much more

---

[27]Carl Schurz, "Thoughts on American Imperialism," in Frederick Bancroft, ed., *Speeches, Correspondence and Political Papers of Carl Schurz* (6 vols., New York and London, 1913), V, 497.

[28]Ray S. Baker and William E. Dodd, eds., *The Public Papers of Woodrow Wilson* (6 vols., New York and London, 1925–1927), VI, 490, 506–507.

terrible since the days of Smyth and Schurz, and even of Wilson, that fear of its consequences seemed all the more justifiable. The isolationists had been forced into the unhappy position of having to minimize the effects of modern technology on the validity of the assumptions of an earlier time in order to sustain their argument about America's impregnability. In regard to the effects of war, modern technology supported their case.

As early as June, 1935, Representative Frank L. Kloeb of Ohio warned his colleagues that "should another major war come upon us, and should we be drawn into it, it would threaten the very existence of future white civilization." Two months later, he reminded a nationwide radio audience of the cost of the First World War: "One hundred thousand killed; 190,000 wounded, at a cost of $23,000,000,000; a post-war cost to this country estimated at $200,000,000,000; business confusion, depression, broken hopes, interminable suffering. . . . These are the lessons that were written us—written in letters of blood across the scroll of chaos." On the floor of the Senate, Bone implored: "Our civilization is at stake. We went through the valley of the shadow of death 17 years ago. In God's name let us not go through another."[29]

Before the year's end, Borah used the facilities of the Columbia Broadcasting System to warn that "if we permit ourselves to be drawn into another foreign war or into a policy which would engage us from time to time in the hazardous enterprise of uncovering aggressors, or chastising supposed national culprits, we shall inevitably experience in time a change in our whole structure of government." Villard pointed out at the same time that "you cannot cure war by war, or do else than debase all mankind in the futile

[29]House, *American Neutrality Policy; Hearings* (1935), 3; *Congressional Record*, 74th Cong., 1st sess., 12661 (August 7, 1935). 13791 (August 20, 1935).

effort to shoot goodness and virtue and your point of view
into those whom you consider erring human beings." The
Nation, commenting editorially on the Italo-Ethiopian War,
warned that "the harm resulting from Il Duce's mad adventure will be slight compared with the havoc that would be
wrought by another world conflict."[30]

In 1936, Maury Maverick declared that, "if war comes,
we are through, and civilization is through—finished. There
is nothing to gain in war—and everything to lose." Harry
Sauthoff of Wisconsin agreed completely. "Many of us believe," he admitted, "that our free institutions could never
stand the strain of another World War; many of us believe
that western civilization would be wiped out; many of us
believe that occidental ideals would perish and be succeeded
by oriental ideals." Involvement in another world catastro-
phe, thought Frank Kloeb of Ohio, would cause "our manhood to be bled white" and result in the ascendancy of "the
yellow race."[31]

The "horrors of war" theme runs like a bloody thread
through all isolationist utterances in the years preceding the
Second World War. Congressional orators warned over and
over again that America's democratic institutions could not
survive the holocaust, that our civilian population would be
decimated and our economy destroyed beyond repair, that
civilization itself might be wiped out. These warnings were
repeated before Congressional committees, in numerous radio
addresses by isolationist spokesmen, in periodical articles, and
in the private correspondence of noninterventionists.[32]

[30]William E. Borah, "Our Foreign Policy," in FDRL PPF 2358;
Villard, "Neutrality and the House of Morgan," *Nation,* CXLI (Novem-
ber, 1935), 555; "Can America Remain 'Unentangled'?" *Nation,* CXLI
(October 1935), 425.

[31]*Congressional Record,* 74th Cong., 2nd sess., 90 (January 6, 1936),
1740 (February 10, 1936), 1485 (February 5, 1936).

[32]See, for example, the remarks made in 1936 and 1937 by Senator

No book written by an isolationist during 1937 was without its reference to the fate awaiting the United States in the event of involvement in war. "It is commonly said," General Hagood insisted, "that another World War would shake the foundations of civilization and would threaten the white man's supremacy. What is there within the range of human events that would warrant the United States becoming party to such a calamity?" Quincy Howe professed to find resemblances between an Anglo-American twentieth century and the last days of the Roman Empire, and warned of the futility of an attempt to rule the world "through a combination of inertia, experience, and armed might." Fascism or communism for the United States, he insisted, marked the end of that road. "There are," Stephen and Joan Raushenbush warned, "anti-democratic forces in the United States. They have never been really united. They probably can never find a better opportunity for uniting, from coast to coast, than during a war."[33]

Congressman Ludlow illustrated his *Hell of Heaven* with

Bone of Washington and Representatives Ludlow of Indiana, Schneider of Wisconsin, Dies of Texas, and Lawrence E. Imhoff and Herbert S. Bigelow of Ohio in *Congressional Record,* 74th Cong., 2nd sess., 2259 (February 17, 1936) and 3532 (March 10, 1936); 75th Cong., 1st sess., 1789 (March 3, 1937), 2685 (March 24, 1937), App. 578 (March 18, 1937), App. 1633 (June 30, 1937), and App. 2335 (August 21, 1937). See also the testimony of Norman Thomas in House, *American Neutrality Policy; Hearings* (1937), 132; Oswald Garrison Villard, "Another Word on Neutrality," *Nation,* CXLIV (May, 1937), 508; M. J. Hillenbrand, "If War Comes Will Moscow Be Our Ally?" *America,* LVII (July, 1937), 295; Edwin M. Borchard, "Neutrality for the United States," *Vital Speeches of the Day,* III (October, 1937), 739; Villard to Hallgren, dtd May 10, 1937, Villard Papers, File 1493; Borah to W. W. Allen, dtd December 17, 1937, Borah Papers, Box 405.

[33]Johnson Hagood, *We Can Defend America* (Garden City, 1937), 293; Quincy Howe, *England Expects Every American to Do His Duty* (New York, 1937), 199, 213–214; Stephen Raushenbush and Joan Raushenbush, *The Final Choice* (New York, 1937), 15–16, 38.

numerous drawings and photographs depicting the horrors of war. He reached this conclusion:

The next war will be a war in which machinery will overshadow man power, with airplanes raining poison and peoples fighting each other with the weapons of wholesale massacre. No longer will active participation in wars be limited to combatant armies on the field of battle. Henceforth whole populations will be involved. It is not to be wondered at that practically every witness before the Senate munitions investigating committee who was interrogated on the subject predicted that the next war will destroy civilization.[34]

During their consideration of the proposal to repeal the arms embargo in the summer of 1939, both the Foreign Affairs and Foreign Relations committees heard additional expressions of these sentiments.[35] The actual outbreak of war in September increased the danger of American involvement and, therefore, further heightened the fears of genuine isolationists. "Nothing," Senator Taft told a Republican rally at Vienna, Illinois, shortly after Hitler's invasion of Poland, "would be so destructive of democratic government as war.... Those who control the present Government apparently believe in a planned economy under Government control. A war policy of confiscation dominated by that

[34]Louis Ludlow, *Hell or Heaven* (Boston, 1937), 147 and *passim*. For the expression of similar views during 1938, see M. J. Hillenbrand, "The Meddlesome Muddle of Foreign Policy Makers," *America*, LVII (June, 1938), 224; Hubert Herring, *And So to War* (New Haven, 1938), 125; Herring, "If War Comes," *Common Sense*, VIII (March, 1939), 13; Borah to A. B. Parrett, dtd February 19, 1938, Borah papers, Box 417.

[35]See particularly the testimony of former Representative Henry C. Luckey of Nebraska, Norman Thomas, Dean Thomas H. Healy of the School of Foreign Service at Georgetown University, General Hugh S. Johnson and L. D. Stillwell of Dartmouth College in House, *American Neutrality Policy; Hearings* (1939), 70, 137, and 305, and Senate, *Neutrality, Peace Legislation, etc.; Hearings*, 281 and 564–565. See also, Borah to J. B. Eldridge, dtd July 24, 1939, Borah Papers, Box 426.

philosophy would create a completely socialized form of life, from which we might and probably never would return to the liberty and freedom heretofore regarded as characteristic of America." In effect, Taft's conservative vision differed only in detail from that presented in a letter Norman Thomas sent to President Roosevelt some weeks later. The leader of the Socialist party insisted:

The method of modern totalitarian warfare is self-defeating in terms of ideal ends. War itself is the only victor. Each particular war begets its more deadly successors. Intolerance, dictatorship, brutality are its inevitable accompaniments and they live on even when exhaustion temporarily stills the guns.

In so far as any ruler or social system will emerge victorious from the present struggle it is likely to be Stalin and his bloody and brutal band of communist totalitarians.[36]

In the second debate over repeal of the arms embargo in October, 1939, Vandenberg described the regimentation and economic dislocation he regarded as the inevitable consequences of war. Bennett C. Clark foretold the probable repudiation of debts and the confiscation of property, and La Follette warned that war kills democracy. Similar statements were made in the House of Representatives.[37]

[36]Kendall A. Hoyt, ed., *A Republican Program: Speeches and Broadcasts by Robert A. Taft* (Cleveland, 1939), 5–6; Thomas to Roosevelt, dtd October 8, 1939, in FDRL PPF 4840. See also Pinchot to Roosevelt, dtd September 19, 1939, Pinchot Papers, Box 66.

[37]*Congressional Record,* 76th Cong., 2nd sess., 97 (October 4, 1939), 329 (October 12, 1939); see remarks of Representatives Shafer of Michigan, Robsion of Kentucky, and Dewey Short of Missouri in *ibid.,* 1144 (October 31, 1939), and 1295 (November 2, 1939). In the months that followed, Senator Wheeler of Montana and General Wood went on record with similar statements, and Norman Thomas attempted to persuade the American Academy of Political and Social Science of their validity. See *ibid.,* 76th Cong., 3rd sess., App. 3676 (June 10, 1940); Norman Thomas, "America's Contribution to an Enduring Peace," *Annals of the American Academy of Political and Social Science,* CCX

Throughout the period of its existence, *Uncensored* pointed with horror to the probable effects of war on America.
It carried a lengthy article entitled "War Breeds Anti-Semitism," warned of the threat to civil liberties posed by the
granting of emergency powers to the president, and noted
that "while militarization of the United States decreases the
danger from fascist forces abroad it fertilizes the soil for
anti-democratic elements at home." It pointed to restrictions
on labor organization and infringements on the rights of
citizens in Canada and Australia as symptoms of a trend
which was an inevitable concomitant of war.[38] "Isn't it hard
to believe," Oswald Garrison Villard asked Porter Sargent,
"that five years from now, or even three years, we may all be
living under a totalitarian machine?... The one way we can
assure our going totalitarian quickly," he maintained, "will
be by going to war ourselves to defeat Hitlerism."[39]

The fears of the liberal and radical isolationists who supported *Uncensored* were summed up by Stuart Chase in
December, 1940. "The consequences to our culture of an
all-out war abroad are simply told—M-Day," Chase wrote,
"the liquidation of political democracy, of Congress, the
Supreme Court, private enterprise, the banks, free press and
free speech; the persecution of German-Americans and
Italian-Americans, witch hunts, forced labor, fixed prices,
rationing, astronomical debts, and the rest." The picture
Chase painted was so black that even Alfred M. Bingham, a

(July, 1940), 45; and Robert E. Wood, "War or Peace—America's
Decision," *Scribner's Commentator*, IX (December, 1940), 81.

[38]*Uncensored*, No. 11 (December 16, 1939), 1–3; No. 12 (December
23, 1939), Supplement "President's Emergency Powers," 2–3; No. 22
(March 2, 1940), Supplement "Canadian Civil Liberties," 1–3; No. 24
(March 16, 1940), Supplement (by C. Hartley Grattan) "Australian Civil
Liberties," 1–2; No. 50 (September 14, 1940), 3.

[39]Villard to Sargent, dtd July 30, 1940, Villard Papers, File 3395.

very recent defector from isolationist ranks, found it necessary to object. "I don't feel as certain as you," he wrote to his friend, "that the consequences would be all so horrible."[40]

The fears of conservative isolationists took substantially the same forms. Early in 1941, the Foreign Affairs Committee considered the Lend-Lease Bill. It heard shipping magnate William J. Grace, chairman of the Citizen's Keep Out of War Committee of Chicago, warn that war meant "the ruin and starvation of depression" and the possibility of dictatorship. Republican members of the Committee agreed in their minority report that "under this bill we surrender our democratic way of life." On the floor of the House, Hamilton Fish charged that "if this bill is passed unamended we will be in this war within 6 months' time, and with it the doom of our free institutions and tying up from now on the destiny of America with the eternal wars in Europe and Asia." "War," asserted George Holden Tinkham, "means the setting up of a complete dictatorship here. It means the abolition of free economics, the imposition of censorship and espionage, in short, the establishment of totalitarian government." Senators Vandenberg, Reynolds, and Taft, among others, echoed these sentiments.[41]

[40]Stuart Chase, "Four Assumptions About the War," *Uncensored,* No. 65 (December 28, 1940), Supplement, 3; Bingham to Chase, dtd January 6, 1941, *Common Sense* Papers. The concept of "M-Day" (mobilization day) haunted many isolationists. See, for example, Colin Chambers, "The ABC of M-Day," *Equality* (June 1940), a reprint of which is in Norris Papers, Tray 34, Box 7.

[41]House, *Lend-Lease Bill; Hearings,* 558–559; *House Reports,* No. 18 (Foreign Affairs Committee), 77th Cong., 1st sess. (1941), II, 2; *Congressional Record,* 77th Cong., 1st sess., 487 (February 4, 1941), 626 and 633 (February 5, 1941), 1107 (February 18, 1941), 1212 (February 20, 1941), 1284 (February 22, 1941), 1299 (February 24, 1941), 1299 (February 24, 1941); speech by Henry Cabot Lodge, Jr. (October, 1940), America First File, Swarthmore College Peace Collection.

As America's movement toward war accelerated visibly, the
warnings of the isolationists became more strident and more
desperate. Colonel Robert R. McCormick of the Chicago
Tribune foretold "a cost of four hundred billion dollars, a
million deaths, and several million ruined lives" if America
entered the war. Harry Elmer Barnes was certain of the coming of fascism, the loss of democracy and civil liberties for
decades, the end of capitalism through debt, taxation, infla-
tion, and state ownership, and a "scapegoat period after the
war which will make Hitler seem a Judophile by comparison,
and will make the Ku Klux Klan of the twenties appear like
a national convention of the Conferences of Jews and
Christians [sic]."[42]

"Mark this," declared Philip La Follette: *"If we go to war
to save democracy in Europe, we shall wind up by losing
democracy at home."* "Our economic system," added John T.
Flynn, "will be broken. Our financial burdens will be in-
supportable. The great war boom will have burst. The
streets will be filled with idle men and women. And the
once independent farmer will become a government
charge....And amidst these disorders we will have the perfect climate for some promising Hitler on the American
model to rise to power with the promise of abundance and
recovery." "I believe," wrote Robert Maynard Hutchins in
Scribner's Commentator in April, 1941, "that the American
people are about to commit suicide."[43]

[42]Robert R. McCormick, "Can America Fight in Europe?" *Scribner's
Commentator*, IX (February, 1941), 90; Harry Elmer Barnes, "Where
Are We Headed?" *Uncensored*, No. 73 (February 21, 1941), 3.

[43]Philip La Follette, "The Arsenal of Dying Europe?" *Scribner's
Commentator*, IX (March, 1941), 87 (italics in original); radio address
by John T. Flynn, delivered March 8, 1941, quoted in Cole, *America
First*, 82–83; Robert M. Hutchins, "America and the War," *Scribner's
Commentator*, IX (April, 1941), 85. See also Charles A. Lindbergh,
Address (New York, 1941), 3; Thomas, *We Have a Future*, 75; Herbert

In October, the Foreign Relations Committee still heard former Senator David A. Reed of Pennsylvania voice his dread of war and its consequences on the social and governmental structure of the United States. It heard Albert Palmer, president of the Chicago Theological Seminary and chairman of the Minister's No War Committee, enumerate these consequences: "the inevitable brutalizing of life, the subversion of truth, the wild waste of public wealth, the starving and drowning and blowing up of fellow human beings," and "a cessation of civil liberty, religious freedom and free speech." Only days before Pearl Harbor, Hiram Johnson lectured a radio audience on the horrors of war and the certainty of financial ruin and dictatorship if America became involved in the Second World War.[44]

Possessed of such fears, the isolationists were largely immune to world events. So long as the European struggle was not entirely one of Good against Evil, and thus a holy cause to which all practical considerations had to be sacrificed, its outcome could not bring any more terrible results than those they believed to be the consequence of involvement itself. The destruction of American democracy through invasion and conquest by a victorious Hitler, the economic strangulation of the United States through German control of the Atlantic and Japanese dominance in the Pacific, and the subversion of the American system of government by internal elements sympathetic to fascism and national socialism

---

C. Hoover, "The Immediate Relation of the United States to This War," in Schoonmaker and Reid, eds., *op. cit.*, 11–12; Burton K. Wheeler, "America Beware!" *Scribner's Commentator*, X (June, 1941), 92; and Wheeler, "What If Germany Seizes the British Fleet?" in Schoonmaker and Reid, eds., *op. cit.*, 194.

[44]Senate, *Modification; Hearings*, 50, 88; Hiram W. Johnson, "Let's Declare Ourselves," *Scribner's Commentator*, XI (December, 1941), 95–96.

were, even in 1941, only possibilities whose likelihood isolationists vigorously denied. The complete transformation of the American way of life upon entry into war, however, the isolationists regarded as certain.

Most Americans no longer shared these views after 1939. Perhaps they had a more realistic conception of the threat the dictators' victory would pose. Perhaps they were merely more confident that America's democratic institutions could survive even total war. In any event, the positions of the minority and the majority had become wholly irreconcilable. The correctness of neither position could be proven conclusively at that time, and both isolationists and interventionists believed their opponents were leading the United States toward certain disaster. The remaining isolationists, therefore, asserted their principles ever more vigorously as war approached America. They believed themselves to be standing at Armageddon—and, in a sense, they were.

IX

RETROSPECT AND PROSPECT

"IN my own mind," Senator Vandenberg confided to his diary some time after the event, "my convictions regarding international cooperation and collective security for peace took firm form on the afternoon of the Pearl Harbor attack. That day ended isolationism for any realist."[1] Vandenberg was right.

Reduced to its least common denominator, the isolationism of the thirties consisted of belief in the amorality of international affairs and the impregnability of the Western Hemisphere which, taken together, made American intervention in a foreign war both unavailing and unnecessary; of the idea that peace-loving nations such as the United States become involved in war largely through the machinations of selfish, greedy minorities; and of the conviction that, since all other countries were amoral, warlike, or vulnerable, it was essential for the United States to adhere to a policy of unilateralism in its foreign relations. Sustaining these attitudes in the face of world events that cast doubt on their validity was the dread of total war and its domestic consequences.

[1] Arthur H. Vandenberg, Jr., ed. (with Joe Alex Morris), *The Private Papers of Senator Vandenberg* (Boston, 1952), 1.

As thus defined, isolationism is devoid of political, economic, or social content. It is neither liberal nor conservative, capitalist nor socialist, Fascist nor Communist, Democratic nor Republican. It was one of the noteworthy characteristics of isolationism during the entire period under consideration that Henry Ford and Kathryn Lewis could serve on the executive committee of the same organization, and that Hamilton Fish could register approval of foreign policy resolutions adopted by the Socialist party.

It has sometimes been asserted that isolationism was largely purged of its nonconservative elements after 1939. The domination of the America First Committee by representatives of the business community and the change of heart evidenced by the *Nation* and the *New Republic* after the outbreak of the Second World War, and particularly after the fall of France, are cited in support of this contention.[2] Yet this assertion ignores the activities of the Communists and of Thomas, Chase, Villard, and other Socialists or near-Socialists after 1939. It does not account for the fact that Beard and Barnes remained staunch isolationists and that other liberals, having lost a forum for their opinions when the *New Republic* decided to support Roosevelt's foreign policy, published the violently isolationist *Uncensored* up to the day of the Pearl Harbor attack. Moreover, it fails to consider that only one leading Progressive, Senator George W. Norris of Nebraska, surrendered his isolationism after 1939, and that men like Nye and Wheeler had supported much of the domestic legislation of the New Deal and cannot be considered as genuine conservatives. Although liberals found it harder to justify their isolationism as time went on, they did not abandon it altogether.

[2]Adler presents this argument in some detail. See Selig Adler, *The Isolationist Impulse* (London and New York, 1957), 295–299.

The fear of war exists to some extent in all men, and the desire for unilateral action is common to most individuals and all nations. The universality of these basic emotions, which combined to form the isolationism of the thirties, makes isolationism permanently attractive and produces at least a nostalgic yearning for it whenever world events become too unpleasant to contemplate with equanimity. But, for the "realists" of whom Vandenberg spoke, isolationism becomes impossible under modern conditions, since the fear of war and the desire for unilateral action must frequently dictate mutually exclusive policies. To act independently and exclusively on one's own behalf satisfies national aspirations and demonstrates national aims. But such a course is a source of danger and an invitation to conflict in a world of competing interests and precarious power relationships.

During the nineteenth century, this danger was minimal because America had no strong neighbors and was guarded on two sides by wide expanses of ocean and on a third by the polar icecap. The isolationists of the thirties relied heavily on their belief in the continued safety of the United States. They consequently regarded assistance to other nations as unnecessary to protect American interests, and, therefore, as a method of weakening this country for the primary benefit of others, and as a policy tending to draw the United States, without compensating benefits, into situations which endangered its security. So long as the illusion of safety survived, the fear of war and the belief in unilateralism could be coherently combined.

Even after 1939, when some aid to Great Britain was deemed advisable, the concept of unilateralism was not abandoned. The conditions under which isolationists were prepared to grant such aid would merely have committed the United States to supplying money and materials which could be readily spared, in the interests of defeating Hitler and thus contributing to America's welfare. Only the Japanese attack on Pearl Harbor, which shattered the myth of American impregnability, destroyed the coherence of the isolationist position absolutely. Vandenberg and his colleagues now realized that unilateral action by the United States was not only ineffective in preventing wars elsewhere in the world— something they had always tacitly admitted—but was no longer able to prevent an attack on America—something they had always vigorously denied.

It mattered little that the area attacked by Japan lay outside the continental United States. The arguments about American impregnability had frequently included references to the safety of Hawaii, Alaska, Puerto Rico, the Virgin Islands, and the Canal Zone.[3] It was apparent, moreover, that any military action against these outlying possessions constituted an attack on the United States under international law and was certain to bring the immediate involvement of this country in war. Since no isolationist seriously suggested surrendering these territories, and since such a suggestion would, in any event, have found little support among the American people, the argument about America's impregnability always included the outlying areas at least by implication. The events at Pearl Harbor laid bare the untenability of the entire argument by showing at least the necessary implication to be invalid. Isolationists were, therefore, forced to choose between a policy of continued unilateralism in the postwar world, and thus the possibility of a future attack, and cooperation with other nations in a system of collective security that might prevent future wars entirely.

The realists preferred the latter alternative. They thus

[3]See, for example, Hanson W. Baldwin, "America Rearms," *Foreign Affairs,* XVI (April, 1938), 444, Robert A. Taft, "Let Us Stay Out of War," *Vital Speeches of the Day,* V (February, 1939), 255, and *Congressional Record,* 74th Cong., 2nd sess., 2261 (February 17, 1936).

committed themselves to putting international relations on the rational and moral basis whose existence they had so long denied. When President Roosevelt took the lead in the formation of the United Nations Organization, Senator Vandenberg lent his unqualified support to the project. Opposition to American membership in the new world body was virtually nonexistent among persons in positions of responsibility and leadership.

Unfortunately, the principle of collective security, which a previously isolationist America had come to embrace by 1942, and which even some of the most confirmed isolationists of the thirties had come to accept, proved to be inapplicable in the postwar era. The Soviet Union had championed collective security as long as Maxim Litvinov served as Foreign Commissar. But it no longer regarded such a system as adequate to defend Russian interests. Instead, the Soviet Union now placed its faith in the expansion of the territory under its control along lines suggested by geopolitical theory. The other European nations which, singly or in concert, had assumed responsibility for order on the Continent since the Congress of Vienna, were too greatly weakened by the Second World War to play this role effectively. In consequence, the United States found itself not merely cooperating with others in the maintenance of world order, but forced into the position of assuming the leadership of one of two developing power blocs.

The Truman Doctrine of March 12, 1947, and the Marshall Plan, first suggested by Undersecretary of State Dean Acheson on May 8 of the same year, marked the second basic change in America's role in world affairs within a decade. Through the intermediate stage of international cooperation, the United States had moved from isolationism to conscious world leadership. Some of the former isolationists applauded even this step. "The greatest nation on earth," said Vandenberg, "either justifies or surrenders its leadership. We must choose. There are no blueprints to guarantee results. We are entirely surrounded by calculated risks. I profoundly believe that the pending program is the best of these risks."[4]

The Berlin Blockade of 1948–1949 and the outbreak of the Korean War the following year clarified the nature and extent of these risks for all Americans. They provided a perfect setting for a new attempt to withdraw from the responsibilities of power. They showed clearly that no rational world order had been established or was likely to come into existence in the foreseeable future, and they etched in strokes too deep to be overlooked the danger posed by the world-wide commitments of the United States. The controversy that followed was again dignified with the appellation "Great Debate." But it was little more than a flurry of protest, which in its nature and its effects demonstrated the final demise of true isolationism.

On November 10, 1950, Senator Taft demanded a "re-examination" of the entire program of American military aid to Europe. On December 12, the former Ambassador to Great Britain, Joseph P. Kennedy, described the foreign policy of the United States as "suicidal" and "politically and morally bankrupt." He urged a withdrawal from "unwise commitments" in Berlin and Korea, and declared the idea that this country had an interest in or a responsibility for the defense of Western Europe to be wholly without foundation. A week later, Herbert Hoover carried the attack on Administration policy still further with his call "to preserve for the world this Western Hemisphere Gibraltar of Western Civilization." The Americas, Hoover argued, were still "surrounded by a great moat," could be made economically self-sufficient, and

[4]Vandenberg, ed., *op. cit.*, 390.

did not need Europe, or the commitment of land forces to Europe and Asia, for their defense.[5]

The echoes of the isolationism of the thirties became even louder when the former President subsequently warned once more against "the eternal malign forces of Europe" and shuddered at the thought of committing a single American to the "quicksands" of Europe and Asia. They reached a crescendo when Taft assured his countrymen: "I do not believe it is at all clear that the Russians contemplate a military conquest of the world. . . . I believe they know it is impossible. It would take them at least a hundred years to build up their sea power."[6]

Yet, for all the debate the expression of such sentiments aroused, there was no evidence of a genuine resurgence of older attitudes concerning foreign policy. Hoover's "Western Hemisphere Gibraltar" was to rely for its safety on outlying bastions in Great Britain, Japan, Formosa, the Philippines, and, possibly, Australia and New Zealand as well. Taft conceded that the United States was engaged in a world-wide battle that had to be fought on a world-wide stage. In *A Foreign Policy for Americans,* he even expressed support for "an effective international organization" as "the most effective assurance of world peace and therefore of American peace." He voiced qualified approval of the Marshall Plan and the Point Four Program, favored some military aid to Western Europe and Nationalist China, and called the At-

[5]Richard P. Stebbins *et al., The United States in World Affairs, 1950* (New York, 1951), 413, 437–440; Joseph P. Kennedy, "Present Policy is Politically and Morally Bankrupt," *Vital Speeches of the Day,* XVII (January 1, 1951), 170–173; Herbert Hoover, "Our National Policies in This Crisis," *ibid.,* 165–167; Herbert Hoover, "We Should Revise Our Foreign Policies," *ibid.* (February 15, 1951), 262–265.

[6]Quoted in Arthur M. Schlesinger, Jr., "The New Isolationism," *Atlantic Monthly,* CLXXXIX (May, 1952), 35, 37.

lantic Pact in its original form a necessary extension of the
Monroe Doctrine to Europe.[7]

Taft showed little enthusiasm for these programs when
they were debated in the Senate. But his book still demonstrated an awareness of the need for an approach to foreign
policy that bears little resemblance to the course he had
championed during the thirties, and thus substantiated his
assertion that "nobody is an isolationist today."[8] The discussion in 1950–1951 was primarily concerned with the extent
of military and economic aid to other nations, not with the
basic necessity for such assistance. It turned largely on the
question of how the cooperation of America's allies might
best be secured, not how America's alliances could be ter-
minated most rapidly.

In any event, no mass support for the Hoover-Taft position
manifested itself. The Democratic party chose the internationalist governor of Illinois, Adlai E. Stevenson, as its
presidential candidate in 1952. The Republican party selected not Taft, but General Dwight D. Eisenhower who,
during his service as commander of the North Atlantic Treaty
Organization forces, had become convinced of the importance
of international cooperation and of the defense of Western
Europe.[9]

The "new isolationism" could not, like the genuine isolationism of the thirties, lay claim to a coherent and logical set
of beliefs. While it might still be maintained that the United
States had no interest in territorial expansion, the other basic

[7]Herbert Hoover, "We Should Revise Our Foreign Policies," *Vital
Speeches of the Day*, XVII (February, 1951), 262–265; Robert A. Taft,
"Safety of the Nation," *Vital Speeches of the Day*, XVII (January 15,
1951), 198–205; Robert A. Taft, *A Foreign Policy for Americans* (Garden
City, 1951), 6, 13–16, 86–88.

[8]Quoted in Schlesinger, "New Isolationism," 36.

[9]Dwight D. Eisenhower, "Defense of Western Europe," *Vital Speeches
of the Day*, XVII (February 15, 1951), 260.

assumptions of the isolationists of the Roosevelt years had become wholly and obviously untenable in the postwar era. Virtually every American saw a moral issue in the conflict between the Communist bloc and the Free World. Neutrality was impossible in any future war, if for no other reason than that the Soviet Union regarded the United States as its primary foe. The United States could clearly not be indifferent to the outcome of any new war in Europe or Asia, since such a war would inevitably affect the world balance of power and, therefore, the safety of the United States. The argument regarding America's impregnability was no longer convincing after the experience at Pearl Harbor and the development of nuclear weapons and intercontinental ballistic missiles.

The "new isolationism" was in reality no isolationism at all. It was, in fact, little more than an emotional outburst by some of the old isolationists, who were trying—and failing—to come to grips with the modern world. It was, in Schlesinger's words, "the last convulsive outbreak of an old nostalgia."[10]

The outbreak came because the responsibilities that go with power are irksome and the task of world leadership is a thankless one. It came, too, because the possibility of total destruction in case of future wars was made all the greater by the advent of the atomic age. Yet, the only country to whom the United States could have surrendered the responsibilities of power in 1951 was the Soviet Union, and this alternative seemed undesirable even to the "new isolationists." Moreover, there was no realistic possibility of avoiding war and its attendant destruction by any other course than that of

[10]Schlesinger, "New Isolationism," 38. Schlesinger regarded the "new isolationism" as a serious threat and emphasized certain of its traditional aspects. But he began with the assertion that "the isolationism of a decade ago is surely dead" (p. 34) and concluded that the new version was a product of nostalgia.

rallying all the noncommunist nations that proved willing into an alliance designed to meet the challenge from the East without equivocation. Under these conditions, there could be no return to nineteenth-century theories and practices, nor to the kind of unilateralism championed by the isolationists of the Roosevelt Era.

This type of unilateralism became obviously unsafe when the Pearl Harbor attack demonstrated that the United States was no longer unassailable. It became pointless when this country emerged from the Second World War as one of two remaining major powers, and when the events of the immediate postwar period made it plain that amicable relations could not be maintained with the Soviet Union. A nation which has little weight on the scale of world politics—such as the United States was by necessity in the early years after independence and by choice well into the twentieth century—can find safety through a unilateral foreign policy that allows it to decide for itself when its vital interests are threatened by events elsewhere in the world. Under such a policy, genuine threats may sometimes not be recognized until it is too late. But a minor power in a favorable geographical position can, in this way, generally avoid conflicts over questions that basically do not concern it.

The vital interests of a major power are automatically threatened by anything its rivals may do to enhance their position. For such a power, unilateralism generally means dispensing with the services of allies without obtaining compensating benefits thereby. Great Britain's status as the dominant world power led it to seek an alliance with the United States during the nineteenth and twentieth centuries and aroused isolationist charges that "England expects every American to do his duty." The Second World War brought about a reversal of roles. It was now in the interest of the

United States to secure reliable allies who could ease the burden of world leadership.

The principal factors which moulded the isolationism of the 1930's still exist, of course. Although depression has given way to sustained prosperity and the economic strength of the United States has been amply demonstrated, although the survival of America's democratic institutions seems certain to all but the radical right, and although the United States is, for the first time in its history, militarily and psychologically prepared to take an active part in world affairs, the advance of military technology has kept alive, and perhaps even deepened, the dread of war and its consequences which was characteristic of the isolationists on the eve of the Second World War. But those who now suggest that the triumph of communism would be preferable to a nuclear holocaust are under no illusion that America's national interests could be promoted or protected by such a course. They hope that many lives and much of Western culture can be saved, but they do not believe, as the isolationists of the thirties clearly did, that the basic institutions of the United States can survive virtually intact. The triumph of fascism which the isolationists were prepared to accept, though not to welcome, in the thirties meant to them the triumph of fascism outside the United States, so long as this country did not link its fate to others through unwise international commitments. Those who now believe the triumph of communism to be preferable to war are certain that this triumph would be world-wide. As a result, they are not unilateralists. They are firm believers in international cooperation and consultation, as the only method that can possibly prevent the triumph of communism without nuclear war.

Those who now consider the United States to be overcommitted and, therefore, urge withdrawal from Vietnam and from other areas where they believe American military assistance cannot be effective are also not unilateralists. Although columnist Walter Lippmann may talk about the necessity for realizing "the limitations of our power" and Senator George Aiken of Vermont may argue that we cannot police the world, their position bears little resemblance to that adopted by isolationists of the Roosevelt era. These men, along with Senators Wayne Morse of Oregon, George McGovern of South Dakota, Ernest Gruening of Alaska, Frank Church of Idaho, and even J. William Fulbright of Arkansas, are sometimes called "neo-isolationists,"[11] but this appellation tends to confuse rather than to illuminate their actual position. They earnestly believe that there are limits to America's power, and that to overstep these limits means courting failure and nuclear war. But they favor American commitment to the defense of Western Europe, are strong partisans of the United Nations, and place their faith not only in continuous consultation with Great Britain and other allies, but in negotiations with the Soviet Union, with China, and with all other governments and organizations whose cooperation is essential for the establishment and maintenance of peace and order in the world. To call the course they propose isolationism is to misread both the history of the thirties and the record of American foreign policy prior to that time.

Indeed, a much better case can be made for the proposition that the direct, if not altogether true, heirs of the isolationist tradition, are those Americans who now decry what they call a "no-win" policy and clamor most loudly for more effective military action. The preference for neutralism of many nations who have benefited materially from American aid, the virtual defection of de Gaulle's France from the

[11]See Henry R. Graff, "Isolationism Again—With a Difference," *New York Times Magazine,* May 16, 1965, 26–27, 98–100. Though Graff does not say so explicitly, his evidence clearly indicates that the "difference" is more significant than any similarities to earlier isolationism.

North Atlantic Treaty Organization, and the failure of Great Britain and other allies to support American policy diplomatically with regard to Communist China and militarily in Korea and Vietnam, have disenchanted many Americans with the ideal of internationalism. Believing these countries to be ungrateful and unreliable, and convinced of the overriding power of the United States, these persons have come to urge this country to defend its own interests in its own way, let the chips fall where they may. They have favored the forcible overthrow of Castro's regime in Cuba, applauded American intervention in the Dominican Republic, and urged a "war for total victory" in Southeast Asia. From the camp of these new unilateralists have come not only increasing opposition to the foreign aid program and other measures for international cooperation, but also demands for resumption of nuclear testing, "defoliation" of the South Vietnamese jungle, and, occasionally, the launching of a preventive war against China.[12]

The "new unilateralism," as expounded by former Senator Barry Goldwater of Arizona, among others, is thus clearly a unilateralism of strength. It is not intended to insulate the United States from world problems, but rather to solve these problems by direct and vigorous action, of a military nature if necessary. It is predicated on the willingness to fight not only in defense of this country and of the Western Hemisphere, but also in defense of an outer perimeter which circles the globe. Although it differs from present American policy in concept and strategy, it bears little actual resemblance to the course proposed during the 1930's, when unilateralism was combined with a policy of avoiding war at almost any cost, and when the suggestion that the frontier of the United

[12]For an analysis of the rise of the "new unilateralism," particularly in the South, see Charles O. Lerche, Jr., *The Uncertain South* (Chicago, 1964), esp. Chapters I and IX.

States was on the Rhine, let alone on the Elbe, the Mekong, or the Yalu, was automatically and indignantly rejected by all isolationists.

Nevertheless, some of the old isolationists find the "new unilateralism" attractive. It incorporates the suspicion of all foreign countries which is second nature to them, and it maintains, with a vengeance, the policy of independence which they have always advocated. The fear that a genuine unilateralism of strength means entanglement and war, a fear that kept even Senator Borah from carrying through on his belligerent stand prior to World War II, has been partly overcome by the fact that the power of the United States has increased to the point where it need no longer fear "dictation" from London, Paris, or other foreign capitals, and that the center of the current crisis is in Asia, where isolationists were always more prepared to fight than in Europe. Moreover, the United States is already so entangled in world affairs that the active course now proposed cannot conceivably add to this involvement but, instead, appears as a means for finding a new, independent position beyond the morass of America's present commitments. As to the threat of war, it is so all-pervasive today that at least a plausible argument can be made for the proposition that a unilateralism of strength may act as a more effective deterrent than other policy options now available.

Yet, like the positions taken by the "better Red than dead" pacifists and the proponents of American withdrawal from Southeast Asia, the "new unilateralism" is not, in any meaningful sense, isolationism. The world has changed to such an extent that the principal elements which made up the isolationism of the thirties can no longer be coherently combined. In the forms in which these elements are now most frequently encountered, they lack the roots which still nourished them a generation ago. They have been transformed into a unilateralism which promises neither relief from the burdens of world leadership nor immunity from world conflicts, and a policy for avoiding war which may ultimately involve the surrender of the American way of life. They thus represent, each in its own way, an abandonment of the traditional American approach to foreign policy. True isolationism, which was the most characteristic expression of that approach, survives only as "an old nostalgia." As a positive, defensible policy it is dead. The years from 1935 to 1941 were the years of its swan song.

BIBLIOGRAPHY

THE most useful sources for expressions of isolationist thought during the period from 1935 to 1941 are the *Congressional Record* and the published reports of hearings held before Congressional committees, particularly the Foreign Affairs and Foreign Relations committees. These documents contain the entire legislative record of isolationism and also present the views of all leading isolationists, both in and out of Congress.

Much additional material can be found in a wide range of popular and scholarly publications. The most useful for this study have been the *New Republic, Common Sense,* the *Nation,* and the mimeographed *Uncensored,* all on the liberal side. On the conservative side, *Scribner's Commentator,* the *Saturday Evening Post,* and *America* were most consistently valuable.

The Franklin D. Roosevelt Papers contain correspondence from leading isolationists, as well as pertinent speeches, handbills, pamphlets, and the like. The Swarthmore College Peace Collection contains the voluminous files of the National Council for the Prevention of War, as well as material on other organizations having some connection, however remote, with the peace movement. The Villard Papers, typical of the material left by the isolationists themselves, contain numerous relevant and interesting pieces of correspondence which add to, but do not alter, the picture to be derived from Villard's published writings. The same comment applies to the Borah Papers. The Amos Pinchot Papers not only contain some valuable correspondence, but also a great deal of America First literature.

The files of the various Congressional committees are incomplete and disappointing, though they occasionally yield some useful items. The *Common Sense* Papers refer only incidentally to the editorial policy of the magazine.

The following is a list of sources quoted or otherwise used in the preparation of this study, and of the most pertinent secondary material:

PRIMARY SOURCES

Manuscript Collections

Harvard University Library, Cambridge, Massachusetts:
  Oswald Garrison Villard Papers
Library of Congress, Washington, D.C.:
  William E. Borah Papers
  Charles L. McNary Papers
  George W. Norris Papers
  Amos Pinchot Papers
  Key Pittman Papers
National Archives, Washington, D.C.:
  House Records, Committee on Foreign Affairs
  House Records, Committee on the Judiciary
  House Records, Committee on Military Affairs
  Senate Records, Committee on Foreign Relations
Franklin D. Roosevelt Library, Hyde Park, New York:
  Franklin D. Roosevelt Papers
Swarthmore College Peace Collection, Swarthmore, Pennsylvania:
  America First Papers
  American League for Peace and Democracy Papers
  American League against War and Fascism Papers
  National Committee for the War Referendum Papers
  National Council for the Prevention of War Papers
Yale University Library, New Haven, Connecticut:
  Common Sense Papers

Public Documents

GERMANY

Akten zur deutschen auswärtigen Politik, 1918–1945, Series D, I (Von Neurath zu Ribbentrop). Baden Baden, 1951.

UNITED STATES

Annals of Congress, 18th Cong., 1st sess. Washington, 1824.

Congressional Record, LXXIX–LXXXVII, 74th Cong., 1st sess., through 77th Cong., 1st sess. Washington, 1935–1941.

Department of State. *Peace and War; United States Foreign Policy, 1931–1941.* Washington, 1941.

House Reports, No. 320, Committee on Foreign Affairs, 75th Cong., 1st sess. Washington, 1937.

——, No. 363, Committee on Foreign Affairs, 75th Cong., 1st sess. Washington, 1937.

——, No. 808, Committee on Military Affairs, 75th Cong., 1st sess. Washington, 1937.

——, No. 870, Committee on Military Affairs, 75th Cong., 3rd sess. Washington, 1938.

——, No. 856, Committee on Foreign Affairs, 76th Cong., 1st sess. Washington, 1939.

——, No. 18, Committee on Foreign Affairs, 77th Cong., 1st sess. 2 pts. Washington, 1941.

House of Representatives, 74th Cong., 1st sess. *American Neutrality Policy; Hearings before the Committee on Foreign Affairs.* Washington, 1935.

——, 74th Cong., 1st sess. *National Munitions Act; Hearings before the Committee on Foreign Affairs.* Washington, 1935.

——, 74th Cong., 1st sess. *To Amend the Constitution with Respect to the Declaration of War: Hearing before Subcommittee No. 2 of the Committee on the Judiciary.* Washington, 1935.

——, 74th Cong., 2nd sess. *American Neutrality Policy; Hearings before the Committee on Foreign Affairs.* Washington, 1936.

——, 75th Cong., 1st sess. *American Neutrality Policy; Hearings before the Committee on Foreign Affairs.* Washington, 1937.

——, 76th Cong., 1st sess. *American Neutrality Policy; Hearings before the Committee on Foreign Affairs,* Washington, 1939.

——, 76th Cong., 1st sess. *American Neutrality Policy; Editorials submitted to the Committee on Foreign Affairs.* Washington, 1939.

——, 77th Cong., 1st sess. *Arming American Merchant Vessels; Hearings before the Committee on Foreign Affairs.* Washington, 1941.

——, 77th Cong., 1st sess. *Lend-Lease Bill; Hearings before the Committee on Foreign Affairs.* Washington, 1941.

Richardson, James D., ed. *A Compilation of the Messages and Papers of the Presidents, 1789–1897.* 8 vols. Washington, 1899.

Senate Reports, No. 118, Committee on Foreign Relations, 75th Cong., 1st sess. Washington, 1937.

——, No. 723, House-Senate Conference Committee on the Neutrality Act of 1937, 75th Cong., 1st sess. Washington, 1937.

——, No. 749, Committee on the Judiciary, 76th Cong., 1st sess. Washington, 1939.

——, No. 750, Committee on the Judiciary, 76th Cong., 1st sess. Washington, 1939.

——, No. 45, Committee on Foreign Relations, 77th Cong., 1st sess. 2 pts. Washington, 1941.

Senate, 74th Cong., 1st and 2nd sess. *Munitions Industry; Report of the Special Committee on Investigation of the Munitions Industry.* 7 pts. Washington, 1935 and 1936.

——, 74th Cong., 2nd sess. *Neutrality; Hearings before the Committee on Foreign Relations.* Washington, 1936.

——, 76th Cong., 1st sess. *Neutrality, Peace Legislation, and Our Foreign Policy; Hearings before the Committee on Foreign Relations.* Washington, 1939.

——, 76th Cong., 1st sess. *War Referendum: Hearings before a Subcommittee of the Committee on the Judiciary.* Washington, 1939.

——, 77th Cong., 1st sess. *Modification of the Neutrality Act of 1939; Hearings before the Committee on Foreign Relations.* Washington, 1941.

Wharton, Francis. *A Digest of the International Law of the United States,* 2nd ed. Washington, 1887.

Books, Pamphlets, and Articles

Adams, John Quincy. "July 4th Address," *Niles' Weekly Register*, XX (1821), 326–332.

Allstrom, Oliver. *The War "Over There" 1917–1918*. Chicago, 1940.

"American Impregnability." *Uncensored*, No. 5 (November, 1939), Supplement.

"American Neutrality," *Living Age*, CCCLI (February, 1937), 555–556; CCCLII (March and April, 1937), 90–91, 183–184.

"Arms and the Men," *Fortune*, IX (March, 1934), 52–57, 113–126.

Armstrong, O. K. "The American Legion and Involvement," *Scribner's Commentator*, IX (November, 1940), 31–35.

Baker, Ray S., and William E. Dodd, eds. *The Public Papers of Woodrow Wilson*. 6 vols. New York and London, 1925–1927.

Baldwin, Hanson. "America Rearms," *Foreign Affairs*, XVI (April, 1938), 430–444.

———. "Impregnable America," *American Mercury*, XLVII (July, 1939), 257–267.

Bancroft, Frederick, ed. *Speeches, Correspondence and Political Papers of Carl Schurz*. 6 vols. New York and London, 1913.

Barnes, Harry Elmer. "Europe's War and America's Democracy," *Virginia Quarterly Review*, XVI (Autumn, 1940), 552–562.

———. *The Genesis of the World War*. New York, 1926.

———. "Where Are We Headed?" *Uncensored*, No. 73 (February, 21, 1941), Supplement.

———. "Why America Entered the War," *Christian Century*, XLII (November, 1925), 1441–1444.

Baruch, Bernard M. "Cash and Carry," *Today*, V (November 2, 1935), 6–7.

———. "Neutrality," *Current History*, XLIV (June, 1936), 33–44.

———. "Neutrality and Common Sense," *Atlantic Monthly*, CLIX (March, 1937), 368–372.

———. *Neutrality and Peace*. Washington, 1939.

Basler, Roy P., ed. *The Collected Works of Abraham Lincoln*. 9 vols. New Brunswick, New Jersey, 1953–1955.

Bausman, Frederick. *Facing Europe.* New York and London, 1926.

———. *Let France Explain.* London, 1922.

Beard, Charles A. *The Devil Theory of War.* New York, 1936.

———. *A Foreign Policy for America.* New York, 1940.

———. *Giddy Minds and Foreign Quarrels.* New York, 1939.

———. "Keeping America Out of War," *Current History,* XLIII (December, 1935), 290–292.

———. "National Politics and War," *Scribner's Magazine,* XCVII (February, 1935), 65–70.

———. "Peace for America—In Time of Peace Prepare for Peace," *New Republic,* LXXXVI (March, 1936), 100–102, 127–129, 156–159.

———. "Peace Loads the Guns," *Today,* IV (June 29, 1935), 3–4, 23.

———, and Mary R. Beard. *The Rise of American Civilization.* 3 vols. New York, 1928 and 1939.

———, and George H. E. Smith. *The Old Deal and the New.* New York, 1940.

———, and George H. E. Smith. *The Open Door at Home.* New York, 1934.

Bingham, Alfred M. *Insurgent America.* New York and London, 1935.

———. "War Mongering on the Left." *Common Sense,* VI (1937), 8–10 (May), 15–18 (June), 11–15 (July).

Bliven, Bruce. "They Cry 'Peace, Peace,' " *New Republic,* LXXXIV (November and December, 1935), 287–288, 352–354; LXXXV (January, 1936), 38–40.

Borah, William E. *Bedrock.* Washington, 1936.

———. "Our Foreign Policy," *Vital Speeches of the Day,* II (October, 1935), 36–38.

———. "Preserving Neutrality," *United States News,* VII (September, 1939), 11.

———. "What Our Position Should Be," *Vital Speeches of the Day,* V (April, 1939), 397–399.

Borchard, Edwin M. "Neutrality," *Southern Review,* II (Autumn, 1936), 238–259.

——. "Neutrality for the United States," *Vital Speeches of the Day,* III (October, 1937), 738–740.

——. "We Can Remain Neutral," *Today,* IV (October 5, 1935), 6, 22–23.

——, and William Potter Lage. *Neutrality for the United States.* New Haven, 1937.

Bradley, Phillips. *Can We Stay Out of War?* New York, 1936.

——. "Current Neutrality Problems—Some Precedents, an Appraisal, and a Draft Statute," *American Political Science Review,* XXIX (December, 1935), 1022–1041.

——. "Neutrality and War," *Amerasia,* I (April, 1937), 78–82.

Browder, Earl. *Democracy or Fascism.* New York, 1936.

——. *Fighting for Peace.* New York, 1939.

——. *The People's Road to Peace.* New York, 1940.

——. *The Second Imperialist War.* New York, 1940.

——, with Bill Lawrence. *Next Steps to Win the War in Spain.* New York, 1938.

Brumback, Oscar. *America, Awake!* Washington, 1936.

"Can America Remain 'Unentangled'?" *Nation,* CXLI (October, 1935), 425.

Capper, Arthur. "Time to Think American," *Scribner's Commentator,* IX (February, 1941), 69–74.

Carter, Boake. *Why Meddle in Europe?* New York, 1939.

Chamberlin, William H. "War—Shortcut to Fascism," *American Mercury,* LI (December, 1940), 391–400.

Chase, Stuart. "Four Assumptions About the War," *Uncensored,* No. 65 (December 28, 1940), Supplement.

——. *The New Western Front.* New York, 1939.

Clark, Bennett C. "Detour Around War," *Harper's Magazine,* CLXXII (December, 1935), 1–9.

——. "Neutrality—What Kind?" *Vital Speeches of the Day,* III (February, 1937), 252–253.

——. "The Question of National Defense," *Vital Speeches of the Day,* V (January, 1939), 216–219.

Cless, George H., Jr. *The Eleventh Commandment.* New York, 1938.

Connally, Tom, and Alfred Steinberg. *My Name is Tom Connally.* New York, 1954.

Crowther, Samuel. *America Self-Contained.* New York, 1933.

Dallas, George M., ed. *The Life and Writings of Alexander James Dallas.* Philadelphia, 1871.

Dennis, Lawrence. "The Highly Moral Causes of War," *American Mercury,* XXXVIII (July, 1936), 299–310.

Detzer, Dorothy. *Appointment on the Hill.* New York, 1948.

———. "What Neutrality Means," *Nation,* CXLI (December, 1935), 642–643.

Deverall, Richard L. "While Europe Races Along the Road to New Wars," *America,* LVII (September, 1937), 583–584.

Downey, William G., Jr. "American Neutrality: Past and Present," *Catholic World,* CXIV (April, 1937), 138–147.

Dreiser, Theodore. *America Is Worth Saving.* New York, 1941.

"Dress Rehearsal for Neutrality," *New Republic,* LXXXV (November, 1935), 4–5.

Dulles, John Foster. *War, Peace and Change.* New York and London, 1930

Eisenhower, Dwight D. "Defense of Western Europe," *Vital Speeches of the Day,* XVII (February, 1951), 258–262.

Eliot, George Fielding. *The Ramparts We Watch.* New York, 1938.

Engelbrecht, H. C., and F. C. Hanighen. *Merchants of Death.* New York, 1934.

———. *Revolt Against War.* New York, 1937.

Fay, Sidney B. "New Light on the Origins of the World War," *American Historical Review,* XXV (July, 1920), 616–639; XXVI (October, 1920, and January, 1921), 37–53, 225–254.

———. *The Origins of the World War.* New York, 1928.

Flynn, Elizabeth Gurley. *I Didn't Raise My Boy to Be a Soldier— for Wall Street.* New York, 1940.

Flynn, John T. "Nazi Economy—A Threat?" *Scribner's Commentator,* X (August, 1941), 19–26.

———. "U.S. Neutrality," *Common Sense,* VI (October, 1937), 8–10.

Ford, Henry. "An American Foreign Policy," *Scribner's Commentator*, IX (December, 1940), 3–6.

"A Foreign Policy for American Democracy," *Common Sense*, IX (July, 1940), 3–8.

Fosdick, Harry Emerson. "My Account With the Unknown Soldier," *Scholastic*, XXVII (November 9, 1935), 9–10.

Frank, Jerome. *Save America First*. New York, 1938.

Gorin, Lewis J., Jr. *Patriotism Prepaid*. Philadelphia and London, 1936.

Grattan, C. Hartley. *The Deadly Parallel*. New York, 1939.

———. *Why We Fought*. New York, 1929.

Hagood, Johnson. "Rational Defense," *Saturday Evening Post*, CCIX (October 24, 1936), 5–7, 40, 43.

———. *We Can Defend America*. Garden City, New York, 1937.

Hemingway, Ernest. "Notes on the Next War," *Scholastic*, XXVII (November 9, 1935), 7–8, 29.

Herring, Hubert. *And So to War*. New Haven, 1938.

Hillenbrand, M. J. "If War Comes Will Moscow Be Our Ally?" *America*, LVII (July, 1937), 294–295.

———. "The Meddlesome Muddle of Foreign Policy Makers," *America*, LIX (June, 1938), 224–225.

Hoover, Herbert. "Challenge to Liberty," in Edwin C. Rozwenc, ed., *The New Deal—Evolution or Revolution? (Problems in American Civilization*, VIII), Boston, 1949.

———. "The Greatest Service the Nation Can Give," *Vital Speeches of the Day*, IV (April, 1938), 407–412.

———. *The Memoirs of Herbert Hoover*. 3 vols. New York, 1951–1952.

———. "Our Foreign Policy," *Vital Speeches of the Day*, V (February, 1939), 258–261.

———. "Our National Policies in this Crisis," *Vital Speeches of the Day*, XVII (January, 1951), 165–167.

———. "We Should Revise Our Foreign Policies," *Vital Speeches of the Day*, XVII (February, 1951), 262–265.

"How to Stay Out of War," *Forum*, XCVII (February, March, and April, 1937), 89–95, 165–170, 249–254.

Howe, Quincy. *Blood Is Cheaper than Water.* New York, 1939.

——. *England Expects Every American to Do His Duty.* New York, 1937.

Hoyt, Kendall A., ed. *A Republican Program: Speeches and Broadcasts by Robert A. Taft.* Cleveland, 1939.

Hull, Cordell. *The Memoirs of Cordell Hull.* 2 vols. New York, 1948.

Hutchins, Robert M. "America and the War," *Scribner's Commentator,* IX (April, 1941), 85–89.

——. "The Proposition is Peace," *Scribner's Commentator,* X (July, 1941), 93–98.

Ickes, Harold L. *The Secret Diary of Harold L. Ickes.* 3 vols. New York, 1953–1954.

"If War Comes," *Common Sense,* VIII (March, 1939), 8–13.

" 'Isolation' vs. 'Collective Security,' " *Common Sense,* VII (February, 1938), 3–5.

Jessup, Philip C. "The New Neutrality Legislation," *American Journal of International Law,* XXIX (October, 1935), 665–670.

Johnson, Hiram W. "Let's Declare Ourselves," *Scribner's Commentator,* XI (December, 1941), 93–97.

Johnson, Hugh S. *Hell-Bent for War.* Indianapolis and New York, 1941.

"Keeping America Out of War," *Common Sense,* VII (March, 1938), 13–16.

Kennedy, Joseph P. "Present Policy is Politically and Morally Bankrupt," *Vital Speeches of the Day,* XVII (January, 1951), 170–173.

Koch, Adrienne, and William Peden, eds. *The Life and Selected Writings of Thomas Jefferson.* Modern Library Edition. New York, 1941.

La Follette, Philip. "The Arsenal of Dying Europe?" *Scribner's Commentator,* IX (March, 1941), 85–88.

Lindbergh, Charles A. *Address.* New York, 1941.

——. "An Appeal for Peace," *Vital Speeches of the Day,* VI (August, 1940), 644–646.

——. "Impregnable America," *Scribner's Commentator*, IX (January, 1941), 3–6.

——. "Our National Safety," *Vital Speeches of the Day*, VI (June, 1940), 484–485.

——. "A Plea for American Independence," *Scribner's Commentator*, IX (December, 1940), 69–73.

——. "Time Lies With Us," *Scribner's Commentator*, XI (November, 1941), 88–93.

——. *"We."* New York and London, 1927.

Lipscomb, Andrew A., and Albert E. Bergh, eds. *The Writings of Thomas Jefferson.* 20 vols. Washington, 1903–1904.

Lodge, Henry Cabot, ed. *The Works of Alexander Hamilton.* Constitutional Edition, 12 vols. New York and London, n.d.

Ludlow, Louis. *From Cornfield to Press Gallery.* Washington, 1924.

——. *Hell or Heaven.* Boston, 1937.

——. *Senator Solomon Spiffledink.* Washington, 1927.

Mallory, Daniel, ed. *The Life and Speeches of the Hon. Henry Clay.* 2 vols. Hartford, 1853.

Maverick, Maury. *A Maverick American.* New York, 1937.

McCormick, Robert R. "Can America Fight in Europe?" *Scribner's Commentator*, IX (February, 1941), 88–90.

Millis, Walter. "The Last War and the Next," *Nation*, CXLII (January, 1936), 95–98, 125–127.

——. "Mars Proposes—Can Uncle Sam Dispose?" *American Scholar*, V (Autumn, 1936), 387–395.

——. *Road to War.* Boston and New York, 1935.

Moley, Raymond. "Easy Steps Toward War," *Today*, IV (October 12, 1935), 12–13.

Murphy, Ray. "Let's Mind Our Own Business," *Scholastic*, XXVII (November 9, 1935), 15, 25.

"Must We Fight in the Next War?" *Nation*, CXLI (August, 1935), 228–229.

"Neutrality," *America*, LIV (January, 1936), 370–371.

"Neutrality and Embargo," *America*, LVIII (April, 1938), 612–613.

Nye, Gerald P. "Preparedness for Peace," *Christian Science Monitor Weekly Magazine,* March 10, 1937, 1–2.

Paine, Thomas, *Common Sense and Other Political Writings,* Nelson F. Adkins, ed. The American Heritage Series, No. 5, Oskar Piest, gen. ed. New York, 1953.

Patterson, Laurence K. "Drifting Toward Armageddon," *America,* LIII (June, 1935), 270–271.

"A Peace Policy for 1935," *Christian Century,* LII (January, 1935), 39–40.

"Positive Neutrality," *New Republic,* LXXXXII (October, 1937), 327–328.

Raushenbush, Stephen, and Joan Raushenbush. *The Final Choice.* New York, 1937.

——. *War Madness.* Washington, 1937.

Roosevelt, Elliott, ed. (with Joseph P. Lash). *F.D.R., His Personal Letters, 1928–1945.* 2 vols. New York, 1950.

Rosenman, Samuel I., comp. *The Public Papers and Addresses of Franklin D. Roosevelt, 1937–1940.* 4 vols. New York, 1941.

Sargent, Porter. *Getting US into War.* Boston, 1941.

Schoonmaker, Nancy, and Doris F. Reid, eds. *We Testify.* New York, 1941.

Seldes, George. *Iron, Blood and Profits.* New York and London, 1934.

Shaw, Albert. "The Progress of the World," *Review of Reviews,* XCV (June, 1937), 6–7.

Simonds, Frank H. *America Faces the Next War.* New York and London, 1933.

——. "John Bull's Holy War," *Saturday Evening Post,* CCVIII (December 21, 1935), 16–17, 57–60.

——. "Shall We Join the Next War?" *Saturday Evening Post,* CCVIII (August 17, 1935), 5–7, 72–75.

Stone, William T. "International Traffic in Arms and Ammunition," *Foreign Policy Reports,* IX (August, 1933), 130–140.

——. "The Munitions Industry," *Foreign Policy Reports,* X (October, 1934), 250–268.

Taft, Robert A. *A Foreign Policy for Americans.* Garden City, New York, 1951.

———. "Let's Mind Our Own Business," *Current History,* L (June, 1939), 32–33.

———. "Let Us Stay Out of War," *Vital Speeches of the Day,* V (February, 1939), 254–256.

———. "Our Foreign Policy," *Vital Speeches of the Day,* VI (March, 1940), 345–348.

———. "Safety of the Nation," *Vital Speeches of the Day,* XVII (January, 1951), 198–205.

Tansill, Charles C. *America Goes to War.* Boston, 1938.

Thomas, Norman. "America's Contribution to an Enduring Peace," *Annals of the American Academy of Political and Social Science,* CCX (July, 1940), 43–49.

———. *The Choice Before Us.* New York, 1934.

———. "The Pacifists' Dilemma," *Nation,* CXLIV (January, 1937), 66–68.

———. *We Have a Future.* Princeton, 1941.

———, and Bertram D. Wolfe. *Keep America Out of War.* New York, 1939.

"The Threat from the Axis," *New Republic,* CIII (October, 1940), 466–467.

Townsend, Ralph. *America Has No Enemies in Asia.* San Francisco, 1939.

———. *Asia Answers.* New York, 1936.

———. *The High Cost of Hate.* San Francisco, 1939.

———. *Seeking Foreign Trouble.* San Francisco, 1940.

———. *There Is No Half-Way Neutrality.* San Francisco, 1938.

Turner, John K. *Shall It Be Again?* New York, 1922.

Vandenberg, Arthur H., Jr., ed. (with Joe Alex Morris). *The Private Papers of Senator Vandenberg.* Boston, 1952.

Viereck, George S. *The Kaiser on Trial.* Richmond, Virginia, 1937.

———. "Mussolini Knew—Twelve Years Ago," *Social Justice,* IA (May 9, 1938), 7.

Villard, Oswald Garrison, *Fighting Years.* New York, 1939.

——. "Issues and Men," *Nation*, CXLIV (January, 1937), 19.

——. "Issues and Men," *Nation*, CIL (September, 1939), 247.

——. "Issues and Men—Another Word on Neutrality," *Nation*, CXLIV (May, 1937), 508.

——. "Issues and Men—Honor to William J. Bryan," *Nation*, CXLI (November, 1935), 583.

——. "Issues and Men—Lansing Self-Revealed," *Nation*, CXLI (October, 1935), 427.

——. "Issues and Men—Neutrality and the House of Morgan," *Nation*, CXLI (November, 1935), 555.

——. "Issues and Men—The War and the Pacifists," *Nation*, CXLI (October, 1935), 455.

——. *Our Military Chaos*. New York, 1939.

Voorhis, Jerry. *Confessions of a Congressman*. New York, 1940.

Wertenbaker, Thomas J. "The Price of Neutrality," *Atlantic Monthly*, CLVLL (January, 1936), 100–108.

Wheeler, Burton K. "America Beware!" *Scribner's Commentator*, X (June, 1941), 88–92.

——. "The American People Want No War," *Vital Speeches of the Day*, VII (June, 1941), 489–491.

——. "Keep America Out of War," *Virginia Quarterly Review*, XVI (Spring, 1940), 279–284.

"Who Cultivate War," *Saturday Evening Post*, CCXI (April 8, 1939), 24, 109.

"Why Commit Suicide?" *Common Sense*, VII (March, 1938), 3–5.

Wood, Robert E. "War or Peace—America's Decision," *Scribner's Commentator*, IX (December, 1940), 76–81.

SECONDARY SOURCES

Periodicals

Public Opinion Quarterly, 1937–1941.

Current Biography, 1940–1941, 1944.

Unpublished Material

Armstrong, John Paul. "Senator Taft and American Foreign Policy, The Period of Opposition." Doctoral dissertation, University of Chicago, 1953 (on microfilm in FDRL).

Cleary, Richard C. "Congress, the Executive and Neutrality, 1935 to 1940." Doctoral dissertation, Fordham University, 1950 (on microfilm in FDRL).

Donovan, John C. "Congress and the Making of Neutrality Legislation, 1935–1939." Doctoral dissertation, Harvard University, 1949.

Kuusisto, Allan A. "The Influence of the National Council for the Prevention of War on United States Foreign Policy, 1935–1939." Doctoral dissertation, Harvard University, 1950.

Moseley, Harold W. "The 'Cash and Carry' Section of the 1937 Neutrality Act." Doctoral dissertation, Harvard University, 1939.

Pechota, Harry L. "Neutrality Legislation of the United States." Doctoral dissertation, University of Southern California, 1939 (on microfilm in FDRL).

Rogers, William C. "Isolationist Propaganda, September 1, 1939 to December 7, 1941." Doctoral dissertation, University of Chicago, 1943 (on microfilm in FDRL).

Witte, William D. S. "Quaker Pacifism in the United States, 1919–1942." Doctoral dissertation, Columbia University, 1954 (on microfilm in FDRL).

Books and Articles

Adler, Selig. *The Isolationist Impulse.* London and New York, 1957.

——. "The War-Guilt Question and American Disillusionment, 1918–1928," *Journal of Modern History,* XXIII (March, 1951), 1–28.

"American Institute of Public Opinion—Surveys 1938–1939," *Public Opinion Quarterly,* III (October, 1939), 581–600.

Bailey, Thomas A. *A Diplomatic History of the American People,* 3rd ed. New York and London, 1946.

Beale, Howard K., ed. *Charles A. Beard: An Appraisal.* Lexington, Kentucky, 1954.

Bemis, Samuel F. "Washington's Farewell Address: A Foreign Policy of Independence," *American Historical Review,* XXXIX (January, 1934), 250–268.

Billington, Ray Allen. "The Origins of Middle Western Isolationism," *Political Science Quarterly*, LX (March, 1945), 44–64.

Burns, Edward McN.. *The American Idea of Mission*. New Brunswick, New Jersey, 1957.

Cantril, Hadley. "America Faces the War: A Study in Public Opinion," *Public Opinion Quarterly*, IV (July, 1940), 387–407.

——, Donald Rugg, and Frederick Williams. "America Faces the War: Shifts in Opinion," *Public Opinion Quarterly*, IV (October, 1940), 650–656.

Carleton, William G. "Isolationism and the Middle West," *Mississippi Valley Historical Review*, XXXIII (December, 1946), 377–390.

Cole, Wayne S. *America First*. Madison, Wisconsin, 1953.

——. *Senator Gerald P. Nye and American Foreign Relations*. Minneapolis, 1962.

Cunliffe, Marcus. *The Nation Takes Shape. The Chicago History of American Civilization*, Daniel J. Boorstin, ed. Chicago, 1959.

De Conde, Alexander, ed. *Isolation and Security*. Durham, North Carolina, 1957.

Divine, Robert A. *The Illusion of Neutrality*. Chicago, 1962.

Donovan, John C. "Congressional Isolationists and the Roosevelt Foreign Policy," *World Politics*, II (April, 1951), 299–320.

Drummond, Donald F. *The Passing of American Neutrality, 1937–1941*. University of Michigan Publications in History and Political Science, XX. Ann Arbor, 1955.

Dulles, Foster Rhea. *America's Rise to World Power, 1898–1954*. The New American Nation Series, Henry Steele Commager and Richard B. Morris, eds. New York, 1955.

Fensterwald, Bernard, Jr. "The Anatomy of American 'Isolationism' and Expansionism," *Journal of Conflict Resolution*, II (June and December, 1958), 125–142, 280–307.

Ferrell, Robert H. *American Diplomacy in the Great Depression* Yale Historical Publications, Studies 17, David Horne, ed., New Haven, 1957.

Fite, Gilbert C. *George N. Peek and the Fight for Farm Parity*. Norman, Oklahoma, 1954.

Gallup, George, and Claude Robinson. "American Institute of Public Opinion—Surveys, 1935–38," *Public Opinion Quarterly*, II (July, 1938), 373–398.

Gilbert, Felix. "The English Background of American Isolationism in the Eighteenth Century," *William and Mary Quarterly*, I (3rd ser., April, 1944), 138–160.

——. *To The Farewell Address*. Princeton, 1961.

Goldman, Eric F. *Rendezvous with Destiny*. New York, 1953.

Graber, Doris A. *Crisis Diplomacy*. Washington, 1959.

Graff, Henry F. "Isolationism Again—With a Difference," *New York Times Magazine*, May 16, 1965, 26–27, 98–100.

Greer, Thomas H. *What Roosevelt Thought*. East Lansing, Michigan, 1958.

Humes, D. Joy. *Oswald Garrison Villard, Liberal of the 1920's*. Syracuse, New York, 1960.

Jacob, Philip E. "Influences of World Events on U.S. 'Neutrality' Opinion," *Public Opinion Quarterly*, IV (January 1940), 48–65.

Johnson, Walter. *The Battle Against Isolation*. Chicago, 1944.

Langer, William L., and S. E. Gleason. *The Challenge to Isolation, 1937–1940*. New York, 1952.

Leopold, Richard W. "The Mississippi Valley and American Foreign Policy, 1890–1941," *Mississippi Valley Historical Review*, XXXVIII (March, 1951), 625–642.

Lerche, Charles O., Jr. *The Uncertain South*. Chicago, 1964.

Link, Arthur S. *American Epoch*. New York, 1955.

Lubell, Samuel *The Future of American Politics*, 2nd rev. ed. Garden City, New York, 1956.

McCoy, Donald R. *Angry Voices*. Lawrence, Kansas, 1958.

McKenna, Marian C. *Borah*, Ann Arbor, Michigan, 1961.

Morgenthau, Hans J. *The Purpose of American Politics*. New York, 1960.

Mugglebee, Ruth. *Father Coughlin*. Garden City, New York, 1935.

Myers, William Starr. *The Foreign Policies of Herbert Hoover: 1929–1933*. New York, 1940.

Nichols, Jeannette P. "The Middle West and the Coming of World War II," *Ohio State Archaeological and Historical Quarterly*, LXII (April, 1953), 122–145.

Osgood, Robert E. *Ideals and Self-Interest in American Foreign Relations*. Chicago, 1953.

Perkins, Dexter. *The New Age of Franklin Roosevelt. The Chicago History of American Civilization*, Daniel J. Boorstin, ed. Chicago, 1957.

Randall, J. G. "George Washington and 'Entangling Alliances,' " *South Atlantic Quarterly*, XXX (April, 1931), 221–229.

Range, Willard. *Franklin D. Roosevelt's World Order*. Athens, Georgia, 1959.

Rippy, J. Fred. *America and the Strife of Europe*. Chicago, 1938.

——, and Angie Debo. "The Historical Background of the American Policy of Isolation," *Smith College Studies in History*, IX (1924), 71–165.

Salter, J. T., ed. *The American Politician*. Chapel Hill, North Carolina, 1938.

——. *Public Men In and Out of Office*. Chapel Hill, North Carolina, 1946.

Savelle, Max. *Seeds of Liberty*. New York, 1948.

Schlesinger, Arthur M., Jr. *The Coming of the New Deal*, Vol. II of *The Age of Roosevelt*. Boston, 1960.

——. "The New Isolationism," *Atlantic Monthly*, CLXXXIX (May, 1952), 34–38.

——. *The Politics of Upheaval*, Vol. III of *The Age of Roosevelt*. Boston, 1960.

Seidler, Murray B. *Norman Thomas: Respectable Rebel*. Syracuse, New York, 1961.

Shenton, James. "Fascism and Father Coughlin," *Wisconsin Magazine of History*, XLIV (Autumn, 1960), 6–11.

Smuckler, Ralph H. "The Region of Isolationism," *American Political Science Review*, XLVII (June, 1953), 386–401.

Squires, James D. *British Propaganda at Home and in the United States, 1914–1917*. Cambridge, Massachusetts, 1934.

Stebbins, Richard P., *et al.*, eds. *The United States in World Affairs, 1950.* New York, 1951.

Taylor, F. Jay. *The United States and the Spanish Civil War.* New York, 1956.

Tugwell, Rexford G. *The Democratic Roosevelt.* Garden City, New York, 1957.

Tull, Charles J. *Father Coughlin and the New Deal.* Syracuse, 1965.

Warren, Harris G. *Herbert Hoover and the Great Depression.* New York, 1959.

Weinberg, Albert K. "The Historical Meaning of the American Doctrine of Isolationism," *American Political Science Review,* XXXIV (June, 1940), 539–547.

——. *Manifest Destiny.* Baltimore, 1935.

White, William S. *The Taft Story.* New York, 1954.

Wilkins, Robert P. "Middle Western Isolationism: A Re-Examination," *North Dakota Quarterly,* Summer, 1957, 69–76.

Williams, William A. "The Legend of Isolationism in the 1920's," *Science and Society,* XVIII (Winter, 1954), 1–20.

INDEX